Long
Promised
Road

Long Promised Road

Carl Wilson, Soul
Of The Beach Boys
The Biography

Kent Crowley

Long Promised Road
Carl Wilson, Soul Of The Beach Boys
Kent Crowley

A Jawbone Book
First edition 2015
Published in the UK and the USA by
Jawbone Press
3.1D Union Court
20–22 Union Road
London SW4 6JP
England
www.jawbonepress.com

ISBN 978-1-908279-84-2

EDITOR John Morrish
JACKET DESIGN Mark Case

Printed by Everbest Printing Co Ltd, China

2 3 4 5 19 18 17 16

Contents

Introduction

HOLLYWOOD, CA, April 1981—Tonight's show amounts to a homecoming of sorts for the crowd, clad mostly in Hollywood's 80s uniform of designer jeans, spandex pants, and satin baseball jackets, who swarm the box office of the Roxy Theatre on a cool spring evening.

Crammed inside the Roxy are rock'n'roll royalty representing nearly three decades of the best American pop music has to offer. They are here to celebrate the solo debut of an artist whose voice and guitar have dominated pop radio playlists for 20 years—yet whose name barely elicits recognition.

The Roxy is the most fashionable of the Hollywood rock clubs and perches atop some of the most sacred ground in rock'n'roll: Sunset Strip. The Sunset Strip actually begins a block west at Gazzarri's on the Strip, just below the point where Sunset Boulevard contours eastward into the stretch Jan & Dean once celebrated as 'Dead Man's Curve.'

In 1981, Gazzarri's serves as flashpoint for a new style of music slowly emerging from the post-punk, disco, and multiplatinum torpor of the late 70s: a brand of raucous heavy metal that will become known as 'hair metal,' encompassing bands like Van Halen, Mötley Crüe, and Ratt. Rowdy, loud, and uncouth, Gazzarri's is the Ellis Island of the Hollywood rock'n'roll scene. Shunned by critics and scorned by rock cognoscenti alike, Gazzarri's is the musical street brawl weeding out the weak before the strong venture further east to the Whisky A Go Go.

Known simply as the Whisky, the club squats on the corner of Sunset Boulevard and North Clark Avenue. A decade earlier, long queues of mostly denim-clad twentysomethings had snaked around the front door of the Whisky for what was in 1970 a guilty pleasure: a chance to see a band who had, in the era before Vietnam, unabashedly celebrated the hedonistic pursuits of the Golden State, including surfing, skirt-chasing, and even food. A small minority—generally devout readers of the *Los Angeles Free Press*, *Rock*, *Crawdaddy*, and *Rolling Stone*—arrived to witness the rumored rebirth of the only American band to rival The Beatles between their American debut and 1967's *Sgt Pepper's Lonely Hearts Club Band*. Yet in a matter of months, The Beach Boys had plummeted from the heights of 'Good Vibrations' and the broken promise of the unfinished *SMiLE* album to sink beneath the awareness of the Woodstock generation. Only when a new generation of pop artists, such as Elton John, Chicago, and America, began acknowledging their debt to the band and its leader Brian Wilson was the stage set for a staggering mid-70s comeback.

Yet, tonight, here in the Roxy, the air crackles with muted electricity. Cool rules as audience members shoot nonchalant glances around the club before the band takes the stage. They are here for Carl Wilson—chiefly remembered as the sweet-faced, chubby lead guitarist in The Beach Boys, now slimmed down, bearded, and grown into stylish manhood. After two decades of serving essentially as The Beach Boys' musical director, and having quietly overcome the substance abuse issues that derailed one brother's career and is destroying the other's life, Carl takes the stage with his new band to promote his recently released solo album. He will be the first Beach Boy to break from the fold and tour to support a solo record.

Sprinkled throughout the club are nearly all of The Beach Boys. A visibly intoxicated, tuxedo-clad Dennis Wilson—rock'n'roll's original wild child—clambers onto a wobbling tabletop and shouts declarations of love and support to his younger brother to the cheers of the crowd. Eternally youthful past-and-future Beach Boy Bruce Johnston stands ready to assist if Dennis tumbles to the floor.

Nearer the stage, placed along the aisle that leads to the backstage area, the notoriously reclusive Brian Wilson sits next to his wife Marilyn. Trembling and perspiring, Brian signs autographs and smiles gamely, even when a silent patron walks up and rudely plops down a stack of old black-label Beach Boys vinyl records in front of him. Brian nods, continues to smile, and dutifully autographs each one while greeting other guests. Of the five founding Beach Boys, three are inside, while Carl's cousin Mike Love arrives fashionably late after the first set.

Nearly everybody here is somebody. Carl's songwriting partner and lead vocalist Myrna Smith began her career as one of Elvis's backing singers, the Sweet Inspirations. She is married to Carl's manager Jerry Schilling—the one member of Elvis Presley's Memphis Mafia that Colonel Tom Parker couldn't fire, because he was Elvis's friend, not his employee. Billy Hinsche, once Carl's brother-in-law, a former teen heartthrob and one of the longest-serving and most talented members of The Beach Boys' backing band, shares the stage. He is the only link between Carl's band and The Beach Boys.

From the opening note, the band renders nearly the entire *Carl Wilson* album, with only Carl's 'Long Promised Road,' from the 1971 *Surf's Up* album, connecting back to The Beach Boys. Wild applause greets the final number as the band exits the stage.

At 34, Carl is celebrating his 20th anniversary as a professional musician and singer—a career that began with an awkward 15-minute performance at the Rendezvous Ballroom in the beachside town of Balboa, California, and led to The Beach Boys' stature as the only American rock'n'roll band to go toe-to-toe with The Beatles.

In the half-decade between 1961 and 1966, The Beach Boys rose from a derided surf band to become America's counterattack to the British Invasion. Then, with the 1966 release of *Pet Sounds*, the band would elevate the disposable teen pap called rock'n'roll to a point where it was taken seriously by artists such as the composer and conductor Leonard Bernstein and the jazz singer and composer Carmen McRae.

Over the next five years The Beach Boys descended from the heights of commercial and critical success to become the first 'oldies' band, serving up paeans to the good old days as America moved into the dark days of Lyndon Johnson and the darker days of Richard Nixon. Despite the fact that Carl, almost alone among the major rock stars of the era, risked his career to stand up against the Vietnam War and the Selective Service System for conscription, The Beach Boys found themselves dismissed by the cognoscenti, all the while releasing some of the most groundbreaking music of their careers.

At the turn of the 70s, with Carl at the helm, they began their resurrection with a new label and *Sunflower*, an album that, in the words of one *Rolling Stone* reviewer, "can finally stand with *Pet Sounds*." Within the next five years, The Beach Boys won the hearts of a new audience of college students who didn't know surf from Shinola, and a new generation of surfers who recognized that—whether or not any of the band actually surfed—The Beach Boys stood fast in celebrating the sport and its environment while the other surf bands disbanded, failed, or adopted fake English accents to survive the British Invasion.

Carl's ability to play an emerging style of electric guitar had launched the band on their way to greatness and put them on their road to redemption a decade later, while he quietly shouldered the burdens of America's first family of musical brilliance and madness.

Now, at the Roxy, the youngest yet most technically accomplished Wilson brother thanks the audience and follows his band offstage. After the show, the crowd slowly rises, jostles, mills, and schmoozes. I find my way to the stage door, where the security guard intercepts me and inquires as to my credentials. This is the era of small independent or 'indie' labels and boutique 'vanity' labels created by the major record companies. I improvise a record company name that sounds suitable and he ushers me backstage.

At the top of the stairs, Carl and Dennis stand in the dressing room doorway. Carl beams and Dennis appears overcome with emotion. I scale the steps and glance inside the doorway into the dressing room. To the left, faces I recognize from dozens of biographies and documentaries about Elvis Presley—the West Coast branch of the Memphis Mafia—lean forward and burst into occasional laughter as Carl's mother Audree holds court, surrounded by Wilsons and Beach Boys insiders.

I wait as Carl thanks Dennis and turns toward the door to check on the activity inside the dressing room. As Dennis turns to leave, I intercept him and ask why he didn't tour to support his excellent *Pacific Ocean Blue* album. He nods, glances at his shoes, and an unintelligible hoarse rasp issues from his throat. Between his shouts of support earlier and the damage wrought by years of smoking and drinking and a punch to the throat that damaged his larynx, he is too incapacitated and too emotional to be understood. While I can't understand what he says, my sense is that he might be expressing regret. I tell him how much I enjoyed his album and thank him, with still no idea what he actually said. He shrugs, offers up a sad smile, and descends the steps, and I am greeted with a smile and a handshake from Carl.

"Mr. Wilson," I say, in my best faux-somebody voice, "wonderful show."

He thanks me, seeming genuinely grateful for my comment.

Carl is well known in guitar circles for owning one of the rarest Fender Stratocasters. Sitting close to the stage, I noticed that the Stratocaster he was playing seems like a good candidate. I ask if that is indeed the one, and he replies that it's actually a newer instrument. I mention that I noticed that he played the entire show without a flatpick, employing more of a jazz guitarist's fingerpicking style. I ask if he's forsaken the pick for fingernails and he shows me his picking hand, explaining that he prefers the softer, warmer sound of fingertips to the sharp percussive attack of nails. He explains how fingertips give him more control over voicing the individual notes of the chords.

As we delve deeper into the discussion, I hear another short burst of laughter echo from the room and realize that I'm monopolizing his time discussing guitar minutiae on what may be one of the biggest nights of his professional life. I thank him. He thanks me for being there and I head down the stairs.

CHAPTER ONE

California Saga

Rock'n'roll lives often begin with family tragedy or break-up. John Lennon, Paul McCartney, and Jimi Hendrix all lost their mothers young and expressed their pain in songs that made the world richer, such as 'Julia,' 'Let It Be,' and 'The Wind Cries Mary.' The gravestone of Phil Spector's father, a suicide, provided him with a title for his first hit song, 'To Know Him Is To Love Him.' Brothers and bandmates Duane and Gregg Allman lost family members to murder.

In this context, the three Wilson brothers, Brian, Dennis, and Carl, were lucky. There was no binding tragedy, and their parents stayed married long enough to bring them up together. Where they were less lucky, perhaps, was in the personality of their father, Murry Wilson, a driven and frustrated man. He was their manager and first producer. Like other bands of brothers, they shared an experience that bound them together and allowed them to soldier on under the toughest of circumstances: they were family, not merely bandmates. Mike Love was family, too: a first cousin but not a brother. That created a rift that would resurface throughout their careers.

Over time, and even within the band, Murry would find supporters as well as detractors, and the portrait of Murry that evolved over the decades changed depending on the teller. In the 60s, while Murry portrayed himself as a stern father overlooking the careers of his beloved sons, The Beach Boys would on occasion make him an object of derision, in songs like 'Cuckoo Clock' and 'I'm Bugged At My Old Man,' and would burlesque his directions during recording sessions with his favorite phrase, "Treble up, guys."

Beginning in the 70s, even excellent journalists like Tom Nolan characterized Murry as an out-of-touch right-winger living in "Nixonian" circumstances and "bomb Hanoi-ish" (supporting the Vietnam War) who still employed execrable anachronisms like "negro artists" when describing his sons' music.[1] In public, though, Murry could be the most gregarious and generous of men, and often the involvement of his sons determined the Murry with whom one dealt at the moment.

During his early days of hustling demos at Hollywood's Gold Star Recording Studios, owner Dave Gold complimented his tie. Murry promptly unfastened the tie and offered it to Gold with his best wishes. When Murry found himself at odds after being fired by The Beach Boys as their manager, he returned to Gold Star to record songs with his friends—including a singing plumber who had fixed his water pipes.[2]

For a generation whose parents were damaged by the deprivations of war and the Great Depression and who were born into unheard-of prosperity, tempered by the looming threat of nuclear holocaust, Murry Wilson served as a prime example of an out-of-touch and overbearing father. After his death, writers and others with real or dubious claims on The Beach Boys' life, legacy, and fortune began trafficking in tales that were once merely legends. There was Murry the abusive father, who pummeled his eldest child so badly that he lost his hearing on one ear. There was Murry the rapacious moneygrubber, who sold out the rights to Brian's songs when the supply of golden eggs evaporated after the *SMiLE* debacle, and who robbed Chuck Berry to give Brian full credit for 'Surfin' USA,' a rewrite of 'Sweet Little Sixteen.'

There was the Murry who denied royalties to Mike Love for 'California Girls' and many other Beach Boys songs.[3] There was the Murry who opposed Brian's partnerships with Jan & Dean and other artists and then recorded an album with his plumber when he had enough 'juice' in the industry to demand his own record contract.[4] And there was the Murry whose draconian demands forced the band to fire him as their manager.[5]

Mostly, though, Murry was viewed as driving his successful sons' career, then derailing it through sheer jealousy when his own career fizzled after a too-brief flirtation with minor success.

In 2005, after surviving decades of drug abuse, mental illness and Dr. Eugene Landy's Orwellian oversight, a recovered Brian Wilson told author Peter Ames Carlin, "My relationship with my dad was very unique. In some ways I was very afraid of him. In other ways I loved him because he knew where it was at. He had that competitive spirit which really blew my mind."[6]

Yet, during Murry's lifetime and afterward, it would be left to his youngest son, Carl, to try to deal with the effects of Murry's often toxic legacy on his two older brothers, both in the musical benefits it wrought and the emotional damage it inflicted. The cost to Carl was to find his own legacy overlooked by all but the most knowledgeable.

In fairness to Murry, his own upbringing was far from idyllic. The Wilsons came originally from New York, leaving there in the early 1800s for Ohio and then Hutchinson, Kansas. From there Murry's grandfather William Henry Wilson moved the family to Escondido in San Diego County to raise grapes, only to return to Kansas a year later.

It took William Henry's son William Coral 'Buddy' Wilson to establish the Wilson clan beachhead in California, leaving behind his wife, Edith Sophia Shtole Wilson, and children, including second son Murry Gage, born in 1917, and daughter Emily Glee, born in 1919.

Buddy came to work the oil fields that stretched out along the southern California coast. By all accounts, Buddy was a difficult and damaged individual who found his employment in the oil fields often punctuated by long stretches of unemployment, due to recurring crippling headaches and alcohol abuse. In 1921, Buddy finally imported his wife and family to California, where they spent their first months living in a tent on the beach in the Orange County oilfields of Huntington Beach.[7] Compared to the sullen and volatile Buddy, said *Endless Summer Quarterly* editor David Beard, "Murry was a boy scout."[8]

"Moody and scattered, plagued by searing headaches and a self-destructive thirst for whiskey," wrote Carlin, "Buddy wandered from job to job to long stretches of unemployment, which he passed grumbling into a glass in a dim barroom. When Edith and the kids finally joined him in

1921, taking the train to the elegant-sounding village of Cardiff-by-the-Sea, he couldn't afford to lease an apartment in town."[9]

Buddy's tendency to abuse alcohol and his frequent bouts of depression are pointed to by historians as the first harbingers of the disorders that would plague two more generations of Wilsons.

In 'A Psychobiographical Analysis Of Brian Douglas Wilson: Creativity, Drugs, And Models Of Schizophrenic and Affective Disorders,' a 2009 paper for a journal called *Personality And Individual Differences*, Dr Stefano Roberto Belli of the Oxford Department of Experimental Psychology, in England, observed that Murry suffered from at least one major depressive episode or MDE. "MDEs are not disorders in themselves but rather are descriptions of part of a disorder, most often major depressive disorder or bipolar disorder," Belli wrote. "After being dismissed as manager of The Beach Boys by Brian [in 1964], Murry took to his bed for a period of between three weeks and a month, with a noticeable loss of motivation: 'He could barely summon the will to change out of his pajamas at first.'"[10]

The resemblance to Brian's frequent and lengthy retreats in the late 60s and 70s is striking. The tendency of the Wilson males to mental illness or self-medication may well have genetic roots. It presents a darker side to the Beach Boys story than the usual sun, fun, and happiness.

The 1930 Federal Census listed the Wilson family, headed by 40-year-old Buddy and 33-year-old Edith, as living in the city of Los Angeles in a rented home on Figueroa Street. Buddy's occupation is listed as plumber. Along with 12-year-old Murry, it lists seven other Wilson children, from the eldest, 15-year-old Elenore, to Charles, estimated to have been born in 1930. Murry was the third born and second oldest son. His closest sibling was ten-year-old Emily Glee Wilson, Mike Love's mother.[11]

By Carlin's account, the Wilson children "marched the thin line dictated by their sour father and stern, demanding mother." When Buddy's anger erupted into violence it was often left to Murry to intervene. When Buddy beat Murry's youngest brother Charles for breaking his glasses, Murry had to physically separate them and drag Buddy out of the house until he sobered up. When Buddy's rage exploded toward Edith, Murry "found himself thrust into the role of his mother's protector, raising his own fists against the father he loved but who seemed unable to love him or anyone else in the family. But if they couldn't talk about their problems, the Wilsons could always sing their way to a kind of amity."[12]

According to journalist Steve Eidem, "Murry loved these times. He even found a guitar and began teaching himself how to play. It was during these musical family get-togethers that Murry decided that he wanted to be a songwriter."[13] Music became the single bond that drew the family together and quelled the violence simmering below the surface of Buddy Wilson's family. Some contend that music's ability to restore a semblance of peace and love in the Wilson family drove Murry's relentless desire to make music his life's calling.

In 1938, while employed at the Southern California Gas Company, Murry met 21-year-old Audree Neve Korthoff, daughter of Carl Arie Korthoff and Ruth Edna Finney Korthoff, whose family came to California from Minnesota. After a courtship, they married and had three sons. Brian Douglas was born on June 20, 1942; Dennis Carl on December 4, 1944; and Carl Dean on December 21, 1946. They settled first in Los Angeles and then into the rapidly growing working-class suburb of Hawthorne in a small two-bedroom ranch house at 3701 West 119th Street.

Murry was exempt from the wartime draft. He had lost an eye in a freak accident while employed by the Goodyear Tire & Rubber Company, which forced him to wear a prosthetic eye. When he returned to work, he tended to overcompensate for his disability, which sparked friction in the workplace. Finally he opened his own business—A.B.L.E. Machinery, which stood for Always Better Lasting Equipment—a combination industrial machinery sales-and-rental operation and tool shop.

Yet for Murry, business was business, and his true calling was music. "There was a lot of music in the house all the time," Carl told an interviewer in 1984. "We had a couple of pianos in the house most of the time. We had three pianos at one time. We also had jukeboxes through the years. So we had a really large cross section of music. We used to sing a lot as a family. Rhythm & blues, as it was called then, was something we loved a lot."[14]

The Wilsons lived in far more modest circumstances than has sometimes been portrayed. In 2013, former Beach Boy and neighbor David Marks, who had rejoined the band in time to celebrate The Beach Boys' 50th anniversary, recalled the Wilson household to journalist Ken Sharp:

"I lived directly across the street from the Wilsons. We both had corner houses. My side of the street was a new tract home development and all the houses were exactly the same in terms of floor plan. On the Wilson side, that neighborhood had been there for quite a while. It was run down. There were no sidewalks. The houses were older and the Wilsons lived in a pretty small, modest two-bedroom home. The boys all shared a bedroom. When they got older, Brian started sleeping in the den more and more, which was a converted garage they had turned into a music room. They had a Hammond B-3 organ, an upright piano, and a little hi-fi in there."

Inside the Wilson home, said Marks, "it wasn't *Leave It To Beaver*. It wasn't *Tobacco Road* either. It appeared to be a poor household, although Murry was successful selling two or three huge machines a year, industrial drill presses and lathes. They were like as big as a car. He would import them from England and sell those to maintain the household. They weren't rich by any means. The outward appearance of the household was happy. The boys were always running around doing something and Murry was on the phone and Audree was wearing the apron in the kitchen. It was pretty typical, actually.

"There was nothing really unusual about it except people probably don't imagine the Wilsons crammed in a tiny two-bedroom house in a poor neighborhood. There was one bunk bed and one cot in the bedroom and it was always a mess … clothes all over the place. They didn't really have any material possessions to speak of, other than the instruments in the music room. All the stuff that you hear about Murry being a prick, for me it was an average normal household. My dad was a prick too, and all the dads in the neighborhood were pricks. The school of parenting for that generation is what I'm describing. It was OK to smack your kid, especially my dad, who was Italian; if you say something out of line you get smacked. If you cause problems you get a beating with a strap."[15]

Murry was a disciplinarian but he also indulged his boys when he had the money. Carl and Dennis got an elaborate Lionel model railway, complete with scenery and houses, one Christmas. Another time, they got a go-kart, which Murry assembled before taking the pair to a track: Dennis, predictably, drove hell-for-leather, while Carl was more sedate. There were also biannual trips to Disneyland.[16]

At the same time, there does not seem to have been much spare money when Murry was building his business. He told *Rolling Stone*'s Tom Nolan that the Wilson family was "all so poor we'd just sit around singing and on occasion drinking a glass of brew. Not the children, the adults. And then I bought a Hammond electric organ, on time, and we'd play duets, my wife and I. And then Brian would get in the act and sing. All they ever heard was music in their house. And on occasion, family arguments."[17]

For decades, most of Murry's musical accomplishments have been ignored or trivialized by writers, with the exception of the performance of his 'Two-Step, Side-Step' on *The Lawrence Welk Show* on the radio. But Murry's musical aspirations and efforts laid the groundwork to turn The Beach Boys from a surf band to the family business to a legend.

In 1951, he formed a relationship with Dorinda and Hite Morgan's Guild Music, recording two songs with a singer named Jimmy Haskell (not the noted arranger). Later that year he wrote 'Tabarin' (a popular name for cabarets or nightclubs in the post-war era) which was recorded and released by The Hollywood Four Flames. An African-American rhythm & blues group, founded in Watts, the Flames featured a young Bobby Day (under his real name Bobby Byrd), who would write the rhythm & blues classics 'Over And Over' and 'Little Bitty Pretty One' and score a major hit with 'Rockin' Robin' in 1958. The Flames would go on to record the rhythm & blues classic 'Buzz, Buzz, Buzz' and a version of 'Gee' (a section of which Brian later appropriated for 'Heroes And Villains').[18]

While *Billboard* magazine gave Murry's song—a slow, jazzy ballad—a dismal review, it was recorded again, with Bob Williams singing with The Red Callender Orchestra, as 'Tabor Inn.' The Flames, meanwhile, followed 'Tabarin' with Murry's 'I'll Hide My Tears.'

In 1952, Welk's orchestra performed 'Two-Step, Side-Step' (capitalizing on a popular dance at the time) on his radio program. In 1954, country singer Bonnie Lou—who was voted one of *Downbeat* magazine's 'Top Five Female Singers' in the 50s and is today a member of the Rockabilly Hall of Fame—covered it on a single, which was followed by other regional versions.[19]

These early efforts present a far different picture of Murry than that of the frustrated white middle-class aspiring songwriter. Murry had begun making connections in the Los Angeles music scene of the 50s, interacting with record company owners, publishers, disc jockeys, and other songwriters like John Dolphin, Art Rupe, and Bobby Day while learning his craft. He wrote for African-American and country & western artists as well as Welk.

More importantly, Murry spent his off hours studying the mechanics of the music business, from writing the song to recording to publishing and then finally to hustling it to other artists and radio stations. As the Wilson brothers pursued their suburban childhood pursuits of baseball, bike riding, and—in Dennis's case—setting fields on fire, Murry had begun blazing the path that would lead to a type of worldwide success that nobody in the 50s could have imagined, not even Elvis.

CHAPTER TWO
Youngblood

Of the three brothers born to Murry and Audree Wilson, only the youngest, Carl, was born in the city the family put on the map: Hawthorne, California.

The only original Beach Boy who qualified as a member of the baby-boomer generation, Carl was, in his mother's phrase, "born 30."[1] As a toddler, he used to mimic the guitar players he watched on the country & western television programs by playing a toothpick.[2] He would grow up to be a cheerful, chubby, calming presence in what seemed to be a textbook suburban household. On the surface, the Wilson household exemplified the post-World War II American Dream; beneath bubbled a seething cauldron of dysfunction.

In the years since The Beach Boys mounted the stage at the Rendezvous Ballroom in Balboa, California, for their debut performance, endless retellings of their story have transformed it into a myth. Four slightly talented suburban teens, led by a half-deaf, half-mad musical genius, and terrorized by an abusive tyrant of a father, sang of sunny good times in America's sunniest state in the happiest time in its history, the 'Camelot' years of John F. Kennedy. They captivated the teenagers of America while the first wave of rock'n'rollers died, went to jail, or did military service. Then an assassin's bullet brought the Camelot era to an end, and America turned to The Beatles and 'Swinging England' for comfort. Too much pressure took its toll on the oldest brother. He retreated to the studio, then scrapped his masterwork. Thereafter, The Beach Boys became America's most successful 'oldies' band, while Brian was slowly rehabilitated, becoming acknowledged as a great artist.

This narrative proved flexible in the retelling, whether to redistribute fortunes, sell soap in mainstream media, or secure dubious places in history for those on the periphery. Yet The Beach Boys' tale of joy, madness, and redemption actually hinged on the one Wilson brother who attempted to carry on the legacy while reining in the dysfunction of his immediate family. Carl steered the family business through long battles with outside forces, notably his brother's renegade psychologist, who hoped to control the fortune that expanded when the band's music became the soundtrack for summer and the lynchpin of his home state's ongoing marketing campaign.

The Wilson family home at 3701 West 119th Street was razed in the early 2000s to accommodate the Interstate 105 freeway. Today California Historical Marker Number 1041 marks the spot, featuring a bas-relief frieze of the photo from the cover of their 1963 *Surfer Girl* album (modified to include original and then later member Al Jardine). The plaque marks "the beginning of an historic musical legacy. The music of The Beach Boys broadcast to the world an image of California as a place of sun, surf, and romance."

The marker commemorates the spot where Brian began writing songs, analyzing Four Freshman harmonies and learning to arrange vocals with his mother, cousin Mike Love, and younger brother Carl. "It was like, 'Mom, make Carl sing,'" Carl recalled. "I was like nine years old and I had to sing. 'No, I wanna play ball.' And Brian would say, 'Mom, make him sing.'"[3]

In the yard, Carl pursued his first passion, baseball, and became so adept at a young age that he beat out his older brother Dennis for a position on a local Little League team.[4] The garage later became the music room immortalized in the ballad 'In My Room'; it was here that David Marks's father Elmer once interceded in a fistfight between Murry and Dennis when Dennis was a teenager.[5] It was here, too, that Dennis suggested to Brian and Mike that they should write a song about his latest passion, surfing, because the dance it spawned was going to be the "latest dance craze." In the same music room, Brian brought his baby brother into their embryonic group, observing that Carl had a high, clear voice that blended well with his own.

Here, too, David Marks invited Carl to bring his cheap Kay guitar along to visit Dave's music teacher, John Maus.[7] (Carl had previously had lessons with Dean Brownel, a family friend from whom he had acquired his middle name. "Dean Brownel was a very technical musician," he recalled. "He used to say of a chord, 'Oh, that's a G-flat third, augmented by a fifth.' We were amused by that, but I was very impressed by his playing. He left his guitar at our house and I learned a few barre chords."[6])

Here, too, future pop star Chris Montez dropped by to visit and make music with his Hawthorne High School classmates.[8] And it was from this house that eight-year-old Carl Wilson walked to a neighbor's back yard and heard Little Richard sing 'Tutti Frutti.'

"I just remember this incredible feeling of excitement in my body," Carl later said. "It was just a really emotional experience. I really didn't know what it was that was going on, I just kind of came on to this really heightened awareness … it really blew my mind."[9]

* * *

The image The Beach Boys projected of California may have been one of, as it says on the plaque, "sun, surf, and romance," but the state had a more complex history and culture than that would suggest. Few cities in the world had the diversity of Los Angeles in the 50s. From a series of native Tongva villages, California became a property of the Spanish crown, then Mexico. Before the discovery of an underground lake in the Cucamonga Valley and the growing of the first successful Navel Orange trees in nearby Riverside in the 1880s, Los Angeles was a frontier cowtown as rip-roarin' and wild as Tombstone or Dodge City. Still basically a small hamlet, it enjoyed the reputation of having the highest incidence of shootings, murders, and lynchings of any town west of the Mississippi.[10]

As workers over decades developed the South Bay ports of Long Beach and Wilmington from the marshy coast west of Los Angeles to become the biggest deep water harbor on the Pacific coast, the City of Los Angeles began importing (many contend 'stealing') most of its water supply from nearby Owens Valley. The fruit industry overtook wheat and cattle farming in the latter part of the 19th century. As the orchards and the South Bay ports gradually took shape, immigrants from every corner of the world beat a path to this new world of abundant sunshine and wide open spaces.

With the major land routes into Los Angeles weaving through the American south, southwest, and Mexico, the guitar-centric musical cultures of Spain and Mexico predominated in the southern part of California, bringing with them the tradition of Mexican *vaqueros* singing soothing ballads to calm the cattle at night and prevent restive herds from stampeding or wandering off into the shoulder-high mustard grass of the foothills. Fusing over time with Irish and English folk traditions, and then swing music, this new hybrid became the 'western' in country & western music.[11]

With the harbors came a vast influx of cultures: Asian, Greek, Chinese, Japanese, Portuguese, Middle Eastern, and others, who brought with them expertise in harvesting the Pacific's bounty. Italian, Mexican, and French immigrants flocked to the vineyards that stretched from Fontana to Hollywood while the Dust Bowl and nascent petroleum industries propelled southern and southwestern Americans down Route 66 to the citrus and deciduous fruit orchards overtaking the counties of San Bernardino, Riverside, Orange, and Los Angeles. African-Americans and white rust-belt refugees carved out their own niches in the patchwork of Los Angeles suburbs as air force, army, and navy bases expanded after the attack on Pearl Harbor.[12]

As soon as sound transformed the movie industry in the late 1920s, a diaspora of trained musicians, composers, and Broadway impresarios such as Frank Loesser traded the rain and snow of New York to set up shop in sunny Hollywood. Soon Los Angeles had its own Tin Pan Alley of coffee shops, drug store soda fountains, and recording studios where songwriters loitered, pitched their wares, and kept their fingers on the creative pulse of the 'city of second chances' to sell their songs to established recording artists and movie and television studios.

The glue holding together Southern California's patchwork quilt of cultures was Latin and its traditions easily joined with what newcomers brought with them: the tradition of providing their own entertainment using portable stringed instruments—guitars, mandolins, violins, ouds, guitarrón (the precursor to the modern bass guitar), and others—that could be carried easily from town to town, house to house, and hauled out on a stage, a store, or a back porch for a night of improvised festivities.

In the 50s, Murry Wilson regularly made the 18-mile drive from the Wilson family home in Hawthorne to the confluence of all of the musical streams that flowed into Hollywood. There he recorded the songs he composed at home while rubbing shoulders with musicians who would pop up time and time again in histories of music and, most notably, his son's careers.

Murry's destination was often Gold Star Recording Studios, which was, in the words of its founder David S. Gold, "a parade of the world." Located in the heart of Hollywood at 6252 Santa Monica Boulevard (Route 66) where it intersected with Vine Street, less than a mile south of the slightly more famous intersection of Hollywood and Vine, Gold Star began its thirty-three-and-a-third years of existence by focusing on the tunesmith trade. That meant recording demonstration records (or 'demos') in its two compact studios for songwriters, whether successful Broadway impresarios like Loesser, aspiring tunesmiths like Jay Livingston and Ray Evans, or a new breed of rock'n'roll songwriter, such as Eddie Cochran, Bobby Day, and Phil Spector.[13]

Dave Gold first met Murry in the hallways of Gold Star in the mid 50s. Over the years Gold would come to know Murry, first as a struggling songwriter, then as his sons' band's early producer, and then upon his return to songwriting with his much-derided *The Many Moods Of Murry Wilson* album.[14]

Gold Star's central location in Hollywood and easy, informal approach to recording led to its becoming a popular networking spot for artists seeking what was new. Musicians, arrangers, and songwriters often dropped by to see who was recording. Meanwhile struggling songwriters availed themselves of the studio's 'Glamor Demo' approach, in which Gold Star engineers and members of the Gold Star family, such as arranger/composer Don Ralke and guitarist/bassist Ray Pohlman, would transform through overdubs a plain piano-and-voice or guitar-and-voice demo into a fully realized recording.

Gold Star later played a role in many key Beach Boys moments: from Murry's early works in the 50s, like 'Leaves,' to some of Brian's first independent productions, such as 'Pamela Jean' by The Survivors, which often ended up reworked on early Beach Boys albums. By the 60s, Brian was a regular at Gold Star, studying his hero Phil Spector. Later he used the studio to begin experimenting with more complex songs and productions such as 'I Just Wasn't Made For These Times,' 'Good Vibrations,' 'Heroes And Villains,' and the seminal tracks for the album that would become *Sunflower*, which he would later complete in his own Brother Studios.

While the engineers at other studios would often work to circumvent Murry's meddling, Murry was part of the Gold Star family and chose Gold Star to record his own album. Stan Ross, Dave Gold's partner, remembered each of the Wilson brothers stopping by and offering to "help out the old man."[15] More importantly, as an independent studio rather than an in-house record label, Gold Star stood at the center of the rock'n'roll revolution in Los Angeles and recorded the artists who later exercised some of the biggest influence on The Beach Boys, such as Duane Eddy, Ritchie Valens, and especially Phil Spector.

To compete with its heavily capitalized competition, such as Capitol, RCA, and Columbia studios, Gold Star focused on building repeat business and positive word of mouth, so it fostered a warm, friendly, creative atmosphere where people like Murry Wilson could be among those he considered his peers in the music community.

"Murry began dropping by Gold Star in the early 50s," said Gold. "He would bring in Audree on most occasions. He was an amateur writer trying to produce a record." Because Murry owned a tool store as part of his business, Gold, a lover of tools who not only handcrafted the bulk of Gold Star's key recording technology but even built the front doors for the business, was "very taken with that," and they conversed frequently.

"My impression of Murry is that he was what would be described as kind of a 'redneck,'" Gold said. In his conversations with Murry, he found Murry to be basically a good heart beating under a gruff exterior: a hard-charging bull in a china shop who could be reduced to tears by beautiful melodies.

"I got the feeling he didn't want to be that way," Gold said. "I know he was very hard on the boys." Murry was also famously generous, however. Returning from a trip to Japan, he found his way to Gold Star to make a gift of expensive silk pajamas to Gold's wife Mitzi.[16]

Part of the Gold Star experience was rubbing shoulders with a wide variety of film composers, songwriters, and musicians, and Gold and Ross facilitated that sense of family by introducing clients to one another to see if sparks might fly, especially if it meant work for the growing Gold Star family.

Two of the key players introduced to Murry's orbit were Ralke and Pohlman. Ralke would go on to produce The Sunrays, the band Murry produced after he was sacked as The Beach Boys' manager, and *The Many Moods Of Murry Wilson*. Pohlman became one of Brian's first-call bassists. "That was Stan's doing," said Gold. "Whenever he got the chance, he would hook people up."[17]

* * *

Even as Murry recorded demos of his songs at Gold Star in the late 50s, a new generation of West Coast rockers hung out in the hallways, making connections in the music business. They included two young artists who would exert a tremendous influence on The Beach Boys' future: Ritchie Valens and Dick Dale.

Today, Valens can be viewed, along with Eddie Cochran, as one of the founding fathers of West Coast rock'n'roll. Ritchie first came to Gold Star in 1958, at the age of 17. There he and his producer Bob Keane cobbled together Ritchie's first hit record 'Come On, Let's Go,' using many of the session musicians from what was then known as the Clique and later became known as the Wrecking Crew, including guitarist/bassist Carol Kaye, drummer Earl Palmer, and guitarist Rene Hall.

The success of Ritchie's follow-up single, 'Oh, Donna,' encouraged Keane to expand his artist list on his newly formed Del-Fi Records. One of his first signings was a young rockabilly singer/guitarist named Dick Dale (formerly Richard Monsour), who performed on local country & western television programs and local rock venues. He had even appeared as a rock star in the 1960 Marilyn Monroe film *Let's Make Love*.[18]

Years before the 1996 film *Pulp Fiction* finally elevated Dick Dale to his long-deserved status as one of rock'n'roll's guitar godfathers, Carl assessed Dale's influence on his own guitar playing in a 1981 interview with Geoffrey Himes. "A lot of stuff that people thought I invented was just the way people played guitar in LA," Wilson said. "At that time Dick Dale was really happening. He played at the Rendezvous Ballroom in Newport Beach. The Bel Airs were playing big dances. Surf music wasn't vocal then, it was guitar bands playing instrumentals in the style of The Ventures. Surf guitar was a real simple, hokey guitar style; they'd play the melody down in a lower register. These kids would buy these huge (Fender) amps, crank them up and those simple little melodies would just roar. But Dick Dale was different from the rest, because he had more control and more bite. Ooh, Dick Dale; that's who you wanted to sound like if you were a guitarist in LA in those years."[19]

The relationship between Dale and The Beach Boys proved mutually beneficial. According to Jon Stebbins, who wrote definitive biographies of both Dennis Wilson and David Marks, Dale owed much of his fame beyond Southern California to The Beach Boys' recordings of his classics, 'Miserlou' and 'Let's Go Trippin'' on their 1963 *Surfin' USA* album. They also reprised 'Let's Go Trippin'' on their million-selling *Beach Boys Concert* album.[20]

"There is no doubt The Beach Boys put the music of Dick Dale into the national consciousness in a big way," Stebbins said. "Millions of kids around the world were digging Dick Dale through Carl, David, and Al that otherwise would never have heard that music until maybe *Pulp Fiction*. Surf guitar lovers should thank Carl Wilson and The Beach Boys every day because they were by far the most effective ambassadors of the genre."[21]

Surfing had been part of Southern California culture since the early 1900s and many notable Southern California athletes, such as Olympians Duke Kahanamoko and Tarzan star Johnny Weissmuller, were often joined out on the waves by young actors like John Wayne or Cliff Robertson. But the realm that Dale ruled actually began on a June day in 1958, when a 24-year-old engineering student from Ontario, California, named Hobart 'Hobic' Alter carried his latest experiment down to Brooks Street Beach in Laguna Beach, caught a wave, and changed the history of a sport and a state forever. He had replaced the traditional heavy carved wooden board with a lighter, cheaper board made from a block of polystyrene foam, covered in fiberglass and resin. Owning a surfboard went from weeks of exacting shaping, glassing, and finishing to a simple trip to a surf shop.[22]

A year earlier, a writer named Friedrich Kohner (later Americanized to Frederick) had immersed himself in his young daughter Kathy's adventures, surfing at Malibu Beach. Barely tipping the scales at 95lbs and only five feet tall, Kathy Kohner found herself nicknamed 'Gidget' ('girl' plus 'midget') by a surfer named Terry 'Tubesteak' Tracy, who along with fellow surfers Mickey 'Da Cat' Dora, Mickey Munoz, Dewey Weber, and others provided the first role models for young California surfers.

Kohner, who had fled Austria to escape the Holocaust, fictionalized his daughter's story into the novel *Gidget* in 1957. By 1959, the book had sold over half a million copies and Columbia Pictures had Kohner write the script for the film version, starring teen idols James Darren and Sandra Dee (who was stunt-doubled in the surfing scenes by Munoz in a blond wig and bikini). It provided the world with a romanticized view of the new surfing culture springing up along the coasts of Southern California. Young Americans flocked to the Golden State from colder American climes as part of a mass migration fueled by Cold War defense spending.

Yet, after the *Gidget* phenomenon and the invention of the modern surfboard, it took a third innovation to complete the trifecta of events transforming Southern California into the sun-and-fun paradise The Beach Boys sang about. Orange County musical instrument manufacturer Leo

Fender provided the third element when he created the first modular or 'stack' amplifier.

Fender didn't play guitar but began his journey in transforming music as a radio repairman. Frequently called upon to repair the amplifiers of working musicians, he sought to develop the most efficient designs possible. Then, recognizing that an electric guitar was essentially an amplifier driver, he focused on the most efficient guitar designs. By 1958, not only had Fender introduced such classic designs as the Fender Telecaster, Stratocaster, Jazzmaster, and Precision Bass, his influence would extend to his fellow instrument makers, who began designing their own solidbody guitars.

Fender stood apart from his fellow guitar builders by focusing on meeting the needs of working musicians, such as blues guitarist Pee Wee Crayton, session guitarist Del Casher, and an up-and-coming rockabilly artist who had recently changed his stage name to Dick Dale. Fender would supply each of them with a prototype or early model and then poll them for their opinions.[23] Not being a musician himself, "he listened to musicians," said guitarist John Jorgenson.[24] Dale suggested that the pickup switch on the Stratocaster be modified to engage two single-coil pickups at once, creating a fatter, warmer sound, similar to the popular 'humbucker' pickups on rival electric guitars (which were essentially two single-coil pickups wired together to diminish extraneous noise).[25]

The guitar, Dale said, wasn't the issue; his problem was that he kept blowing up his amplifiers. So, one evening in 1961, Fender and his associate Fred Tavares traveled the nearly 30 miles from Fullerton to the Balboa Peninsula in Newport Beach to a beachside ballroom, where they navigated through moving clusters of surfers stomping the hardwood floors to the driving rhythms of Dick Dale & His Del Tones.[26]

Fender listened. The next day he returned to his factory in Fullerton and changed music forever, creating the Showman amplifier, which allowed lead guitar to be the dominant voice in a group. In time it would make Carl Wilson the leader of the touring Beach Boys.[27]

CHAPTER THREE

Seems So Long Ago

When Carl Wilson died, in 1998, friends, fans, and the media mourned him as an angel or a saint; yet few wondered how a home environment that had produced one of the world's most important and damaged musicians, and another who embodied the 'sex, drugs, and rock'n'roll' lifestyle, could have produced a man who was by all accounts the essence of gentleness, humility, and warmth.

In his youth, those closest to Carl marveled—in fact, worried—that he never seemed to lose his temper and kept everything bottled up inside. In his older years, as the children, wives, and ex-wives of band members proliferated, he was known as 'Papa Bear' for the way he assumed the oversight of the offspring of his brothers and cousins.[1]

"He had a way of disagreeing with you in the kindest way," said Stephen W. Desper, a long-time Beach Boys sound engineer and the designer of Brother Studios. "I must say, I never saw him get mad, or angry, or shout, or come undone. He was the leader during Brian's illness because he was so stable, steady, solid, and strong in the way he handled adversity. His competence gave the group confidence, a most needed attribute during those times when the group seemed to be on a downturn. He always retained that confident attitude."[2]

Gerry Beckley, America guitarist and future partner in Beckley-Lamm-Wilson, saw a slightly different side. "I know he had some hard edges. And I saw them, and I could see Carl getting riled up, but very, very rarely."[3]

The childhood that shaped Carl Wilson varied from the one that shaped his brothers Dennis and Brian, largely because there was so little of it. At 14, he was recording songs with the band that became The Beach Boys. By the age of 16, he was a guitar star. When he was 18, he assumed the role of onstage musical leader of the band that stood as America's greatest hope to dethrone The Beatles.

The usual answer to the question of Carl's nearly imperturbable geniality is that Dennis inherited Murry's volatility and Carl inherited Audree's sweetness. He was always close to his mother and he was apparently her favorite. She told Carl's wife Gina that he didn't start talking until he was three.[4] Another idea is that, if Brian poured his pain into music and Dennis released his with sex and mischief, Carl found comfort in food, contributing to the weight issue that caused the shy and sensitive boy to be bullied mercilessly by neighborhood children with nicknames like 'porky.'[5]

Throughout his career, journalists or insiders treated Carl's weight cavalierly. Brian once wrote a song about his fat brother and recorded it on his Wollensak tape recorder.[6] In interviews or profiles of the band, writers made a point of noting Carl's preference for jump suits to ameliorate any vestiges of baby fat or remarked that the appearance of 'chubby little Carl' worked against The Beach Boys developing a viable image in the 60s.[7]

Before they were The Beach Boys, they were high school athletes. Brian excelled in football and baseball, Mike ran track, and the Love family produced not one but two celebrated college and professional basketball players: Mike's brother Stan Love and nephew Kevin Love. Dennis surfed (Mike would learn later) and Al Jardine, another Hawthorne High boy, could claim that Brian cost him his football career when a play went awry and left Al limping off the field with a broken leg. While David Marks was too young to pursue high school sports (he was still in today's equivalent of middle school when he joined the band), he more than anybody matched the image of a surfer with his slender frame and bushy blond hair. While Carl demonstrated an early talent for baseball, his opportunity to develop as an athlete diminished with each new Beach Boys success.

Incidentally, Carl was born left-handed, but throughout his life played guitar right-handed.[8] While left-handers comprise only ten percent of the population, left-handed musicians seemed to exercise a disproportionate influence on the music of the 60s. Paul McCartney played his bass and guitars strung for a lefty (or 'mirror image'), and Ringo Starr always said that being a left-hander playing a right-hand drum kit gave him a unique approach not shared by drummers playing the correct line up. While Carl's hero Dick Dale and Jimi Hendrix were both lefties, Dale strung his guitar as a right-hander would and played his instruments upside down, with the bass strings below the high strings.[9] Paul Simon, Ritchie Valens, and Mike Bloomfield were, like Carl, lefties who played right-handed.[10]

Brian's love for music and the emotional release it provided was common knowledge among friends and family when he commandeered family members to sing his arrangements around the piano. Carl's proved to be a more private passion, jamming with David Marks or Chris Montez, or sitting alone learning chords and figures from Duane Eddy and Chuck Berry records in a home where pianos ruled.

Carl himself left few clues to his childhood. In the song 'Seems So Long Ago' on his 1981 debut album *Carl Wilson*, the lost childhood Carl laments seems far removed from the inferno of familial dysfunction often portrayed in biographies of the band or its individual members. With Myrna Smith helping him shape his lyrics, as Tony Asher had done with Brian's *Pet Sounds* songs, Carl conjures a gentle tableau of his childhood, recalling the trees in the Wilson yard, his mother's "sweet smile" and how his father "worked so hard." He sings of "the good times we shared" and how much his parents cared, which is not the usual story told about life with Murry Wilson. But there is a reminder, too, of the moral guidance he received and which he took to heart: "to not do wrong."

Children in larger families often find when growing up that the parents they recall and their childhood memories are often far different than the recollections of their siblings. In interviews, Carl was always careful to mention his parents' support, noting that Murry sold his business to focus on The Beach Boys' career. In the liner notes to The Beach Boys' 1964 album *All Summer Long*, while each of the other Beach Boys reveals his personality in the short paragraph appearing above his name, Carl, as always, quietly assumes the role of caretaker and caregiver that would distinguish his life:

"It's been a while now, but it seems like we just started out yesterday. I still get that overwhelming feeling when we're announced to come onstage. And a fantastic ovation—you could never know how much we appreciate them. To Mom and Dad: Brian, Dennis and you: I hope you are proud of us. You know we owe so much to you."[11]

Much of those differences in the parent-child relationship can be attributed to the fact that parents do learn over time. It is a common axiom that the oldest child is the one parents 'make their mistakes on.' This would be especially true in the Wilson home, where Murry's role model for fatherhood was the distant, disagreeable, and volcanic Buddy; Audree's father was by some accounts a stern presence in the home.

In larger families, older children are shanghaied into the child-rearing process by being given small doses of parental authority to accomplish small tasks, such as getting one's brothers or sisters ready for bed or a family outing. Older siblings, particularly in homes such as the Wilsons', will often band together in common cause to protect one parent against another or to protect one another.

Whatever can be said about the relationship between Brian and Murry, it was one of anything but neglect. Given Brian's early musical gifts, and the possible guilt Murry may have felt when Brian was diagnosed with 90 percent hearing loss in his right ear, Brian was in many ways the 'fair-haired' child.[12] Even Murry's detractors marvel at the attention and resources he lavished on his oldest son, which included buying him a car and building him his own music room.[13]

With only two years between them, it was often left to Dennis—who would go on to be the band's sex symbol and the songwriting partner of Charles Manson—to co-parent Carl. While miles of ink have been lavished on Brian's mental disorders and chemical addictions, most music journalists, with the exception of Dennis's biographer Jon Stebbins, have been content to accept Dennis at face value. Yet over the years, even casual Beach Boys insiders saw indications in Dennis of what would today probably be diagnosed as Attention Deficit Hyperactivity Disorder (ADHD). According to the National Institute of Mental Health, ADHD "is one of the most common childhood disorders and can continue through adolescence and adulthood. Symptoms include difficulty staying focused and paying attention, difficulty controlling behavior, and hyperactivity (over-activity)."[14]

Alternatively, Dennis might have suffered from Oppositional Defiant Disorder, displayed by children who are overly stubborn or rebellious and refuse to obey rules, or Bipolar Disorder, "in which extreme mood swings go from mania (an extremely high elevated mood) to depression in short periods of time."[15]

Brian marveled at Dennis's nervous energy and physicality even when it created issues in the studio. During the overdubbing of vocals on 'Wouldn't It Be Nice,' Brian found himself fretting for hours on how to capture Dennis's vocal part, as Dennis would frequently lose focus on the microphone and glance around the studio during recordings. Brian finally struck upon a solution by having Dennis cup his hands over his mouth to keep his attention focused on the mic.

Throughout his life, Dennis was known to swing from extremes of generosity to violence and he is often considered the 'real' Beach Boy as he embodied the hedonistic, sensation-chasing life that The Beach Boys celebrated in their songs: surfing, fast cars, and girls—lots of girls.

While Brian attempted some pop psychologizing in his liner note for the *All Summer Long* album, Dennis clearly reveled in his role as the wild child of the band: "Hi. They say I live a fast life. Maybe I just like a fast life of driving my Sting Ray and XKE, playing the drums, and meeting so many girls and guys (especially girls). I wouldn't give up this life for anything in the world. It won't last forever either but the memories will. Thank you for writing so many great letters. I hope I can answer them soon. I'll see you in your town."[16]

Of the three brothers, only Dennis would confront Murry. His nervous energy and mischievousness served as a lightning rod for Murry's frustrations and anger, touching off long simmering emotions in Murry's damaged psyche. Many contend that Dennis suffered the most at Murry's hands.

Tough, impulsive, and fearless, Dennis could on occasion be cruel to Carl, too, as older brothers are wont to be. You can hear this on the March 1965 overdubbing session for the single version of 'Help Me, Rhonda.' This is the recording later known as the 'I'm a genius, too' session, after the phrase an inebriated Murry used as he tried to hijack the recording. Carl finds a chair so he can add a guitar overdub to the mix. Dennis asks if Carl is going to sit, then taunts him, saying "You've got the biggest butt in the world."[17]

Yet as Jon Stebbins points out, "Dennis often threw himself in front of his dad to protect Carl. I don't think Carl ever forgot that." And while Dennis could tease Carl about his weight, Stebbins adds, if anybody else did they would face the wrath of the middle Wilson.[18]

David Marks recalled a time when he and Dennis explored a tunnel near the Wilsons' home. Dennis enlisted Carl in the effort, then abandoned him and left him crying.[19] Yet on those occasions, said Stebbins, "Dennis would inevitably go back."[20]

Being the youngest, Carl not only witnessed the turmoil in the Wilson household from the greatest distance, he learned from it. Just as Brian deconstructed The Four Freshmen's harmonies and Gershwin's chords from an early age, Carl analyzed the interactions of his family—noting how a word or a look could set Murry off, and how his mother Audree managed to cobble together semblances of peace to keep the family whole. More importantly, in a home where peace was often a rare and valuable commodity, Carl better than anybody understood the fragility and mechanics of peace, as well as, most importantly, the need for it.

In the Wilson household, music proved to be the greatest facilitator of that peace. Nuclear and extended family musical gatherings were hugely important in the Wilson home, and all of The Beach Boys spoke freely of how the sound of his three young sons harmonizing on songs like 'Ivory Tower,' a hit in 1956, could reduce Murry to tears.

Brian was the dominant personality in the Wilsons' music-making.

"Music was the only domain in which [Brian] Wilson showed especial intelligence, and was the only domain where he expressed creativity," wrote Stefano Belli. "Interestingly, music is an area of Wilson's life that seems to be strongly related to various aspects of his schizoaffective disorder."[21]

Meanwhile, from an early age, mischief proved to be Dennis's territory. "We called him 'Dennis the menace' and he was always causing trouble," said David Marks. "He was considered the neighborhood bully in a way … there was always something going on with Dennis and the police."[22]

Once they became a band, The Beach Boys didn't back away from encouraging and even promoting Dennis's wild-child persona. His drumming gymnastics and mugging for the crowd proved indispensable in whipping up the hysteria that accompanied Beatlemania-era performances. (When Glen Campbell joined the band briefly in 1964, he was told to not concern himself too much with the band's performance because the audience probably wouldn't be able to hear him over the screaming.[23]) The highlight of The Beach Boys' early performances was often Dennis's rendition of Dion's 1961 song 'The Wanderer' (later included on their 1964 *Beach Boys Concert* album), which proclaimed the joys of casual sex and fast cars.

Yet in a family of athletes and sex symbols, Carl's weight issues, along with his family's dysfunction, may have played a deeper role in the development of his self-image. In an interview about the career of the great comedy team Laurel & Hardy, Oliver Hardy's widow Lucille revealed a heartbreaking secret about the actor who left a legacy of joy, love, and laughter few comics or actors could claim even today. As she applied or removed makeup, Hardy—the 'fat one' of the team—would often place his hands gently on her shoulders, glance at his reflection in the mirror with his face screwed up somewhere between scowling and quizzical, and sigh, "How can you love me? How can you love someone who looks like this?"[24]

With a musical genius for a brother, in a house that valued music, and another brother who was a sex symbol in a rock'n'roll band, Carl came to

The Beach Boys without any clear sense of entitlement and, as the youngest and least damaged, a stronger sense of caring for family, even when they started other families.

"Carl Wilson was an angel," said Brian's first wife, Marilyn Wilson Rutherford. "He was not perfect, but pretty close. He was a caring, loving brother-in-law and I could always depend on him to back me up on anything and everything. We understood each other. He was the best uncle to (Brian's daughters) Carnie and Wendy and had them in his lap driving when they were very little. He appreciated their talents. He told me he was very happy for me when I met my husband, Daniel Rutherford. He cared for him very much and Daniel felt the same way about him. He was generous … a good loving father to (his sons) Jonah and Justyn. It is still very hard to think of him being gone."[25]

Yet Desper, who probably spent more one-on-one hours with Carl than anybody outside the family, recalled a bigger influence on Carl that overrode the others. He references a YouTube video in which Carl sings 'God Only Knows' at a wedding, accompanied only by former brother-in-law and Beach Boys touring band member Billy Hinsche, signing off with "God bless you," quietly into the microphone. "The last three words Carl says shine a bright light on the nature of the man. He and I have had many talks about God, the nature of God, man's relationship with God, and all those heavy topics. Carl was a man of God."[26]

That had always been the case. In 1967, Brian was asked to sum up his brother. "Wow, I can hardly express the great admiration I have for Carl. He's the most truly religious person I know. He's completely at peace with himself and the world and he radiates this."[27]

* * *

In 1961, historian Paul I. Wellman published *A Dynasty Of Western Outlaws*, revealing "a long and crooked train of unbroken personal connections" that link the famous outlaw gangs of the Old West to the gangsters of the 1930s such as Pretty Boy Floyd. For a generation of Southern California rockers,

Ritchie Valens served similarly influential in launching a dynasty of West Coast rockers who came of age in the early 60s.

Thanks to the hit film *La Bamba*, Ritchie Valens is today celebrated as the first Latino rock'n'roll star, yet his impact on Southern California music far transcended his ethnicity. While the film portrayed Ritchie as hailing from the usual migrant experience, Ritchie was a pure product of Southern California who grew up in the rougher neighborhoods of Pacoima in Los Angeles County. He initially refused to record 'La Bamba' because he was worried that Mexican-Americans would be offended by his singing traditional folk material with an American accent; and he spoke very little Spanish.[28]

In fact, the portrayal of Ritchie as a migrant worker in the California fruit orchards irked his producer Bob Keane. "Nobody in the Valens family picked fruit," Keane said. "His mother worked in a machine gun factory."[29]

In his short career, Valens laid the template for a decade of Southern California artists to come. He was a songwriter who often brought pieces of song into the studio to be polished and cobbled together into finished numbers. His records employed seminal studio techniques that would later became staples of the recording process and used top-flight session professionals who would frequently appear on Phil Spector, Chris Montez, and Beach Boys recordings, including Carol Kaye and Earl Palmer. His hit records such as 'Oh, Donna,' 'Come On, Let's Go,' and 'La Bamba' were more than mere archiving of a live performance—they were stand-alone pieces of performance art.

With the exception of Chuck Berry and Eddie Cochran, the vast majority of rock stars in the first wave of rock'n'roll were either pianists like Fats Domino or singers like Elvis Presley who essentially accompanied themselves on rhythm guitar. Ritchie was a guitarist. Early on, he replaced his green Harmony Stratotone electric guitar with what was, in 1957, the latest in electric guitar technology: the Fender Stratocaster. Then he began experimenting with instrumental pieces, with songs like an electrified flamenco classic, 'Malaguena,' the bluesy 'From Beyond,' and the proto-surf

'Fast Freight' (where he was billed as Arvee Allens). The success of Ritchie's early Del-Fi singles enabled his producer Bob Keane to take on a young rockabilly singer and—in Keane's own phrase—"avant garde" guitarist named Dick Dale.[30]

Ritchie was to have a direct influence on Carl, thanks to a Hawthorne neighbor named Chris Montez and an Inglewood guitar teacher named John Maus, who would change his name to John Walker when he formed The Walker Brothers.[31]

Known as 'Zeke' for his given name of Ezekiel Christopher Montanez, Hawthorne High alumnus Montez would kick off his career as a singer with his 1962 rocker 'Let's Dance.' Later he joined Herb Alpert's A&M Records stable of jazz- and Latin-influenced artists such as Wes Montgomery, The Tijuana Brass, and Sergio Mendez & Brazil 66. There he had a string of jazzy, understated hits such as 'Call Me' and 'The More I See You.'

When they were classmates, instead of superstars, not only did Montez attend classes with the two older Wilson brothers, he often stopped by the Wilson household for informal jam sessions with Brian and Carl. "They lived about eight blocks from where I lived," Montez said. "I'd go play with them and we'd jam. Brian would be on the organ … and Carl would be on guitar. We'd jam and I remember it was never any 'This is a song I wrote,' we just played what was playing on the radio."

At the time, Chris and Carl were "novices," said Montez. "We did the best we could. We thought we knew something, but we didn't know that much. Basically, if you knew how to strum it and sing a song, you were all right."[32]

Montez provided The Beach Boys' first and most direct link to Valens. A devout Valens fan, he scored his first hit with the Valens-flavored rocker 'Let's Dance,' recorded at Gold Star with Carol Kaye and Leon Russell backing him.

More importantly, Montez had the great fortune to bump into his idol at a local dance before Ritchie's tragic fatal plane crash. The flustered Montez expressed his love for Valens's music to his idol, then added that he, too, was a singer. Valens listened politely and encouraged Montez in his musical pursuit. "I shook his hand and he was really nice to me," said Montez. "I said to myself, 'If I ever get a hit record or become famous like him, I will treat people like he treated me: kind.'"[33]

Yet it would be John Maus, rather than Montez, who introduced Ritchie Valens's guitar techniques to The Beach Boys. Maus was slightly older than Carl and neighbor and fellow guitarist David Marks, and often performed on bills with Valens. "John was like a protégé of Ritchie Valens," said Jon Stebbins.[34]

Maus would soon start using the surname Walker. In 1964, he formed The Walker Brothers with Scott Engel and Gary Leeds, who also changed their names. They achieved considerable local success as the house band at Gazzarri's nightclub in Hollywood, before setting off to London and scoring hits with songs like 'The Sun Ain't Gonna Shine Anymore' and the Burt Bacharach and Hal David classic 'Make It Easy On Yourself.' They would go on to sell more than 23 million records and make three albums and ten singles before breaking up in 1968.[35]

Carl told Geoffrey Himes, "The kid across the street, David Marks, was taking guitar lessons from John Maus, so I started, too. David and I were about 12 and John was only three years older, but we thought he was a shit-hot guitarist. John and his sister Judy did fraternity gigs together as a duo. Later John moved to England and became one of The Walker Brothers. That was really a beautiful time; David and I would go to John's house after school for our lessons. He showed me some fingerpicking techniques and strumming stuff that I still use. When I play a solo, he's still there."[36]

Before he became one of the most important members of The Beach Boys' touring band, and Carl's occasional songwriting and producing partner, Billy Hinsche studied Carl when, as lead guitarist for Dino, Desi & Billy, he found himself on tour with The Beach Boys. Interviewing Carl in 1981, he learned that Carl named Chuck Berry and Maus as his major early influences, "because I was most involved with him as far as playing."

Carl explained, "I took guitar lessons at an accordion studio. There was a guitar teacher there, and I took lessons from him for a couple of months, but it was too boring 'cos I was just reading notes—stuff like 'Yankee Doodle Dandy.'"[37]

When Carl found out Marks was also taking guitar lessons, he was invited to sit in with Maus and Marks, and Maus's influence, through Carl, would extend into Brian's songwriting.[38] "The funny thing was that his house was almost directly across the street from the accordion studio," said Carl. "He had a Stratocaster that I thought was really fantastic, and we used to sit in his room and jam; it was really just casual."[39]

David Marks recalled those early sessions and how Maus also channeled Valens's influence. "John was acquainted with Ritchie Valens, so John taught us how to do that strum which you can do on our ballads like 'Surfer Girl' and 'In My Room,'" said Marks. "He also taught us how to do the Chuck Berry boogie and how to play single string leads—he was a tremendous influence on our playing. He learned from Ritchie Valens how to strum on songs like 'Oh, Donna.' That was a big influence on a lot of our ballads, so we took that strumming technique and applied it. That was a very valuable thing that John was telling us.[40]

"I was ten and Carl was twelve and we had just gotten our guitars and we just met John; he lived down the street on Inglewood Avenue. We were in the right place at the right time to have known John—he was an invaluable part of The Beach Boys. I credit him with introducing the electric guitar to The Beach Boys because they were pretty much going in a Kingston Trio direction with acoustic instruments."[41]

CHAPTER FOUR

Boogie Woodie

Before it described a style of music born from ragtime, stride piano, and blues, the term 'boogie' meant 'rent party,' a method used by poor African-Americans living in tenements to raise money to pay their rent during hard times. For a small entry fee, neighbors gathered at an apartment to spend the evening dancing and singing until the rent was paid; that was soon followed by another neighbor throwing another party.

Because most of the pianos in the homes hosting the boogie were cheap and of poor quality and most of the musicians were unschooled, boogie-woogie music developed as a physically demanding style of music. Its sheer volume was produced by the physical strength of the player, and it drew upon all of the player's improvisational resources to keep the music going through the night. Boogie-woogie reached its peak in the years spanning the Great Depression and the end of World War II.

Boogie-woogie differed from the styles that preceded it in two key respects. Firstly there was the role of the left hand in driving and emphasizing the rhythm, using a repeated figure called an 'ostinato' (making boogie-woogie a 'two voice music' as the right hand played and embroidered the melody). Secondly it incorporated blues techniques and scales into what was a fusion of pre-blues styles.

The challenge Carl, Al, and David Marks all faced was that, unlike the vast majority of bands emerging in the 60s, The Beach Boys built their style on a piano-based boogie-woogie foundation rather than on guitar-based blues. The seminal instrumental (or 'instro') hits of the surf music era, from Dick Dale's 'Let's Go Trippin'' and The Tornadoes' 'Bustin' Surfboards' to The Surfaris' 'Wipe Out,' were all compositions built on 12-bar blues structures, as was one of the acknowledged hits of the pre-surf era, 'Bulldog' by The Fireballs.

The Beach Boys' early surf instrumental efforts, like 'Beach Boys Stomp,' 'Stoked,' and 'Surf Jam,' were essentially 12-bar blues workouts. Even surf music's regional rival in the Los Angeles basin in the early 60s, known as the Eastside Sound after the Hispanic area from which it emerged, relied heavily on blues architecture for hits like The Mixtures' 'Stompin' At The Rainbow.'

As singer Linda Ronstadt discovered in 1993, while recording a version of Jimmy Webb's song 'Adios' with Brian Wilson (for which Brian provided as many as 15 vocal parts), when he needed to clear his head or think through a complicated passage, he would sit down at a piano and play a raucous boogie-woogie song in a different key. Then he would return to the microphone to perform his harmony parts flawlessly. You can hear the style, played as a piano and organ workout, on 1963's 'Boogie Woodie' on the *Surfer Girl* album.[1]

Ronstadt's experience casts light on one of the keys to Brian's music: his mother Audree specialized in boogie-woogie piano playing and imparted her love for the form to her eldest child. "Audree taught boogie-woogie piano," said David Marks, "and we automatically adapted it to guitar." The legacy of Audree's contribution to Brian's songwriting is that Brian adopted the essentials of boogie-woogie, particularly that of the moving left hand coloring the chords on the right by changing the root notes.[2]

During downtime on a 1964 Australian tour with The Surfaris, their saxophonist Jim Pash studied Brian's writing style, noting that the moving left hand enabled Brian to reshape chords into more complex voicings than conventional playing styles, in which the left hand often plays the root note of the chord or simply mirrors the right hand chord. Brian, noted Pash, would form a basic C chord on the right while overlaying different notes on the left, resulting in a series of complex chords.[3]

The difference between guitars and keyboards is the physical layout of the playing area. With pianos, a series of white keys—called the naturals— are interspersed with black keys called flats and sharps, each voicing a single note: to form a chord, notes are depressed with both hands. On a guitar, chords are formed as shapes built from a series of notes fingered at the same time with just the fretting hand.

In the early years, The Beach Boys adapted the songs written by Brian by redistributing the piano notes, with the rhythm guitar playing one rhythmic part and the lead guitar playing a similar part further up the neck, as illustrated in Mike Love's "this is how The Beach Boys go about making a record" introduction to 'Little Deuce Coupe,' seen on the 1964 NBC performance known as the lost concert.

Breaking down a complex song was common among guitar bands. Carl's beloved Ventures arrived at their first hit by taking a solo jazz guitar instrumental (first by Johnny Smith and then by Chet Atkins) and breaking the melody out of the chord to produce 'Walk, Don't Run.'[4] However, this meant that Carl, Al, and David (and additional guitarists in The Beach Boys like Ed Carter, Jeffrey Foskett, and Billy Hinsche) would have to command a far larger vocabulary of chords and chord voicings than most rock'n'roll guitarists while possessing a better understanding of the role each note played in the chord. This type of knowledge was a prerequisite for jazz players—whether big-band maestros like Count Basie Orchestra guitarist Freddie Green or combo guitarists from Charlie Christian to Grant Green—but the first generation of rock guitarists seldom strayed from conventional major and minor chord forms.

Brian's fusion of boogie-woogie and jazz chords produced a style of music that many guitarists found daunting. As Stefano Belli wrote, "That Wilson employed novel approaches in composition is evident from his use of unconventional instrumentation and compositional methods, which make heavy use of bizarre and idiosyncratic harmonic progressions."[5]

Carl can be regarded as one of the pioneers of the first school of guitar playing created for and by single-note soloing, and utilizing volume, distortion, and outboard effects. But performing the songs Brian wrote forced Carl to forsake the benefits of the surf guitar revolution and instead adopt the approach of the earlier big-band jazz guitarists.

Few people knew Carl's musicianship more intimately than Stephen Desper, who worked with The Beach Boys as their primary recording and sound engineer during the critical years after *Pet Sounds*. Fewer still had Desper's wide range of exposure to the greatest guitarists of the era, such as Frank Zappa and Jimi Hendrix. (Desper commanded the live sound console at the Monterey Pop Festival, only yards away from where The Jimi Hendrix Experience ended their American debut with Jimi torching his Stratocaster onstage.)

Carl, wrote Desper, "could play the instrument in the dark—which means he did not rely on looking at the frets to place his fingers. He could transpose on sight. He could change keys at will. In Carl's hands the guitar was not a technical device to be harnessed or overcome to get music out of. Rather the guitar was a gateway to the music.

"Carl was unchallenged by any guitar, bringing the best out of any instrument he might pick up and play. Carl must have owned around 100 various guitars—solid body, six-string acoustic, 12-string acoustic—some for recording only and some for the road.

"I never saw Carl manhandle any guitar, always returning it to its case after playing. If the roadie was busy, he would clean his own instrument after a show. If a string broke on stage, he could improvise around the missing string. His ability to tune the guitar superseded any electronic tuner and took into account the human element of emotion that a mechanical tool lacks.

"Although you never saw Carl do it, he could also 'trick' play the guitar: behind his back, upside down, and with one hand. He could also play the guitar with a violin bow for special effects. He was also good at playing the [pedal steel] guitar, but for recording usually used a professional."[6]

Yet, while Carl may have sacrificed his reputation as one of the pioneer guitarists of the 60s to the complexity of Brian's songwriting, his approach did yield occasional humorous results. When guitarist Jeffrey Foskett first joined the touring Beach Boys, he sought to impress his hero Carl with his intimate knowledge of the block chords, intervals, and rhythm figures used by Carl in the early days of the band. Carl stopped him. "You have six strings," he said. "I suggest you use them all."[7]

* * *

As Carl and David mastered the chords and figures they learned from John Maus, folk music had overtaken rock'n'roll as the music of choice for young people, with groups like The Kingston Trio and The New Christy Minstrels scoring hits. The folk boom hit the entertainment world so quickly that when The Kingston Trio won a Grammy Award, in 1958, it was in the country & western category; as yet there was no category for 'folk.' Yet folk music's attraction was the lyrics, which were generally sung over simple chord changes on acoustic instruments, accompanied by additional acoustic instruments such as banjos, mandolins or string basses. Hardcore folkies disdained electric guitars and the disposable teenage music it accompanied.

Dick Dale, meanwhile, had already recorded some rockabilly singles for Bob Keane's Del-Fi label when tensions rose between Keane and Dale's father, James Monsour. So Dale rode his motorcycle down to his favorite surfing spot, the Wedge on Newport Beach's Balboa Peninsula.[8] One evening he encountered a young folk singer named Nick O'Malley, performing folk classics on a Fender Jazzmaster guitar in a small beatnik club called The Prison Of Socrates. In rapid succession, they formed a band, now called Dick Dale & His Del Tones, and began merging folk, rockabilly, and rhythm & blues into a new guitar-driven hybrid. Their base was a dance club, across the street from the Prison Of Socrates, called the Rinky Dink Ice Cream Parlor & Nightclub.[9]

This quiet corner would give birth to a new type of folk music: surf music. It was with this instrumental music that The Beach Boys would always be compared with as they were forging their own very different sound. It was the source of considerable animosity against them from within and without the surfing world. "We were sitting there in the Rinky Dink Ice Cream Parlor and we were playing in the summer time," recalled O'Malley. "And what kind of audience did we have? We had surfers."[10]

Surf music began as a basic guitar-based dance music that required little more than one or two amplifiers and a drum kit. One of the earliest and most important bands, The Bel Airs, didn't even have a bass player. With the basics of guitars, amps, and drums in tow, surfers going to impromptu dances or surf film showings now had a music that was easier to set up and perform than any previous style.

The myth that one had to surf to perform this music only grew after The Beach Boys attained massive success. When the original generation of light board surfers found themselves crowded out of their favorite surfing spot by amateurs, they immediately blamed songs that exhorted "let's go surfing now" and condemned The Beach Boys—only two of whom actually surfed—as false prophets.

In June of 1961, Dale signed a lease and pulled permits to perform in the Rendezvous Ballroom. Built on the ocean front a few steps west of the Prison Of Socrates, the two-story building featured a mezzanine and balcony with a dance floor spacious enough to accommodate about 3,000 people. When Dale, his band, and his father opened the club, he performed to a crowd of 17 surfers. But soon they had their own dance: the surfer stomp.[11]

A year later, two members of the Santa Ana-based band The Paramours, Bill Medley and Bobby Hatfield, changed their name to The Righteous Brothers. Using many of the same musicians who performed surf music at the beachfront ballroom, they debuted their first single, 'Little Latin Lupe Lu,' at the Rendezvous. It gave the ballroom the double distinction of being the home of surf music and of blue-eyed soul. The rhythm & blues rave-up immediately resonated with the surf crowd "because kids could do the surfer stomp to it," Medley said.[12]

Before the opening of the Rendezvous, surfing had spawned a lifestyle and a fashion trend, thanks to *Gidget* and a cottage industry of filmmaking. Filmmakers such as Bud Browne and Bruce Brown would show surf films such as *Going My Wave* and *Barefooted Venture* in local auditoriums, theaters, and even churches, using local rock'n'roll bands to provide live instrumental backing. Originally, said The Bel Airs' drummer and producer, Richard Delvy, "surf music was for dancing and to be played behind a surf movie."[13]

In the six months between Dale's first set and his moving off to larger venues, Dale's association with Leo Fender yielded the first 'stack' or modular amplifier, with the Fender Showman.[14] The Showman paved the way for guitars that could generate greater output and greater distortion. Greater distortion led to sustain and for guitarists, sustain is the Holy Grail. Sustain elevates the guitar out of the percussion category by allowing it to play long, sustained notes like violins, reeds, or brass instruments. And the search for sustain led to the Fender Reverb unit.

Fender had been experimenting with adapting the Hammond organ's reverberation system to accommodate a human voice when Dale "plugged my Stratocaster into the reverb and played some of my instrumentals. It was the icing on the cake. Only then did my Fender Reverb sound become associated with surf music."[15]

As the amplifiers grew more powerful, guitarists found that kicking the sturdy reverb unit also produced a long, low crashing sound like a wave. Together, they enabled Dale and other guitarists to attain Dale's dream of reproducing the experience of surfing, with what Dale called "the 'boom' of the barrel and the hiss of the lace."[16]

For the first time in the history of music, the lead guitar was king. In the space of a few months, Dale and Fender transformed the guitar to the point where it would eventually become the most popular musical instrument on the planet. In doing so, Dale laid the groundwork for subsequent guitar forms to follow, such as heavy metal, and spawned an army of lead guitar-driven rock'n'roll bands. The lead guitar finally had a voice—they called it surf guitar.[17]

Unfortunately, contemporary recordings were unable to contain the volcanic impact of Dale's performances with records like 'Let's Go Trippin',' 'Miserlou,' and 'Hava Nagila.' His influence remained primarily on guitarists and didn't extend far beyond Southern California. But in

Hawthorne, just an hour's drive away, Carl Wilson listened and learned. His ability to master surf guitar and its complicated signature technique (called wrist tremolo or 'double picking') enabled the vocal band he was forming with his brother, cousin and neighbor to enter into this new world of rock'n'roll called 'surf music.'

Carl's ability to supply what was essentially a doo-wop group with the requisite driving instrumentals put The Beach Boys on the ground floor of an emerging musical craze, rather than the dying folk or white doo-wop genres. In due course, the band's innovative harmonies, Brian's complex chords and melodies, and Mike Love's Chuck Berry-influenced lyrics would supplant the surf guitar's role as the sound of surf, at least as it was seen by the world beyond Southern California.

As 1961 wound to a close, on the heels of a homemade record written by his older brother Brian and cousin Mike at the behest of brother Dennis, Carl Wilson and his father visited a Hawthorne music store and brought back a Fender Stratocaster and a Fender Showman amplifier. They were just in time to ride a wave of new music to untold success.

CHAPTER FIVE

Carl's Big Chance

For John Lennon and Paul McCartney, the historic moment began with an introduction at a church fete. For Jagger and Richards, it was a chance meeting at a railway station. For Stills and Young, their careers began with an encounter in the midst of a Hollywood traffic jam followed by a low-speed car chase.[1] Yet for The Beach Boys, stardom began with scattered seeds rather than a decisive moment. As Carl recalled in 1983, "Brian had been fooling around at the piano for years, picking apart those Four Freshmen songs and putting them back together again. He would make me, my mom, and Mike sing the harmonies he had figured out. He'd make us do that for hours. Then one day he got it in his imagination that he could do simpler, more direct music: rock'n'roll. He thought he could put together a band and make music like we heard on the radio."[2]

What makes The Beach Boys unusual in the history of pop music is that they started out as a singing group who later learned their instruments. And it is in this respect that their surf music origins are significant.

The entry requirements for surf bands were not high. The Surfaris, who recorded 'Wipe Out,' began as four high school age boys who formed a band with a backline consisting of a drum kit and one Fender Bandmaster amplifier. Because the Bandmaster had four inputs, they were able to plug two guitars and an electric bass into it and learn a smattering of instrumentals, mostly culled from The Ventures and Dick Dale's *Surfer's Choice* albums. For school dances, back yard barbeques, and showings of surf films in 1961, surf music delivered the most music for the least investment and any guitar players with a rudimentary knowledge of basic chords could easily master the instrumental hits of the day.[3]

History proved to be kind to The Beach Boys. Surf music along the Orange Coast, where Dick Dale ruled, and the South Bay, where The Bel Airs led the charge, was still a developing regional phenomenon. Bands like The Tornadoes and The Chantays came to the Rendezvous or the Bel Air (later the Revilleaire) in Redondo Beach and carried the idiom inland, where the relative availability and affordability of Fender instruments, compared with their more established counterparts like Gibson, Gretsch, or Guild, meant that kids with generous parents, paper routes, or lawn mowing jobs could purchase and learn a fine instrument in far less time than before.

In the summer of 1961, Al Jardine, an accomplished folk singer, standup bassist, and guitarist musician around Hawthorne, persuaded his friend Brian Wilson to start a singing group. Brian suggested he include his brother Carl and his cousin Mike Love. In late August, Al took the fledgling group, with Dennis Wilson in attendance, into the studios of Hite and Dorinda Morgan, owners of Guild Music, Murry Wilson's music publisher.

Dorinda Morgan liked the harmony-vocal sound but expressed regret that the boys had not come up with anything original. Dennis told her that surfing was the new craze and that Brian had written a song about it (it had begun as a school music exercise). The would-be group went home to set about completing and rehearsing it.

Over Labor Day weekend, at the start of September, Murry and Audree left for a trip to Mexico City. The group rushed down to a music store on Hawthorne Avenue and spent their food money on renting instruments, including a standup bass for Al. They also got a generous contribution from Al's mother, performing an impromptu a capella 'Their Hearts Were Full Of Spring' (made famous by The Four Freshmen) for her to close the deal.[4]

When Murry and Audree returned home, Murry barely contained his fury at what the boys had done—until they played him their song, 'Surfin'.' In an October 1971 article in *Rolling Stone* magazine, Murry recalled what happened next, in his own inimitable style.

"Dennis made them write it. He told them, 'Write a song about surfing.' He bugged them. He was an avid surfer. He'd disappear every Saturday and

Sunday he could, without cutting the lawn—you might put that in, too—without cutting the lawn. He loved the sport."

Encouraged by Murry, the future Beach Boys set off to record some demos for the Morgans. One of them was 'Surfin'.' In their original configuration, Carl played guitar, Al played bass, and Brian played a snare drum with a pencil—covering it with his shirt to mute the volume. Lead singer Mike stood at one microphone while the rest of the band clustered around a second.[5]

"We sounded so shitty at first," Carl later lamented. "We were so shaky and lame. After all, I was just 14 and a sophomore in high school."[6]

According to Murry, "They kept saying to Mr. Morgan, Hite Morgan, my publisher, 'We've written a song about the surfing sport and we'd like to sing it for you.' Finally he agreed to hear it and Mrs. Morgan said, 'Drop everything, we're going to record your song. I think it's good.' And she's the one responsible."

Murry quickly cut a deal with a small independent label called Candix Records, whose owners neglected to inform him that they were teetering on the verge of bankruptcy. While the band originally hoped to call themselves The Pendletones (in honor of both the Pendelton shirts favored by surfers and The Del Tones), they unpacked the first shipment of their records to find that one of the label's executives had renamed them Beach Boys—omitting 'The.' At one point they nearly became The Surfers.[7]

"It came out on the Candix label," said Murry, "and it was played on three stations in LA every hour, 24 hours a day. Sam Riddle introduced it on KDAY, and Russ Reagan—a well-known producer and record figure, who was then handling Candix and who gave them the name Beach Boys—got it on KFWB and KRLA. And it went to 76 on the Top 100 chart."[8]

In the 60s, Los Angeles boasted dozens of small independent labels like Candix, Downey, and Del-Fi, and getting a song recorded and pressed was a far simpler affair than it would be in the post-Beatle era. In the early 60s, airplay was the issue; disc jockeys wielded enormous power to make or break a band, but enterprising musicians could always find ways onto the charts.

In the 60s, each radio station compiled its own list of current hits drawn from polling local record stores and from the number of calls requesting the songs through the switchboards. Bands often mobilized armies of friends and neighbors to pepper the stations with phone calls and left stacks of records at local record shops, then sent friends in to buy the entire stock. The record store then reported to the radio stations about a new record that sold out in a matter of hours or days, and a hit was born.

In an effort to circumvent pressing plants that were reportedly owed money by Candix, a second pressing on the X Records label followed in December. Then more Candix pressings followed, keeping record collectors occupied for the next five decades.[9]

Essentially a doo-wop tune, the only connection between the song 'Surfin'' and surfing itself was the lyrics; Carl's Kay guitar is barely audible. They weren't the first to celebrate the brave new world of California beaches in a doo-wop tune; the San Bernardino-based The Pentagons (who once boasted singer Al Wilson of 'Show And Tell' fame as a member) released 'Down At The Beach' in April of 1961.[10] Yet the band found themselves called The Beach Boys, and with the surfer stomp the latest dance craze in Southern California, and with airplay already bubbling up on local Los Angeles stations, there was no place for them to go except surfin'.

* * *

As 'Surfin'' began its ascent of the local and then national charts, the band now faced a problem that would confront Crosby, Stills & Nash in 1969, when they produced their first album—they had a hit record they could sing, but they couldn't play.

To make matters worse, of all of the friends and family mobilized to call radio stations to request 'Surfin',' one missed out on the excitement. Carl's long-time jamming partner, David Marks, felt left out, especially since he had been part of the Wilsons' musical circle since the beginning. Carl and Dennis had 'adopted' David as a friend and, in Dennis's case, a partner in petty crime. More importantly, David idolized Brian and often stood by the window spying as Brian carefully deconstructed chords and Four Freshman harmonies on the piano.

Transforming a doo-wop group into a surf band posed the first problem for The Beach Boys. In the beginning, the band comprised only a piano player, a rhythm guitarist, and a string bassist (Dennis was still considered only a vocalist). This was hardly the foundation for a group who would be a surf band, whether they liked it or not.

Audree solved one of the first problems by insisting that Dennis be included as a drummer, apparently despite Brian's objections. Mike then acquired a saxophone, a staple of the early surf bands, who included a generous helping of rhythm & blues songs like 'Tequila' and 'Night Train' in their set lists.[11] Brian moved Al, who was already an accomplished folk guitarist, on to rhythm guitar. He took over on bass, acquiring a Fender electric instrument and mastering it quickly.

The final piece of the puzzle fell into place when Carl replaced his Kay guitar with a three-color sunburst Fender Stratocaster with a rosewood fretboard. When Fender first introduced the Stratocaster it featured a maple fretboard with a thicker neck. By the late 50s, the Stratocaster came equipped with a slimmer neck, which made it far easier for younger guitar players to master.

More importantly, the Stratocaster and the designs that it inspired, such as the 'tilt-waist' Fender Jazzmaster and Jaguar models, offered features that easily accommodated the emerging surf sound. Rather than a 'set' or glued-in neck, Stratocaster necks were bolted on to the body, which many players felt added sufficient tension for the lower strings to roar rather than twang. The single-coil pickups produced searing razor-sharp highs, whereas humbucker pickups offered a warmer, mellower higher register. These designs helped surf guitarists like Dick Dale create the sounds that allowed guitarists to capture the power and intensity of a breaking wave.

In the wake of recording 'Surfin',' the newly named Beach Boys comprised only two accomplished musicians—Carl and Al—and three others learning their instruments. Now they set out to become a band. Rehearsals began at the Wilson home, and as soon as the band had mastered some of the rudimentary surf tunes of the time, such as 'Let's Go Trippin'' and 'Mr Moto,' Murry wangled an intermission performance at the Rendezvous Ballroom in Balboa immediately after the single's release.[12]

For The Beach Boys and the few who remember their maiden performance, on Saturday, December 23, 1961, it was by all accounts a brief and dismal affair. The band was horribly nervous. "The only boys who weren't were Mike and Alan—and probably Carl, because Carl is basically a musician," recalled Dorinda Morgan. "He gets so involved in his music that he forgets about the crowd."[13]

The headliner, Del Tones guitarist Nick O'Malley, witnessed what he remembered as awkward newcomers dressed in white pants and short-sleeved dress shirts.[14] Some recall the show lasting as little as 15 minutes and containing only 'Surfin'' and the single's B-side, 'Luau' (written by Bruce Morgan, son of Dorinda and Hite Morgan). Dorinda Morgan recalled Brian feeling "humiliated" by the audience's lack of interest.[15] In retrospect, some claimed The Beach Boys were rejected by the surfing audience and scorned as the "Hollywood version" by light-board surfers.

'Surfin'' and 'Luau' were both primarily mid-tempo vocal songs, and 'Luau' sounded suspiciously like advertising agency travelogue lyrics superimposed over The Coasters' 'Poison Ivy.' ("Let's do 'Luau'" became a running joke during informal jam sessions.)[16] The two songs stood at odds with the fast, loud, aggressive guitar styles audiences had come to expect at the Rendezvous, which by that point had hosted probably all of the major surf guitarists of the era, such as Norman Sanders, Jim Masoner, Dave Myers, and others. Standing onstage with three-fifths of the band still learning their instruments, one might say that with that first performance The Beach Boys brought a switchblade to a gunfight.

For Beach Boys fans and historians, that first performance is an odd curio. For decades afterward, The Beach Boys exiled the memory of it to what politicians call the 'memory hole' and claimed their actual debut occurred a week later, on New Year's Eve at the Long Beach Municipal

Auditorium. The occasion was a Ritchie Valens Memorial benefit headlined by Ike & Tina Turner, Gene McDaniels, Frankie Avalon, and others.

With 'Surfin'' just beginning its ascent up the charts, The Beach Boys turned their attention to becoming a performing band—and within weeks faced their first major hurdle.

"After 'Surfin'' the boys were off the air and they couldn't get back on the air," Murry told Tom Nolan. "No one wanted them; they thought they were a one-shot record. Al Jardine hit the road and enrolled in dental school. Mr Morgan [who produced 'Surfin''] and I went to Dot Records and cooled our heels in the foyer. Nobody would talk to us. We went to Liberty, and the big shots were too busy to see us. And finally I asked Mr Morgan, 'What'll we do?'

"He says, 'I don't know, Murry, you're their dad and manager, lots of luck to you.' And he says goodbye. And that cost him $2,700,000, that statement. It cost him $2,700,000."[17]

* * *

For decades, Al Jardine seemed a reluctant warrior: the only non-family member in the band, an outsider who ended up with the flu during the photo shoot for *Summer Days (And Summer Nights!!)* and who groused about the burdens borne by musicians when the other band members discussed the music and their fans.[18] In later years, when Carl and Mike generally agreed upon start times and set lists, many Beach Boys touring band members recall it was Al who would demand changes in the set lists to reduce the number of lead vocals he had to sing.[19] Yet Al's role in the band's formative months proved crucial. At first, he was the most accomplished musician in the band. He was the band's first bassist and he would go on to play bass on many Beach Boys hits that were later credited to Brian or members of the Wrecking Crew.[20] As a vocalist, Al sang lead on The Beach Boys' second number one single, 'Help Me, Rhonda,' and often substituted for an absent Brian on vocals and bass. But besides being outside the family, Al viewed himself as a musical outsider as well.

While Al and Brian shared a love of folk harmony bands like The Kingston Trio, Brian was at heart a jazz composer. Mike, Carl, and Dennis, meanwhile, shared a common passion for Chuck Berry and the raucous rhythm & blues records issuing from their transistor radios. A dyed-in-the-wool folkie, Al later admitted, "I'm one of those three chord guys. I like music that has nice melodies and tell good stories."[21]

Songwriter Harlan Howard, who penned such classics as Patsy Cline's 'I Fall To Pieces' and Ray Charles's 'Busted,' famously described country music, which evolved from folk, as "three chords and the truth." The truth was in the lyrics. Al would later admit that he had come late to appreciating the complexity of Brian Wilson's music because of his background in folk music's three chords, simple melody, and focus on lyrics. "I didn't appreciate the musical substance," he said. "I was more involved with the lyrics."[22]

After the band's fourth performance, at the Mesa Presbyterian Church in Hawthorne on January 25, and a recording session on February 8, Al Jardine quit The Beach Boys. The usual story is that Al left the band when he felt that The Beach Boys were on the path to being one-hit wonders, and when the rehearsals and benefit gigs were producing no income yet still detracting from his studies. When he turned in his notice, the single 'Surfin" was still making its steady ascent up the local KFWB Fabulous Forty Survey, where it would reach a peak of number four. Meanwhile, 'Surfin" had received its first mention in *Billboard* magazine, where it charted at number 118 in the second week of January and peaked at number 75 in the week ending March 24. Likewise, *Cashbox* magazine called it the 'Hit Pick of the Week' for the week of January 27, and it would peak at number 85 in March.

Jardine's departure from The Beach Boys occurred at a crucial juncture in the band's career. For the first six weeks of their existence, The Beach Boys had performed only at a handful of venues—mostly local benefit shows at churches or local recreation centers—and were ready to start moving on to paying gigs. More importantly, while surf music dominated the music scene along the coastline, the style had just begun breaching the inland cities beyond the beach towns and—like it or not—The Beach Boys were riding the crest of the wave.

On February 16, 1962, The Beach Boys commenced a two-night stand at the Rainbow Gardens nightclub, located at 150 East Monterey Avenue in Pomona, one of the centers of the Latin-flavored rhythm & blues known in Los Angeles as the 'Eastside sound,' which dominated the music scene in the eastern portion of Los Angeles County. Like the Rendezvous, the Rainbow Gardens began as a popular nightclub featuring some of the biggest names of the big-band era in the 1940s before transitioning to rock'n'roll in the 50s. Musician and historian Mark Guerrero called it one of the "quintessential and classic places for Latin music, rhythm & blues, and Chicano eastside sound bands."[23]

As 1962 dawned, "surf music was coming in," said Dr Leroy 'Zag' Soto, then bassist with one of the most popular Eastside bands, The Mixtures.[24] At the Rainbow Gardens, The Beach Boys served as the 'break band' for The Mixtures, so named because they were a racially mixed band—a rarity at the time. According to Jon Stebbins, the band's performance (for which they were paid $150) didn't exactly resonate with the primarily Latino fans of The Mixtures.[25]

"Segregation was a big thing at that time," said Soto, who had begun performing in predominantly African-American high schools with a teenaged drum prodigy named Bernard 'Pretty' Purdie. Soto recalled that at this point, The Beach Boys had abandoned the dress shirts and adopted the Pendleton shirts and black slacks uniform they favored in the first part of their career. Yet The Beach Boys continued to share bills with The Mixtures at the Rainbow Gardens and 'Pop' Leuder's Park in Compton, a largely African-American community near Hawthorne. "They weren't well received—racism was big time at that time," Soto added. "Whites didn't go into black neighborhoods."

Reduced to a quartet, The Beach Boys were performing before racially mixed audiences, opening for a racially mixed band, at a time when mixing races at an entertainment venue could lead to violence. Soto remembered

The Mixtures "would play El Monte Legion Stadium and the fights would break out with knives. People would shout 'play louder!'"[26]

The two bands didn't socialize after the gigs, probably because, as The Surfaris' Jim Pash pointed out, leader Brian spent every available minute rehearsing the band's harmonies backstage, while Murry watched over the band hawk-like and ensured the drinking, carousing, and skirt-chasing were left to bands without stern parental oversight.[27]

Yet what impressed Soto and his bandmates was The Beach Boys' harmonies. "They were great; they were one of the first bands where harmonies were great," Soto said. "There was not a lot of that with rhythm & blues bands, who specialized in the raucous high energy sounds of artists such as Screamin' Jay Hawkins."

As a bassist, Soto also paid close attention to Brian's bass playing. "It was surfer music, but I liked some of the stuff he had."[28]

Times were changing and The Beach Boys were on the cutting edge of that change. The success of 'Surfin'' ensured that The Beach Boys would go on to bigger and better gigs, which proved problematic for The Mixtures when their manager suggested they learn to play surf music, telling them "surf music was just moving up—he would like for us to play a little whiter."[29]

Al's departure happened at the right time, or so it seemed at first. Shackled to surf music by dint of their name and the theme of their hit record, The Beach Boys now had the opportunity to become an actual surf band. At one point, the band was reported to have invited Paul Johnson, guitarist with the Bel Airs and composer of 'Mr Moto,' to join the band, but Johnson declined, as Jim Pash later explained, because he "wanted to play surf music."[30]

The pressure was on. 'Surfin'' continued its climb up the national charts and surf music—real, lead-guitar-driven surf music—broke its coastal bonds and raged down the Santa Ana Canyon and eastward from Redondo Beach. More and more bands picked up Stratocasters, tube reverbs, and big Fender amps and produced music in which the most singing involved was to exhort the audience to shout "Let's go trippin'."

It was at Carl's behest that the three Wilson brothers solved their problem by taking a short walk across the street and inviting David Marks to fill Al's spot.[31] The move proved critical. Brian no longer had an ally in pursuing folk harmonies, and Carl's long-time jamming partner now anchored the rhythm guitar spot. Marks—a devout rock'n'roller with roots in blues and jazz—brought a new energy into the band and a stronger command of the techniques of rock'n'roll and surf. While the 13-year-old Marks adequately covered Jardine's harmony vocal style, his biggest contribution was to unleash the rock'n'roller in Carl. The guitars now held their ground against the singing voices at the exact moment in history when the lead guitar was becoming the voice of rock'n'roll.

CHAPTER SIX

Let's Go Surfin' Now

When David Marks replaced Al Jardine in early 1962, it finally put The Beach Boys on course to be considered a legitimate guitar-driven surf band; only for them ultimately to redefine the idiom from a guitar style to a vocal style. More importantly, it marked the point at which Carl—now 15 and still in high school—began sharing the spotlight and the pressures of leadership with Brian and Mike.

With Marks on board, The Beach Boys found themselves playing at some early surf film showings, including one of Bruce Brown's *Surf Crazy*.[1] Immersed in the South Bay culture of film shows and surfer stomps, Marks was ready to be a part of the revolution.

Where the guitar in folk music supported vocals, the rhythm guitar in surf music supported the rhythm section: drums and bass. For that reason, electric guitarists explored the percussive and percussion elements offered by the combination of guitar, amp, and outboard reverb. Most guitarists in surf music used the heavy or medium weight flatwound guitar strings favored by Dick Dale. Preferred by jazz guitarists for their durability and ability to hold a tuning for long stretches of performing, flatwound strings are created when a flat ribbon of wire is wound around a metal core to create a smooth surface. Many surf guitarists including Dale often replaced the third string with a lighter unwound string to facilitate the bends and slurs favored by Chuck Berry-influenced guitarists. Yet Carl and David stuck with the heavier wound third string in order to attain what Marks called "a thuddy, dead sound to get a more percussive sound. We hardly ever changed them."[2]

The band incorporated more instrumentals into their set list, which now included two Dick Dale tunes and a smattering of rhythm & blues hits like The Coasters' 'Riot In Cell Block Nine' and Ray Charles's 'What'd I Say,' which became Carl's signature vocal rave-up. "Carl would sing 'What'd I Say' and we'd just jam on it," said Marks.

Now the band ventured into a far wider range of performing opportunities. "We played with a bunch of crazy people," said Marks. "There was this band called The Pyramids, they shaved their heads; The Crossfires, who later became The Turtles; and Dick Dale. We played the Aragon Ballroom at Pacific Ocean Park, and shared the bill with Preston Epps at Pandora's Box."[3] It was there that Brian met a 15-year-old aspiring singer named Marilyn Rovell, whom he would marry.

For all of the odium heaped on Murry Wilson for the way he drove the band in the early years of their career, one has to consider that for their first few months, The Beach Boys generated little enthusiasm—and often outright derision. In the spring of 1962 they returned to play Hawthorne High School, alma mater of Brian, Al, and Dennis, and where Carl was still a pupil. It was not a happy homecoming: many students objected, and others took up a collection to hire a more capable band.[4]

Nonetheless, the band that, for the first few months, could barely master the reasonably forgiving 'Mr Moto' by The Bel Airs had slugged away and turned themselves into an actual surf band capable of performing even daunting instrumentals such as 'Miserlou,' which soon became a staple of their set list and featured on the *Surfin' USA* album. In fact, after Dick Dale became a Capitol artist in 1963, the company rushed to put out a compilation of surf tunes by Capitol artists and mistakenly used Carl's version of 'Miserlou' rather than the master's.[5]

'Miserlou' often proved to be the make-or-break point for novice guitarists. Dale recorded the song after one of the surfers in his audience challenged him to play an entire song on a single string. Drawing on his Lebanese background—the song is a traditional Middle Eastern piece— and borrowing a picking technique used on the oud, Dale's 'Miserlou' was one of the most demanding of the popular surf tunes. It required the player to double-pick the entire song while keeping the beats and the meter correct. It was also played on single strings from open E (both high and low) all the way up past the octave, rather than laterally across the fretboard, which reduces pressure on the arm. In the 60s, Carl's version would outsell all others.[6]

In 1962, relentless gigging and rehearsing transformed The Beach Boys from a barely adequate rock'n'roll band to a band promoters hired. Unlike many pop acts of the day, The Beach Boys were a totally self-contained band and were able both to perform their own music and to back up acts like vocal duo Dick & Dee Dee. At one show they backed Sam Cooke and Lou Rawls—a terrifying experience for a new band of white, suburban high school kids.[7]

"They were the kings and we didn't know what the hell we were doing," Marks said. "We just got up and played our covers and our little surf tunes." Marks remembered that Cooke and Rawls, who were accustomed to working with some of the finest musicians in the nation, were taken aback when they found their backing band consisted of "these little white kids."

Marks said that the invitations to back other artists on the bills were flattering at first, but gradually the band realized they were "being used." However, gigging up and down the coast and throughout Los Angeles and neighboring counties forged The Beach Boys into a band willing to take on all comers. Once, after finishing a set in Newport Beach to a nearly empty auditorium, they asked where the crowds were. They were told most of the kids in town were attending a concert by a rival surf band—a local Orange County outfit called The Centurions—just a few miles away.

Emboldened, The Beach Boys showed up to check out the competition and found the stage empty as their rivals took a break in the parking lot. The Beach Boys clambered onstage and hijacked their rivals' instruments. Hearing 'Johnny B. Goode' issuing from the open doors of the club, the band rushed in to reclaim their instruments. The charge was led by a particularly offended and lubricated member of the road crew. The Beach Boys surrendered the instruments, but the roadie chased Mike Love into the parking lot hurling curses and threats until Mike—a high school track star—outran him.[8]

Unfortunately, as the tale circulated, the fight grew grander and more violent with each retelling. Soon The Centurions had acquired a reputation as the band that beat up The Beach Boys. It was to cost them dearly. Nobody wanted to play with a band who had attacked another band onstage.[9]

* * *

As The Beach Boys' command of live performance grew with each gig and 'Surfin'' still clung to the pop charts, Brian brought them into the studio for a new round of songs. On February 8, 1962, the band recorded seminal versions of 'Surfin' Safari," Surfer Girl,' and a Carl Wilson-penned guitar instrumental known as both 'Beach Boys Stomp' and 'Karate,' due to an unfortunate and ill-timed 'Tequila'-like shout midway through the song and at the end. 'Beach Boys Stomp' echoes many of Carl's influences at the time: Duane Eddy, The Ventures, Bill Doggett's 'Honky Tonk,' and even a phrase of muted notes recalling Ritchie Valens's 'Fast Freight.'

Another session at Western Recorders, with Chuck Britz helming the console, yielded a second version of 'Surfin' Safari,' along with the Brian Wilson/Gary Usher ballad 'The Lonely Sea' and '409,' the first of many Beach Boys 'car songs.'[10] Britz recalled, "Carl was pretty young and very naïve. He played excellent guitar." The band edited in a sound effect recorded on David Marks's tape recorder for '409.' It involved Usher revving up his motor in the Wilson driveway late enough to wake the neighborhood—and Murry.

With Candix out of business, Brian and Murry hit the bricks again. With a hit record under their belt, they took demos of new Beach Boys songs, including 'Surfin' Safari' and '409' (a Chevrolet Impala with a 409 cubic inch engine, one of the most powerful cars in production in 1962) to Capitol Records. Capitol was one of the biggest of the Hollywood recording companies and boasted Frank Sinatra, Nat 'King' Cole, and The Kingston Trio. They played the demos for Capitol producer Nick Venet.

"Nick acted real cool," Murry recounted later. "He says, 'You come back in an hour and we'll let you know if we want you to be Capitol recording artists.' He didn't act like he was too excited.

"So we walked out of there, and I said, 'Brian, let's make them wait five minutes, you know, let's don't act too eager.' This is the truth. And we got back in an hour and five minutes. In the meantime—we found out later—Nick Venet rushed across the tower on the 12th floor, raced across the offices, burst in on Gilmore and says, 'Boss, I've got a double-sided smash for Capitol.' And he was right."[11]

"The day the record came out it was a hit," Venet recalled. "The record just broke all kinds of sales records in New York City and everything for [Capitol] that year. The Beach Boys became very important."[12]

More importantly, as the surf music craze cooled in late 1963 due to oversaturation (even Bo Diddley, Freddie King, and Henri Mancini recorded 'surf' albums), songs about cars took over as the way to celebrate teen life. As the band's chief lyricist, Mike Love recognized early on that everybody didn't have an ocean, but everybody drove a car. With '409,' once again The Beach Boys put themselves on the cutting edge of a musical craze. While most of the 'car songs' were simply rock'n'roll songs with lyrics about racing and, in some cases, simple inventories of desirable speed technologies (such as the later 'Custom Machine'), they actually extended the life of the surf music era. Non-surf guitarists availed themselves of the Fender Reverb and moved to lighter gauge guitar strings bringing out the twang associated with rockabilly and later country music. As more bands found they could successfully market themselves as 'surf bands' by cranking up their reverb units, and Hollywood began exploiting the surf scene, the original coastal surf communities turned their backs on surf music. It would be 'car songs' that extended the idiom's life just long enough to keep The Beach Boys and their growing retinue of friends on the charts for the critical year ahead.

Had they started a year earlier, without the surf cachet, The Beach Boys would have been viewed as either a folk harmony group or part of a brief renaissance of white doo-wop, previously the province of bands like Randy & The Rainbows ('Denise') and The Reflections ('Just Like Romeo And Juliet'). Both these idioms would be swept away by either the surf music revolution or Beatlemania. With the possible exception of The Four Seasons, who had been performing under various names since the early 50s and had an average age of 29 when they first charted with 'Sherry' in 1962, there was no-one at the center of the pop music marketplace. Only surf hovered on the horizon as a possible 'next big thing.'

Had they begun a year later, their survival would not have been assured. The level of musicianship in surf bands had risen considerably in the brief period following Dale's tenure at the Rendezvous. Even in the latter half of 1961, surf bands were few and far between. Yet by 1962, with the introduction of the Fender Showman and Reverb units and the introduction in 1962 of the Fender Jaguar, a new style of lead-guitar-based music spawned a new school of lead guitarists. Surf bands popped up everywhere, from bands like Glendora's The Surfaris to experienced rock'n'roll bands like The Cascades or the Inland Empire's The Tornadoes (which at one point featured two lead guitarists: Norman 'Roly' Sanders and future guitar designer Wayne Charvel)[13] who quickly adopted or wrote guitar instrumentals.[14] Even a young guitar prodigy like Larry Carlton cut his teeth playing on sessions by a surf band called The Challengers.

Yet in that first year between their opening performance in 1961 and the dawn of 1963, when Brian began fashioning the record that would become 'Surfin' USA,' The Beach Boys began as a raw group of barely competent musicians and emerged as seasoned professionals. They were just in time to become a phenomenon—an actual surf band capable of performing even the most daunting of the surf instrumentals while singing the harmonies on Brian's increasingly sophisticated songs.

Now a fully self-sustaining band, capable of backing up major rock artists and with a hit record under their belt, The Beach Boys rushed to the Capitol Tower in Hollywood to commence a marriage clearly not made in heaven. Many of the issues The Beach Boys would confront over the next decades were the result of being a band of talented musicians led by a genius.

"Brian had all the odds against him ever having more than two hit records," recalled Nick Venet. "Brian was a square peg in a round hole. Brian was five years too early with his business thinking, with his creative thinking, and yet he made it. But he suffered for it. And I'm sure he's paying for it today."[15]

* * *

Less than a year after the future Beach Boys piled into Brian's car to spend their parent's food money on musical instruments, the band signed their first contract with a major record label. It marked the beginning of a long and often contentious relationship.

"The people at Capitol didn't like my dad at all because he really gave them a hard time if he thought that something was unfair," Carl recalled in a 1971 interview. "A lot of the executives didn't like him at all. Which is perfectly understandable, but we were his kids, you know?"[16]

In 1962, the signing was a coup for any band, let alone a surf band. The idea of a self-contained band that wrote and performed its own material was a fairly new one for the record business in the early 60s. Bands like The Crickets or The Fireballs generated their own material, but once they had scored a hit, record companies would generally try to develop the lead singer as a solo artist, as happened to Buddy Holly.

More importantly, in the early days, while surf bands generally performed vocal music, the records released by record companies were usually their instrumental versions, leaving the individual performers anonymous for the most part. Some surf music producers, like Richard Delvy and Bob Keane, employed session players and had the bands learn their parts from records—a charge that would taint The Beach Boys' reputation for decades. This approach served two purposes: it cut costs in the studios (Keane often complained that he used to drive as far as the Huntington Beach pier to pull musicians out of the surf and get them into the studio) and gave the producers control over the band.

Capitol was a powerhouse label like RCA or Columbia, with its own studios, unlike the labels that generally gambled on instrumental surf tunes, like Del-Fi or Aertaun. They generally farmed out their recording to independent studios such as Gold Star, Pal Recording Studios, or Western/United.

The summer of 1962 set the scene for much of the friction in The Beach Boys' future, and laid the groundwork for Carl's eventual takeover as leader of the performing band. Brian had begun writing songs with lyricist Gary Usher earlier in the year, their partnership yielding '409' and 'The Lonely Sea.' But after hearing KFWB disc jockey Roger Christian discuss their record on his radio show, Brian introduced himself and sparked his next songwriting partnership. Christian loved fast cars and wrote poetry. After his program, he and Brian repaired to a coffee shop called Aldo's, behind the radio station, where they feasted on hot fudge sundaes and scribbled out lyrics that became 'Don't Worry Baby,' 'Little Deuce Coupe,' 'The Little Old Lady From Pasadena' and several of the songs for The Beach Boys' 1963 album *Little Deuce Coupe*.

Christian was described by Bruce Johnston, already a figure on the surf music scene, as a "gear head."[17] He was a car enthusiast with a vast technical knowledge blessed with a literary gift as well—something that none of the other Beach Boys seemed to possess at the time. Yet in a matter of months, Brian's decision to bring in outsiders as lyricists resulted in a shift in the balance of power within the band. With Carl and his friend and jamming partner David anchoring the guitars, and a second hit record about surfing on the horizon, Carl's role in the band expanded. As for Brian, writing with Usher and Christian in lieu of Mike solidified his power as the band's songwriter and downplayed the team of Wilson and Love. And while Gary Usher had no love for Murry (nor Murry for Usher), Christian was eight years older than Brian and found Murry to be an honorable man.

Mike's role in the band, though, extended farther than writing lyrics and singing. He provided a balance to Brian's shyness and sensitivity. In the beginning, though, his biggest contribution was to act as Brian's protector against the overbearing Murry. When Murry deflated Brian's ego, it was often left to Mike to repair the damage. When Murry confronted The Beach Boys on contentious issues, it was often left to Mike and Dennis to calm him down.[18]

Mike alone accepted Murry's challenge to learn to surf, but he made an unfortunate choice when it came to adopting an instrument. In 1961, saxophones were staples of surf, rock'n'roll, and rhythm & blues bands, but they were to become the first casualty of the surf music revolution. Brian had fortunately chosen the bass, while drums provided a beneficial outlet for Dennis's nervous energy. Carl and David found themselves on the ground floor of the emerging musical style that made the lead guitar the voice of rock'n'roll.

Saxophonists were less fortunate. The Chantays of 'Pipeline' fame began their career with saxophonist Jim Frias, then saw the future. At an Orange County battle of the bands, Chantays guitarist Brian Carmen escorted Frias into the audience and asked, "What do you hear?"[19]

"I hear guitars," Frias replied, "only guitars."

This was the band's way of informing Frias that his services were no longer required. The big amps and reverbs of surf music soon rendered saxophones redundant.

With Brian working with outside lyricists and Mike's instrument of choice fading (although he reportedly thanked the road crew member who lost his saxophone), Mike found his influence within the band contracting. Together, Carl and Mike provided the team that kept The Beach Boys popular, then solvent, with Carl handling the musical direction and Mike connecting with the audiences. But the choices made in that first six months of 1962, to stick with surf music and keep the Beach Boys name, would come back to haunt the band in the future.

In July 1962, about a month after the release of 'Surfin' Safari' b/w '409,' The Beach Boys were filmed at the Azusa Teen Club for a film called *One Man's Challenge*, a documentary about the opening of a teen club in this San Gabriel Valley suburb. The band (still sporting their Pendeltonesera Pendelton shirts and three-color sunburst Stratocaster front line) lip-synched to their newly recorded single. According to Keith Badman, the band's appearance was a happy accident—they had already been booked to perform at the club and were asked to be in the film because they were already on site with their instruments.

Narrated by Roger Christian, the black-and-white educational film was shot by Glendora-based photographer Dale Smallin. In September, he would begin managing a neighborhood surf band called The Surfaris (named after 'Surfin' Safari' but a different band than that with which The Beach Boys shared the stage at their Rendezvous debut). Smallin co-produced their 'Wipe Out' b/w 'Surfer Joe' single with Paul Buff at Buff's Pal Recording Studios in nearby Rancho Cucamonga, and provided the comical 'witch's cackle' for the opening of the A-side, a song The Beach Boys would record nearly a quarter of a century later with The Fat Boys, in one of the first collaborations between pop and hip-hop artists.[20]

In October 1962, The Beach Boys issued their first Capitol album, *Surfin' Safari*. Today it is viewed as a charming relic, a showcase for the emerging songwriting team of Wilson and Love, or as an example of surf music as garage rock interspersed with an occasional guitar instrumental. It also reveals The Beach Boys as far more of a democracy at the start of their careers than would be the case later, with Mike, Brian, Dennis, Carl, and David contributing lead vocals (Carl and David share 'Summertime Blues').

Carl also offers a surf instrumental: 'Moon Dawg.' One of the most important songs in the history of surf music, it always comes with an asterisk and marks the first step in the myth of The Beach Boys not playing their own instruments on record.

Originally written by guitarist Derry Weaver and released by The Gamblers on World Pacific Records in 1960, 'Moon Dawg,' backed by 'LSD-25,' is generally considered to be one of the very first guitar instrumentals of the surf music genre, despite the fact that it contains wordless harmonies. Weaver began with a band called The Moon Dogs (their name reportedly inspired by the blind New York street musician and composer Moondog, who performed in a Viking helmet). After that band broke up, Weaver went into the recording studio with his former bandmates and session players to record a song that would become a staple of surf bands throughout the early 60s. His musicians would go on in subsequent years to become members of the reigning Los Angeles bands, including The Mothers Of Invention, Canned Heat, and even The Beach Boys: future Beach Boy Bruce Johnston played piano and future producer Nick Venet provided the dog howls.[21]

And here is where the mystery begins: Weaver was part of the early LA music scene that orbited around Gold Star and included a pre-surf Dick Dale, Eddie Cochran, and songwriter Sharon Sheeley, who wrote 'Poor Little Fool' for Ricky Nelson. Even though Carl was the most instrumentally accomplished member of The Beach Boys, union sheets indicate that Venet imported Weaver to play guitar on the *Surfin' Safari* sessions that produced 'Summertime Blues,' 'Land Ahoy,' 'Ten Little Indians,' 'Little Miss America,' 'The Baker Man,' 'Chug-A-Lug,' 'Cuckoo Clock,' 'Heads You Win,' 'County Fair,' and 'Moon Dawg' (credited as 'Surf Dawg' on the sheets).

Venet told Beach Boys historian Stephen McParland that Weaver wasn't even present for the *Surfin' Safari* sessions: he had put the guitarist's name on the session sheets to secure session pay for himself. Using fictitious session players to give producers a bonus was not uncommon at the time, and is one reason session logs from the period are considered suspect by historians. However, some contend that Weaver did indeed perform the solo on The Beach Boys' version of 'Moon Dawg.'

"Venet did provide the dog growls on 'Moon Dawg,' as he had done on The Gamblers' recording," said John Blair. "But Weaver's Hollywood address and his Social Security number were both included on the session sheets, not Venet's."[22] According to author Peter Reum, who interviewed Nick Venet long after the sessions, Venet "indicated that Derry Weaver had played the lead guitar on the ['Moon Dawg'] session, duplicating his work on his single from 1960 on World Pacific."

If Weaver repeated his solo on 'Moon Dawg,' then it means that the

LONG PROMISED ROAD • 71

solo most surf music historians regard as the first surf music instrumental is repeated on *Surfin' Safari* by its composer, making it a rare historical artifact and placing The Beach Boys at the heart of the surf music scene. If it is Carl playing the solo, then it is the opening salvo of a career that probably sold more surf guitar instrumentals at the time than any other guitarist. The answer to the mystery is likely the latter. "The guitar sounds like a Carl Wilson solo," wrote Reum. He also praises Carl's work on 'The Shift,' the throwaway ditty about a dress style—not a car song—that closes the album. Reum writes "there is a nice Carl Wilson guitar solo on the song that is probably the highlight of the record."[23]

However, in a rare display of foul-mouthed anger, in the famous 1971 *Rolling Stone* article 'The Beach Boys: A California Saga,' Carl said, "I must say Nick Venet is really full of shit regarding us. He did an interview with a large magazine, the *Saturday Evening Post*, and he really lied his balls off in it. See, actually, he hardly had (anything) to do with the group. He would be in the booth and he would call the take number, and that was about it ... Brian didn't want anything to do with Venet."[24]

Venet, said David Marks, "went through the motions but he didn't really do anything. He was very ineffective as far as producing. Brian pretty much ignored him. Carl was funny, he used to make fun of Nick constantly, he'd make fun of his accent or make fun of the fact that he was not doing anything. When we first did *Surfin' Safari, Surfin' USA*, and *Shut Down Volume 2* at Western, I think Murry got his way a few times. He was obsessed with the guitars being all trebly, which actually benefited the sound overall. You've gotta give Murry a little credit there, but for the most part Brian was very frustrated with Murry interfering with his musical expression. Brian knew what he wanted before he would go into the studio."[25]

A photo from those Capitol sessions shows an additional guitarist in the studio playing with Carl and David, who some say could be Venet or could be Weaver. Either way, 'Moon Dawg' offers the first glimpse into the 'Beach Boys vs Wrecking Crew' debate and illustrates how music historians are often stymied by inaccurate or falsified paper trails. More importantly, it reveals fatal cracks in the myth that The Beach Boys were merely 'Brian's puppets' rather than fully involved partners in his creations.

Surfin' Safari stands as the first of The Beach Boys' 'orphan' albums— albums that are often dismissed, disregarded, or disrespected because they fail to carry the 'Produced by Brian Wilson' imprimatur.

Yet as Reum points out, "The album has a primitive but clear quality to it that belies the time in which it was recorded … The Beach Boys' musicianship on *Surfin' Safari* is basic, but competent. Dennis kept a solid backbeat on the album, and Carl's lead guitar is a major strength. As a slice of teenage life in Southern California in the early 60s, this album hits the bullseye."[26]

As 1962 ebbed into 1963, the band that was ignored at its first show now boasted three hit singles—'Surfin',' 'Surfin' Safari,' and '409'—and an album deal with a major label in less than a year, and was preparing for its first tour.

Meanwhile, in September, four British musicians had recorded a song that would be rejected by Capitol, The Beach Boys' label, even though they had recorded it for Capitol's parent company in the United Kingdom. The song was 'Love Me Do.' Thus began a rivalry that produced some of the decade's greatest statements and put The Beach Boys on the path to becoming 'America's band.'

CHAPTER SEVEN

Dance, Dance, Dance

"Our heads were spinning," David Marks later recalled to journalist Ken Sharp. "It just happened so fast and it was really exciting. We were presented with various temptations and opportunities to be naughty and we took them. We were rowdy kids in the neighborhood before we were The Beach Boys. Nothing was gonna change us. It just opened up the door for us to be even more mischievous. When you're a young teenager and you're making lots of money, there are a lot of opportunities to drink. There were no drugs around but we did drink. There weren't really a lot of groupies. Most of the kids that came to the shows were little girls."

According to Marks, the band's road manager at the time facilitated Mike's and Dennis's conspiracy to deflower 16-year-old Carl and 14-year-old David with a prostitute in a hotel.[1] However, for The Beach Boys it was mostly work. Rock bands in the 60s had lifespans measured in months. They could recover from one dud single (as The Beach Boys had done with their second Capitol single, 'County Fair'), but two duds in a row meant back to the bars.

"In those days the tours were grueling. It wasn't like you jumped into a limo and went to a five star hotel and then did your 90 minutes," recalled Marks. "You had to rent a U-Haul truck and a Chevy station wagon and drive 500 miles and you stayed at crappy motels and then you played for hours. You did three or four 45-minute sets at the high school dance. For the most part it was really hard work and the accommodations sucked. It wasn't that glamorous."

During one drunken episode on a hotel balcony, Mike actually saved David's life when Marks, trying to impress some girls on the balcony below, leaned too far over the railing and plunged backward. Love caught him by the ankle before he went completely over. "I probably would have died," Marks said.[2]

They may have felt exploited, but acting as the backup band for other artists on tour did wonders for The Beach Boys, expanding their musical horizons and providing new musical opportunities. The Beach Boys occasionally shared the stage with Jan & Dean, a singing duo whose first hit records like 'Baby Talk' and 'Heart And Soul' charted in 1959 and 1961 respectively. At one show, the duo ran short of material and suggested they all reprise some of The Beach Boys' material. The next day, Jan & Dean invited the whole band into the recording studio where the duo produced their own versions of 'Surfin'' and 'Surfin' Safari,' backed by The Beach Boys.

As the friendship grew, Brian gave the duo a preview of two new songs he had written: the opening chords and chorus of a song called 'Two Girls For Every Boy'; and the song planned for The Beach Boys' next single, a rewrite of Chuck Berry's 1958 hit 'Sweet Little Sixteen,' but with the lyrics rewritten to replace Berry's favorite cities with a list of the most desired surfing beaches in Southern California.

Jan Berry added lyrics to the first song and changed the title to 'Surf City'; it would reach number one in July 1963. The latter became 'Surfin' USA' and reached number three in May. During an appearance on a late-night dance show hosted by disc jockey Sam Riddle on one of Los Angeles's local networks, The Beach Boys posed in front of a curtain with a surfboard, mimicking the cover of the 'Surfin' Safari' single, while they lip-synched to 'Surfin' USA.' Carl glanced over at Mike and laughed after lip-synching Brian's falsetto part. It was all a new experience and they were very amused by it.

The success of the one-two punch of 'Surf City' and 'Surfin' USA' would be felt throughout the surf music community. Now, with Jan & Dean taking a similar approach to The Beach Boys, surf music would no longer be defined as a guitar style, but a vocal style. Soon, instrumental bands like The Surfaris found themselves learning how to sing like The Beach Boys, and the blistering single-note solos of surf guitar retreated back to a chord-based support style, with only an occasional solo to rest the singers' voices.[3]

'Surfin' USA,' followed by the success of the flip side, 'Little Deuce Coupe,' also augured the biggest change for the band. Brian's falsetto now distinguished The Beach Boys' sound; it was displayed in full on The Beach Boys' *Surfin' USA* album, released in March 1963. Brian was an expert in double-tracking or 'doubling' vocals. The technique had been used since the early recordings of Les Paul, and generally served to smooth out the rough edges and weak spots in performances.

Now, The Beach Boys displayed a new confidence; with a series of hit records under their belt, the hard work and experience started to pay off. While Carl, Dennis, and Mike had all taken lead vocals on the first album, Brian now sang lead on three of the album's best tracks: 'The Lonely Sea,' 'Farmer's Daughter,' and 'Lana,' while Carl cut loose on four instrumentals, including his own 'Surf Jam' and Brian's 'Stoked.'

Carl's style began to change with 'Surfin' USA.' He swapped his Stratocaster for an Olympic white Fender Jaguar, a guitar with a shorter neck and more distinctive sound.[4] Later, after Al got a red Stratocaster and had it painted white, the rest of the band followed suit, and white became the official color of The Beach Boys' hardware. In fact, when guitarist John Daly signed on as lead guitarist to support Carl's first solo tour in 1981, he was asked to paint his Fender Vibrolux Reverb amp white, "because it was The Beach Boys' color."[5] While Al had suggested the Kingston Trio-style candy-striped shirts, Carl soon began contributing as the band's fashion maven. He had already inveigled the band to all get their hair cut by trendy Hollywood hair stylist Jay Sebring (later a victim of the Manson Family).[6]

As The Beach Boys' success grew, so did Brian's influence. He managed to convince Capitol President Voyle Gilmore to allow him to produce The Beach Boys' records outside of Capitol's in-house studio. Gilmore, probably happy to avoid dealing with Murry and wanting to please one of his biggest moneymakers, agreed.

Throughout the year, Brian had already produced outside records at

Gold Star and Western studios: 'Pamela Jean' by The Survivors, for instance, and 'Revolution' by Rachel & The Revolvers. Now, Brian would be in charge, with no interference from Nick Venet.

The next album, *Surfer Girl*, marked the end of The Beach Boys as a surf band. Now, Brian's roots—The Four Freshman, Stephen Foster, boogie-woogie, even George Gershwin—were on display. Dick Dale and Chuck Berry took a back seat. There are only two instrumentals on the album: 'Boogie Woodie' (a piano and organ workout, showing off Brian's boogie-woogie skills) and 'The Rocking Surfer,' in which Carl offers a single guitar break in what is otherwise another organ workout.

Yet, as *Surfer Girl*—both the single and the album—hit the streets in July and September 1963, a new challenge for The Beach Boys rose up in their own back yard. According to conventional histories, The Beatles' appearance on *The Ed Sullivan Show* in February 1964 wiped out the surf music that had dominated local radio playlists for nearly two years. Yet the radio stations that served Los Angeles and adjacent San Bernardino, Riverside, and Orange counties had given The Beatles their first real shot at chart success more than six months before that first appearance.

The version of The Beatles' introduction to Americans accepted by most historians goes like this. In mid November of 1963, a Washington DC teenager named Marsha Albert prevailed upon her local radio station to play their fourth single, 'She Loves You.' The song had previously been played on a 'Rate The Record' segment of *American Bandstand*, where host Dick Clark dismissed the band and their haircuts. (Clark was a partner in the record label that released two early Beatle singles, but then he owned a piece of everything in rock'n'roll in those days and may not even have known they were the same band.) Nonetheless, the *Huntley-Brinkley News Hour*, and *Tonight Show* host Jack Paar, began covering the United Kingdom phenomenon of Beatlemania in advance of the band's first visit to the States.

However, California had already discovered the band. Disc jockeys in the three key AM radio stations that serviced San Bernardino, Riverside, Northern Orange, and much of Los Angeles counties gave the first two

Beatles discs sporadic airplay until June of 1963, when the band's third single, 'From Me To You,' began working its way up all three stations' charts. By mid July, 'From Me To You' had gone from 'wax to watch' (a radio term for a new record with potential) to charting as high as number seven on the KFXM charts and number nine on KMEN. There it rivaled nine surf-themed chart entries (including 'Beach Ball' by The City Surfers, featuring future Byrds founder Roger McGuinn and pop star Bobby Darin), yet it was unable to dislodge the higher-charting 'Wipe Out' by The Surfaris and Jan & Dean's 'Surf City.'

Nobody is sure where Carl first discovered The Beatles—either listening to the radio at home or on the 1964 Australian tour with The Surfaris—but all agree he was the first Beach Boy afflicted with Beatlemania. As he had with rhythm & blues and Chuck Berry, Carl would be the one to infect Brian with enthusiasm for the new sound.

* * *

In September of 1963, on the drive from Chicago to The Beach Boys' New York debut, David and Murry clashed one too many times. They had had a stormy relationship. David was upset that Murry had forced the band to set and strike their own equipment (Carl and David's Showman amps weighed about 120lbs each, plus the additional weight of the reverb units), weary of the endless penalties and fines Murry imposed for cursing onstage, and chafing under Murry's strict rules. He decided to strike out on his own. "I was kind of going off in my own direction musically," said Marks. He would stay in the band until mid October, when Al Jardine took over as his long-term replacement.

At first, having David in the band had been a boon, especially since he, like the Wilson boys, had been introduced to boogie-woogie by Audree and shared influences and guitar teachers with Carl.

"We played together every day and our guitar playing blended, not unlike the vocal blend of the Wilson brothers," Marks said. "Our blend and the way we played off of each other sounded like one guy. We would do our little nuances to complement each other. We were trying to play like our heroes but we couldn't, so it came out our own, raw, garage kind of sound. When you're young and you're trying to emulate someone and you can't really do it, when it comes out as your own style, that's the ideal thing; and that's what happened with us. But then we started hearing other people trying to play like us."[7]

The Beach Boys' sound, said Jon Stebbins, "didn't come out of the den at Hawthorne." It had only crystalized after Al had dropped out, to be replaced by David. "The Beach Boys were thought of in their earliest conception as a vocal group like The Four Freshmen or The Lettermen. They were not really thinking of themselves as a rock band. Who was a freestanding rock band back then? There really wasn't a band like that. The Beach Boys really created the template of that kind of band."[8]

As time went on, however, David's presence in the group proved problematic for Carl. They were old friends and jamming partners, and had developed the musical sympathy guitarists develop over time, but the old surf instrumentals were growing less important to the band and the songs and vocals more important. Brian began looking more to Carl for leadership in the band, as performing (especially with Murry as manager) proved too much of a distraction to his songwriting and producing.

Even at 16, Carl was, in Brian's words, "the Rock of Gibraltar of the group. He would say, 'Come on guys, let's quit clowning around and get to work.'"[9] In most bands, the drummer sets the beat and counts off the song, but for the duration of The Beach Boys' career, it would be Carl's responsibility to count off the tunes and keep the rhythm 'in the pocket.' As Carl's leadership grew, Murry required him to be the onstage morality police, reporting back to his father, especially when David gleefully muttered obscenities into the microphone just to aggravate the old man. "Murry gave Carl instructions to document when I used dirty lyrics in the shows. I shared a microphone with Carl, and on a dare I would lean over and shout some profanities and Carl would get all mad and yell 'Fifty dollars! That's fifty dollars!' which was a helluva lot of fucking money back then."[10]

To make matters worse, The Beach Boys were now playing to thousands of fans, not hundreds, and Carl often found himself starstruck when sharing the stage on package tours with major acts like Marvin Gaye and Little Stevie Wonder.

Meanwhile Brian was increasingly unhappy in his role in the touring band. On September 14, 1963, Brian asked Al Jardine to replace him at a show in Sacramento. Jardine was working in an aircraft plant at the time. "Al, you gotta come back," Brian implored him. "It's driving me nuts—my dad is driving me crazy."[11]

Jardine returned to the position he had originally held in The Beach Boys: bass and harmony vocals. At times that fall, Al also replaced Brian on lead vocals, while Brian spent his time in the studio.[12] By the end of 1963, Brian had released three hit albums and three top ten singles with flip sides that charted as well. After the departure of David Marks, and with Brian in attendance, Al would finally switch to rhythm guitar. Photographs of a 'Y-Day' event, sponsored by the YMCA at the Hollywood Bowl in November, show Al performing on a borrowed Gibson SG, carefully paying attention to Carl's hand positions.

"We thought we were through when Brian stopped touring with us," said Marks, who still had a few gigs to play. "Alan came back and saved the day. He was our hero."[13] However, saving The Beach Boys after abandoning them nearly two years earlier didn't improve Al's status with Murry. "He made my life a living hell," Jardine later admitted.[14]

Meanwhile, however, the compliant and awkward youngest brother whom Al had sung with in 1961 had become a seasoned and confident rock star. Given the sales figures their first three albums had achieved, Carl could be considered one of the best-known guitarists in the business.

The style of rock'n'roll The Beach Boys delivered changed considerably in 1963, in large part due to the *Surfer Girl* album, the first to bear the credit 'Produced by Brian Wilson.' To most of the world, The Beach Boys were surf music, and the while the album art and lyrics all shouted 'surf,' little was left of the instrumental surfing sound, save for tonal glimpses in Carl's guitar solos. Brian had begun incorporating more sophisticated influences into his music. 'Our Car Club' echoed the Afro/Cuban rhythms of Herbie Hancock's 'Watermelon Man,' 'The Surfer Moon' floated on a frothy orchestral arrangement, and 'Your Summer Dream' was nothing if not a perfect romantic musical interlude for a film musical or Broadway show.

More importantly, with Al replacing Brian and David leaving to pursue his own musical vision, the pressures of onstage leadership were now divided between Mike and Carl. Mike, whose saxophone playing diminished with each album, focused on developing his frontman role. Carl now stood as the musical heart of a band who—unlike their transatlantic rivals—didn't cover Broadway hits like 'Till There Was You,' they wrote their own.

In September, the band had returned to Gold Star with Brian's new girlfriend Marilyn Rovell, her sister Diane, and cousin Ginger Blake to rework as a single a song Brian originally wrote for their upcoming *Little Deuce Coupe* album. 'Be True To Your School' featured part of the Hawthorne High fight song (actually the song 'On Wisconsin' with modified lyrics). Beach Boys insiders laughed up their sleeves at the band's exhortations to "let your colors fly": Dennis had been expelled from the school for fighting, and Carl for leaving class to go to the bathroom without permission.[15]

The new arrangement of leaving Brian at home much of the time, so he could write, seemed to work. As the final weekend of November 1963 approached, he put the finishing touches on a sad, haunting ballad that had come to him late in the week and packed up his gear for a show in Marysville, California, on Friday night. The next day, November 22, at about 10:30am on the West Coast, news flashed that President John F. Kennedy had been assassinated in Dallas, Texas.

The Beach Boys' concert promoter Fred Vail urged the band—in true Murry fashion—to bite the bullet and go on with the show, but they canceled their performance in Sacramento the next night. Brian and Mike repaired to Brian's office, where Mike penned what may have been the best lyrics of his career to create 'The Warmth Of The Sun.' Surf bands with an average age of 19 years old didn't address earth-shaking events with sad songs, and any record company that valued its bottom line would have balked at any attempt to do so at a time when rock'n'roll was just entering its second decade, so Mike captured the band's and the nation's sorrow metaphorically in terms of a lost love that teenagers would understand.

However, the rescheduled show in Sacramento proved to be a far happier affair for the band. On December 21, the band celebrated Carl's 17th birthday by singing 'Happy Birthday' onstage, and Capitol set up equipment to record the program. When the local disc jockey scheduled to introduce the band didn't appear, Murry told Vail to go out and introduce them. Vail's introduction, "From Hawthorne California, to entertain you tonight…" opens up what became one of The Beach Boys' most successful albums: *Beach Boys Concert*.

The concert marked nearly two years to the day since the band's debut, and now Capitol Records prepared to lavish unheard-of sums to produce a gatefold album—generally reserved for Broadway musical cast recordings—with a special insert of concert photos. The band had generated millions in sales for Capitol Records, which had broken new ground in the industry by allowing their 21-year-old leader to produce records in studios of his choice—not the label's—with little supervision by a staff producer.

They had delivered three albums and four double-sided hit singles and would finish out the year with the Christmas classic 'Little Saint Nick.' Their former local surf band rivals were now being herded into recording studios and forced to sound like The Beach Boys just to survive. The Beach Boys, meanwhile, felt confident enough to taunt their national crosstown rivals by singing "Four Seasons/you better believe it" on 'Surfers Rule,' a song in which the future 'America's band' celebrate the joys of graffiti, defacing public property, and illegal street racing.

The year 1963 belonged to The Beach Boys, and Carl Wilson darted around town in his new blue 1964 Pontiac Grand Prix. It would grace the cover of their first 1964 album, *Shut Down Volume 2*, next to brother Dennis's Chevrolet Corvette. But trouble brewed on the home front. Even with two hit albums on the charts, the strain began to show on Brian. He missed a series of shows in Hawaii in June 1963 and was now also spending time producing other artists, such as The Honeys and The Survivors. Murry was becoming unbearable, and David's departure created instability in the performing band. Unbeknown to the band, their own record company prepared to invest the vast sum of $40,000 in The Beatles.

The Beatles' signing would challenge—and briefly topple—The Beach Boys' empire. And that would only be one front in a two-front war, with the second starting in their own back yard. They called it the 'Wall of Sound.'

* * *

In the late summer of 1963, Brian Wilson was driving around Los Angeles, listening to the radio, when disc jockey Wink Martindale introduced a new record, by a group called The Ronettes. It was 'Be My Baby.' The verses didn't move him, but when the chorus kicked in—"So won't you be / Be my little baby"—Brian screeched to the side of the road and listened closely to a song that would change his life for ever. "What a great sound, the Wall of Sound," he said later. "Boy, I first heard this on the car radio and I had to pull off the road. I couldn't believe it. The choruses blew me away. The strings are the melody of love. It has the promise to make the world better."[16]

Fortunately for Brian, while his first encounter with Phil Spector's music occurred on that hot Los Angeles street, he'd known about Spector's 'instrument'—his favored studio—for years. The Wall of Sound was the sound of walls, and those walls were the custom-designed and handcrafted echo chambers of Hollywood's Gold Star Recording Studios. Even the cement compound that coated the walls was custom-designed by studio co-owner Dave Gold to mimic the acoustic qualities of the rest room in his father's Los Angeles tailor shop. Brian had first visited Gold Star with his father Murry while he was still in high school.[17] He used the studio for some early Beach Boys records and would use it for many of his early outside productions, such as 'Pamela Jean' by The Survivors which, with rewritten lyrics, became The Beach Boys' 'Car Crazy Cutie.'

Spector came to Gold Star to record his band The Teddy Bears singing

'To Know Him Is To Love Him.' He had attended the same high school as co-owner Stan Ross and knew that Gold Star's main attraction, after the sound, was its ability to help develop new artists build repeat business.

Spector grew up in New York as a happy, chubby boy in a family of four until his world ended on a spring morning in 1949 when his father parked on a nearby street just five miles from the Spector home and ran a hose from his tailpipe to commit suicide. Young Phil was devastated. His mother Bertha moved to the predominantly Jewish area of Fairfax in Los Angeles, where Phil took up jazz guitar and created The Teddy Bears with his friends Marshall Leib, Harvey Goldstein, and Annette Kleinbard.

After the success of 'To Know Him' and the relative failure of the follow-up album, Spector apprenticed himself to two transplanted Angelenos in New York, Jerry Leiber and Mike Stoller. Their studio of choice was the far more capacious Mira Sound, and there Spector would produce a string of hits.

However, returning to Los Angeles to record 'He's A Rebel,' Spector overestimated Gold Star Studio A's ability to accommodate the larger number of musicians he was accustomed to in New York. So many musicians showed up for the session, they found they had to stack their instrument cases in the hallway.[18]

When the musicians, about a dozen in all, started playing, the resulting cacophony proved to be a "train wreck," said Ross. So session engineer Larry Levine took the embarrassed Spector aside and showed him how to transform a train wreck into a wall of sound by introducing echo from one of the two custom-built chambers.[19]

The combination of the compact space, which in engineer Levine's phrase "melded" the sound, and the introduction of echo at the recording—rather than mastering—stage helped weave the disparate sounds into a single harmonic and rhythmic pulse over which Spector could overlay crystal-clear vocals. Moreover, Gold's handcrafted recording console and various other studio technologies enabled Spector to stack instruments, vocals, and orchestral 'sweetening' to minimize the noise and sound degradation inherent in the analog recording process.[20]

However, Spector found in the recording process an added gift: when two signals with similar frequencies and timbres merge, they create a sonic 'seam,' the same way that merging watercolors create a third color. It was this 'whole greater than the sum of its parts' approach that caught Brian's ear. When Brian applied the concept to his own recordings, he referred to these 'greater than the sum' tones as his "pet sounds."

Brian had long been aware of the role session musicians played in the Los Angeles recording scene. Murry had struck up friendships with many of them. Brian's contemporaries, Jan Berry and Richard Delvy, frequently used session players to accelerate their sessions and provide distinctive instrumentation. Berry, for instance, used dual drummers Hal Blaine and Earl Palmer on his Jan & Dean singles.[21]

Brian later claimed that Phil Spector made him think in terms of making records rather than just songs and David Marks admitted later that he felt Brian never wanted to be a Beach Boy, but a songwriter/producer like Spector.[22] But while Brian had already recorded a handful of independent singles, all had failed to chart, while his Beach Boys productions seemed to succeed effortlessly. Brian's introduction to the Wall of Sound sparked his greatest growth as an artist. At the same time, it created a schism in The Beach Boys that was never healed, by spawning the myth of The Beach Boys as Brian's puppets.

It was not something Carl accepted easily. "No we are not just Brian's puppets," he said. "Brian plays the major creative role in the production of our music, but everyone in the group contributes something to the finished product. It's not like an orchestra translating the wishes of the conductor. We all have a part to play in the production of the records."[23]

Yet as Brian sought to ease out of The Beach Boys' touring band and into the producer's chair full-time, he found his plans interrupted by The Beatles. At least for a while, The Beach Boys would be one again.

CHAPTER EIGHT

Good Timin'

On New Year's Day, 1964, The Beach Boys gathered in Western Recorders studio in Hollywood to record their next single, 'Fun, Fun, Fun,' a lighthearted rocker about a girl who tells her father she's going to take his Ford Thunderbird to the library to study and instead barrels around town challenging the boys to races and making "the Indy 500 look like a Roman chariot race." It possessed all of the elements of a Beach Boys hit record: fast cars, pretty girls, and good times unleashed by 12 bars of Carl's signature Chuck Berry-derived lead guitar.

Yet 'Fun, Fun, Fun,' the anchor single on the album that would become *Shut Down Volume 2*, augured a change in Brian's production approach. "We first started using session players on songs like 'Fun, Fun, Fun,'" Carl said later.[1]

The single's flip side, a reworking of Frankie Lymon & The Teenagers' 1956 hit 'Why Do Fools Fall In Love,' found Brian taking the band into Gold Star studio for his first Wall of Sound effort. Drenched in Gold Star's echo, it also featured a stunning a capella break on the bridge to remind the listener that *this* was The Beach Boys. While Brian clearly worshipped Spector, 'Why Do Fools Fall In Love' was a cast gauntlet, not a homage. The album would also feature 'Don't Worry Baby,' which Brian had written as a possible Spector single, but demurred when Ronnie Spector told him Phil wouldn't record it without rewriting it to get a co-writer credit.[2] In a rare 1970 interview in *Rolling Stone* with future Beach Boys manager Jack Rieley, Brian said he always felt that 'Don't Worry Baby' served as the best showcase for The Beach Boys' vocals and harmony.[3]

Carl, meanwhile, believed that the secret of the group's harmony was that their "vocals were voiced like horn parts, the way those R&B records made background vocals sound like a sax section. They're all within the same octave; that's really the secret to it. We didn't just duplicate parts; we used a lot of counterpoint, a lot of layered sound."[4]

For *Shut Down Volume 2*, Capitol began marketing the band as more of a 'hot rod' or 'car song' band than a surf band. The word 'surf' appears nowhere in the songs and only in passing in the album's liner notes, as if to acknowledge that surfing was the past and hot rods the present.

'Fun, Fun, Fun' may have been a teenage slice-of-life song lyrically, but musically it took The Beach Boys into adventurous territory for a rock'n'roll song. "'Fun, Fun, Fun,'" said Carl, "starts so simple with that three-chord verse, but when you get into the chorus, the harmonies really stretch. It goes E to A-flat minor to A, B, A, A, A-flat minor and then a B suspended over the A. It spreads the harmony because it doesn't do what you think it should do. It resolves but it doesn't. The song is in E, but the instrumental break is in B and then it flip-flops to end the song.

"My dad said, 'That tag sounds too funny, that high part sounds too weird. That part might make the song only go to number 13.'"[5]

Murry was wrong. Even with America in the throes of Beatlemania, 'Fun, Fun, Fun' topped out at number five on the *Billboard* charts in March, one position higher than their previous single 'Be True To Your School.'

At the time of *Shut Down Volume 2*, The Beach Boys in the studio and onstage consisted of the five original members, yet it would feature more Carl lead vocals than any other Beach Boys album until 1967's *Smiley Smile*. Carl alternates verses with Mike on Richard Berry's 'Louie Louie,' originally recorded in a Los Angeles garage by his band The Pharaohs. The song scored a hit for The Kingsmen in 1963, which later became the definitive version, but for *Shut Down Volume 2*, Carl and Mike unleash their LA rhythm & blues roots to deliver a rendering faithful to the original.

Carl's other lead vocal is 'Pom Pom Playgirl,' another high school slice-of-life, with Carl at the end saying, "Shake it, wave those pom poms all around…" and finally "Wow." 'Pom Pom Playgirl' reveals the distinct influence of the throat-ripping vocals popular in rockabilly and rhythm & blues, especially the vocal work of his hero Dick Dale. (The style got a full workout on The Beach Boys' live performance of 'What'd I Say.')

For the band's now customary instrumental outing, Carl delivers 'Shut Down, Part II.' Following Brian's lead on 'Fun, Fun, Fun,' he takes one of the most beloved changes for guitarists, a 12-bar blues in the key of A, then departs from the traditional form in bar 10 by including four beats of F, a half-step (semitone) up on the expected E.

The Beach Boys had interrupted the recording of *Shut Down Volume 2* when, on January 15, 1964, they commenced a two-week tour in Australia and New Zealand with Roy Orbison, The Surfaris, and other acts. Hundreds of frenzied fans greeted their arrival at Sydney Airport.

The Beach Boys immediately struck up a friendship with The Surfaris, who hailed from their home county of Los Angeles and whose drummer, while not related, was named Ronnie Wilson. One night during the tour, The Beach Boys grabbed The Surfaris' saxophonist Jim Pash, handed him a bass guitar and draped him in Brian's stage shirt as Brian failed to show up in time for their set. The terrified Pash, who was younger than Carl but the same height as Brian, informed them that he didn't play bass. Carl shrugged and told him to just stand there and look like Brian, as they wouldn't be heard over the screaming fans anyway. When Brian did arrive, moments before showtime, he quickly retrieved his shirt and bass and said, "I just wanted to see what you guys would do without me."

Pash interpreted this as Brian's none-too-subtle reminder to the band that he was still in charge, but after that the band invited Pash into their inner circle, with the young Surfari often shadowing Brian to divine his songwriting methods. One day, as Brian sat at the piano working on a song, he glanced over at Pash with a wry smile and joked, "I could write a fart and it would be a hit."

One evening during the tour, Pash accompanied the band to a local theater, where they showed a clip of The Beatles at the Royal Variety Performance in London on November 4, 1963, where Lennon quipped,

"The people in the cheaper seats, clap your hands; and the rest of you just rattle your jewelry."

Pash recalled that the band cringed at The Beatles' raw harmonies. Carl and Brian in particular mocked the dry, flabby guitar tones emanating from The Beatles' backline of Vox amplifiers. Only Al, Pash said, seemed concerned, saying, "I think they've got something there."[6]

That "something" became apparent a few weeks later, when The Beatles arrived to perform the first of three shows on the variety program *The Ed Sullivan Show* on CBS television. The next morning in Hollywood recording studios "the phones just stopped ringing," said Stan Ross.

The difference between The Beatles' first chart-topping hits in Southern California in the summer of 1963 and the Beatlemania of 1964 clearly involved two major factors. The first was the recent assassination of John F. Kennedy in Dallas. For weeks, somber black-and-white images saturated newspapers and television (at that time offering only three network channels and a smattering of regional stations). However, there was more than the emotional toll of Kennedy's death in play. Americans had difficulty digesting the 'crazed lone assassin' theory, and many harbored suspicions that the Cold War was turning into a real war. Kennedy's successor, Lyndon Johnson, inspired little love or trust that, if Kennedy's death was an act of war, it would be a war America could win. The sudden shift from reports of nonstop mourning and anxiety to shots of shrieking, joyous teenage girls infesting airports proved too strong a tonic for the media to ignore.

Furthermore, unlike The Beach Boys, who had slugged their way to success over the course of two years, learning their craft in full view of the record buying public, The Beatles arrived on American shores ready to show off the sum total of their career to that point. Their first Capitol album *Meet The Beatles!* nearly qualified as a 'best of' compilation of the two albums and four singles The Beatles had already recorded. *Meet The Beatles!* contained only one cover tune (Meredith Willson's showstopper from *The Music Man*, 'Till There Was You') and 11 Lennon/McCartney originals. On the English version, released two months earlier, six of the album's 14 tracks were cover tunes.

For decades, the historical and critical assessment of The Beach Boys has been heavily influenced by comparisons with The Beatles when, in fact, they sprang from two different sources. The Beatles consisted of three songwriters and a producer and worked in the record company's home studio, whereas Brian handled both the songwriting and production details for his band. Capitol had to make back its investment in The Beatles or be viewed as the American company that let The Beatles get away.

Carl was the first Beatlemaniac in The Beach Boys. "He fell in love with them from day one," said Jon Stebbins. "Carl was the biggest Beatles fan on earth." One of the biggest effects The Beatles had on The Beach Boys was that Carl switched to a Rickenbacker 12-string semi-hollowbody guitar.

When the Beatles' film *A Hard Day's Night* premiered in the Bay Area in advance of its Los Angeles premiere, Carl chartered a private plane and invited David Marks—now playing with his own band—along. "The immediate reaction was they each bought a 12-string Rickenbacker," said Stebbins. "That's when Carl switched. Carl was a giant Beatles fan ... and Dennis, too."

Carl's switching to a 12-string changed the course of his solos and the texture of The Beach Boys' overall sound. "Carl had a very unique style in the way he attacked the guitar," said Stebbins. "He could throw a little timing interplay with his fills: almost jazzlike. His fills and solos almost had a jazz feel to them. They're not straightforward, but they're always 'in the pocket.' It's a subtle thing. There is something that he does that is unique to Carl. He's still using the Chuck Berry fingering, but it's in his right hand and in its feel."[7]

One key difference between rock'n'roll and jazz is that in rock, the drums maintain the rhythm, whereas with jazz, the rhythm instrument (whether a guitar or a piano) keeps the beat while the role of the drums is to play a bit ahead of the beat to propel the rhythm forward. With brother Dennis learning his instrument in the early days, and a revolving door of rhythm guitarists, Carl merged the roles of both rhythm and lead guitar into one. His solo on 'Don't Worry Baby' consists of beautifully timed rhythmic block chords clipping against the rhythm, whereas 'She Knows Me Too Well,' from 1965's *The Beach Boys Today!* album, builds tension with a subtle lower-register single-note solo that closes by revisiting the chords as the vocals rise in the background.

Once The Beach Boys proceeded beyond surf music, Carl adapted his lead guitar role in the band into one unique to The Beach Boys. Rather than stepping forward with a flurry of single notes to explore the chordal, melodic, or rhythmic possibilities in the song, and to rest the singer's voices—the original role of the lead guitar—Carl managed to develop a more orchestral concept that suited Brian's approach to composing arranged records rather than simply writing songs to which instruments were later added.

* * *

As The Beach Boys returned from Australia and prepared 'Fun, Fun, Fun' for release in February of 1964, they found The Beatles' albums and singles effortlessly careening up the pop charts and radio playlists. Meanwhile, Beatles merchandise devoured shelf space at local drug stores and five-and-dimes.

Once The Beatles had breached America's walls, a torrent of English bands followed. Record companies balked at signing or even investing in records by American acts. Many American rock'n'roll bands—especially the surf bands—began dialing down the instrumentals and ratcheting up the vocals. Some did their best to look and sound English. For instance, Southern California's The Goldtones promptly rechristened themselves Thee Sixpence.

As The Beatles began locking in the pop charts for what would eventually be a historic three-month run, a big change came in how record companies viewed their acts. The Beatles' sudden and seemingly endless stream of celebrations of love and romance made the teenage slice-of-life scenarios favored by The Beach Boys seem quaint and provincial. When The

Beach Boys celebrated the joys of sports and fast cars, they sang from a male perspective about things important to males. Yet the clear message of the British Invasion, led by the charming, well-dressed, and well-coiffed Beatles, was that girls drove the record market. As had happened with surfing, The Beach Boys found themselves shackled to an image—that of the 'guys' band.' They were red-blooded, suntanned all-American boys, and the girls were screaming for English gentlemen.

While The Beach Boys suddenly, in Brian Wilson's words, "felt unhip," the British Invasion served to galvanize the band and Brian's commitment to it. [8] If they were a 'guys' band,' so be it—they would show those charming English blokes exactly what being a badass American was all about.

As they entered their third year as a band, The Beach Boys had weathered three different band formations: the first with the original five, the second with David replacing Al, and the third with six Beach Boys. Now back to the original five, with Brian recommitted to the band, The Beach Boys entered the studio to record the single that, along with Louis Armstrong's 'Hello Dolly' and Mary Wells's 'My Guy,' would finally break The Beatles' stranglehold on the record charts.

Fortunately, the pressure on Carl was easing. While Brian pursued his songwriting and independent productions back in California, on tour Carl served twin roles as Brian's musical lieutenant and Murry's morality policeman. More importantly, Brian's piano-based songwriting approach and increasing sophistication had gradually eroded the role of the guitar over the course of the three albums he'd produced. No longer front and center, as it had been on *Surfin' USA*, by *Surfer Girl* the guitar had been relegated to a support instrument as Carl and Al struggled to adapt Brian's increasingly complex chords to simpler guitar positions. Just as they had when they had to become a surf band, The Beach Boys prepared to confront The Beatles and capitalize on their strengths for a record that would be leaner, meaner, and more macho than ever: 'I Get Around.'

Before that, in the early spring of 1964, 'Fun, Fun, Fun' rose to number five on the charts, disproving Murry's prediction that the single wouldn't crack the top ten. Nonetheless, rumors swirled that some Capitol Records executives considered cutting The Beach Boys loose and concentrating on English bands instead. Many in the band, meanwhile, viewed Murry as out of touch in this new world of new music.

The Beach Boys now added television to their list of accomplishments, recording segments for *The Steve Allen Show* and an episode of *American Bandstand* where they arrived on set only to discover that host Dick Clark expected them to stand in a row in front of a curtain and lip-synch to 'Don't Worry Baby,' without instruments. Watching the program a month later, Carl cringed. "When we saw how we looked, we died a thousand deaths. It was awful," he said.[9]

On March 14, The Beach Boys arrived on a soundstage at NBC studios in nearby Burbank to play live for a show later known as the lost concert, because the tapes disappeared for 35 years. The recording would be spliced together with other recordings by The Beatles and singer Lesley Gore and shown in movie theaters.

With Mike carrying his saxophone and Carl clutching his Jaguar, the band takes the stage and Carl counts off 'Fun, Fun, Fun.' They perform their choreographed stage moves based on the surfer stomp, which itself was based on an early dance called the Stroll. The awkward lead singer, who once simply stood nervously behind the microphone, now proves to be a seasoned entertainer, dancing and burlesquing the lyrics to 'Long Tall Texan' to the audience's delight.

"Now we'd like to show you how The Beach Boys go about making a record," says Mike, introducing 'Little Deuce Coupe.' The band play the introductory bars, coming in one by one. Carl seems genuinely startled at the applause his introduction generates and mouths "thank you" to the audience. Next comes 'Surfer Girl.' As evidence that Brian thought in terms of writing records, not songs, the band manages the trick of seeming to fade out the number, rather than giving it a solid finish. Later, the band reveal their Los Angeles rhythm & blues roots by cutting loose on a raucous rave-up on The Rivingtons' 'Papa-Oom-Mow-Mow.' The onstage leadership of the band becomes clear as Carl waits patiently for Mike to conclude his patter with the audience before counting off 'Hawaii' from the *Surfer Girl* album.[10]

The concert reveals a confident band that at this early stage already boasted enough hits to be able to leave several out: 'Surfin' Safari,' 'Surfin',' and even the recent hit 'Be True To Your School' didn't make the final cut. In the 70s, Carl would lament these concerts as The Beach Boys' 'human jukebox' era, but the audience clearly didn't care.[11] And, despite later efforts to promote various incarnations of 'new, improved' Beach Boys, the audience would always have the final word.

As The Beach Boys' success grew, attempts had been made by the band to reduce Murry's involvement. He still had A.B.L.E. Machinery to deal with and asked others to take over the onstage oversight of the band. At one point, he even asked David Marks's father Elmer to travel with them. But time and success had transformed the 'little surf band' into America's challenge to the British Invasion. They now saw Murry's guidance growing less supportive and more intrusive and meddlesome.

By the beginning of April 1964, The Beatles had accomplished a historic feat in achieving the top five singles on the *Billboard* charts and, a week later, boasting a total of 14 songs in the *Billboard* Top 100. As Brian prepared The Beach Boys' first post-Beatlemania response—their next single, 'I Get Around'—Murry's criticism and hectoring drove Brian to snap in the studio. Grabbing his father by the collar, Brian screamed "You're fired … Do you understand me? You're fired."[12]

The next day, The Beach Boys formally incorporated as Beach Boys Entertainment Enterprises Inc., with Brian, Mike, Dennis, and Carl as directors and corporate members. They hired Murry's accounting firm Cummings & Currant to handle the corporation's finances.

Shocked, Murry returned home and climbed into bed, where he stayed, according to various accounts, anywhere from one week to a month. The repercussions of that firing would haunt The Beach Boys for decades. Murry's bed episode provided the first hint that, rather than just being difficult, he might be suffering from a genuine mental illness that would be mirrored in Brian's behavior in later decades. However, there is no evidence that Murry or his family ever sought treatment. In the 60s, mental illness was still considered a taint on the family and individuals, and frequently misdiagnosed. When it was diagnosed, doctors often employed questionable methods to 'cure' the illness, such as shock therapy. The most common treatment among middle-class Americans was to hope the affliction merely ran its course and went away like a cold.

This was the end of the Hawthorne period. Shortly afterward, Audree and Murray bought a new house in Whittier, then found they no longer wanted to live in it together. Carl was disturbed by the sad sequence of events: the loss of the old family home, which remained empty, and the end of his parents' marriage.[13]

Murry's firing sparked another popular Beach Boys myth, which served to blemish whatever little good was left of Murry's reputation: that a vindictive Murry created a band called The Sunrays to compete with The Beach Boys, complete with identical candy-striped shirts and four-part harmonies. In fact, it was Carl who first brought The Sunrays—then called The Renegades—to Murry's attention. Their first meeting with Murry occurred nearly six months before Murry's firing, when David Marks was still in the band.

Now a professional entertainer, Carl had left Hawthorne High School to attend Hollywood Professional School. But he was still living at home in Hawthorne when one of his new classmates, named Eddy Medora, invited Carl and Dennis to see his band The Renegades, based in Pacific Palisades.

Early in The Beach Boys' career, they had shared a stage with The Renegades during a performance at UCLA's Dykstra Hall. "They played one gig with us. 'Surfin'' was just busting out and so they changed their name to The Beach Boys," said Medora, saxophonist with The Renegades. "So yes, we played together but we didn't know each other at that time."

But now The Renegades were Carl's classmates. "Every Friday you were able to perform, whether you were an actor, actress, whatever. We would perform and Carl went crazy. Carl and Dennis went absolutely bonkers over our band," said Medora.

Carl approached The Renegades and informed them that Murry was looking for another band to manage, although Medora joked, "Yeah, you just want your dad off your back—which was probably part true."

The Renegades, said Medora, "were a blues band. Our repertoire was B.B. King, Ray Charles, T-Bone Walker, King Curtis … it was sort of cool, though, because when we started to do the Sunrays gigs, we'd pull one of those songs in and the audience would freak out and say, 'Why are you guys playing that kind of stuff?' And we'd go back and say, 'That's what we were weaned on.'" Early on, the band had recorded sides with producers Larry Marks and Kim Fowley, before meeting Carl at school. Carl already knew Medora's bandmate Rick Henn and they introduced him to the rest of the band: guitarist Steve O'Reilly (later replaced by Byron Case), keyboard player Marty DiGiovanni, and bassist Vince Hozier.

Not only did Medora find Carl in no hurry to hook his father up with another musical pursuit, he found him to be gentle and shy, so he tried to accelerate the meeting with Murry by hooking Carl up with cute girls he knew.

"First of all, I kept setting Carl up with these girls. So I said, 'When are you gonna introduce us to your dad?'" Carl, said Medora, would reply "Dad's been busy, Dad's been this, Dad's been that."

"Then he said, 'Why don't we go to the prom again?' I said, 'Carl, I'll set you up with the girl you want to go with.' He bought me a tux, shirt, shoes. He went out and bought a brand new 1964 [Pontiac] Grand Prix, white leather seats, turquoise blue … and it was just incredible, a fun time."[14]

Carl brought the band over to the Hawthorne house to find four of The Beach Boys rehearsing and David arguing with Murry. They set up their equipment and performed a handful of their best songs. Even though Murry effused that the band was great, he laid out terms for managing them. The first was to learn four- and five-part harmonies. "If you listen to me," he told the band, "you will have a record in six weeks."

Murry began by offering the band the basics in constructing harmonies and microphone technique and said "I want you to go home and write and write and write." Henn took part of a chord progression from one of Medora's songs and transformed it into the first big Sunrays' hit 'I Live For The Sun.'

Murry also introduced the band to some Capitol Records executives, who encouraged them to change their name, feeling The Renegades sounded too rebellious. When Capitol executives winced at having another harmony band competing with The Beach Boys, fearing it would confuse their marketing efforts, Murry and Capitol executive Alan Livingston created a new imprint called Tower Records (for the Capitol Tower on Vine Street, Hollywood), although they were on the Capitol label everywhere else in the world.

Murry took the band to Gold Star studios, where he matched them up with arranger and producer Don Ralke to produce two hit singles, 'I Live For The Sun' and 'Andrea' (inspired by an attractive stewardess they met on a flight).[15] Ralke fused equal parts gentleness and genius and was often suggested to Gold Star's more demanding customers, like Murry. His work so inspired Henn that the young singer and songwriter abandoned his rock star dreams to pursue a lifetime of composing and arranging.[16]

The Murry that The Sunrays worked with was very different from the one portrayed in the media. Over the years, they became his stoutest defenders. "There's got to be one chef in the kitchen cooking," Medora said. "You get too many chefs and you get a lot of arguments and that's what happened with Murry and his sons.

"You can ask all five of us. [We] never saw a bad side of Murry. He was eccentric, he would get upset in the studio, but we understood that, because he was spending a lot of money to try and make records. He wanted it his way, and I think that's where he and Brian got into it. The talent end of it. Brian was out there writing with Van Dyke Parks and Roger Christian, these other people, and Murry wasn't writing with anybody, so he wasn't growing as a writer.

"We wrote a song called 'Our Leader.' It's a tribute: we gave it to Murry for Christmas Eve. That night it was snowing and cold and he busted up like a little baby. We went in the studio and wrote it: we didn't know what to give a guy that was worth millions of dollars. We cut the track all ourselves, and if you listen to the lyrics, it's almost religious. If the guy was a tyrant, obviously we wouldn't have taken the time to give him a gift like this. We would have written different lyrics."[17]

On their 1966 Murry Wilson-produced album *Andrea*, The Sunrays addressed an issue that had rapidly engulfed the nation. In the Latin-flavored Rick Henn song 'A Little Dog And His Boy,' they sing of a small dog that is informed his master has "gone away / Fighting in a foreign land."

The war in Vietnam was under way. It would soon encroach upon the world of The Beach Boys.

CHAPTER NINE

All I
Wanna Do

In May 1964, The Beach Boys released 'I Get Around' b/w 'Don't Worry Baby,' still considered one of the best double-sided singles released in the 60s. It resonated with American boys who suddenly felt left in the dust by the British Invasion.

"I'm getting bugged driving up and down the same old strip / I gotta find a new place where the kids are hip," seethed Mike's lead vocal. The Beach Boys' first response to the British Invasion amounted to a musical counterattack. By July, it had become The Beach Boys' first number one single, with 'Don't Worry Baby' charting in the Top 20 as well. Featuring odd tempo changes over jazz chords, 'I Get Around' threw down a musical and lyrical gauntlet to their rivals across the pond.

Described by David Beard, editor of *Endless Summer Quarterly*, as "the perfect machismo recording of all time," 'I Get Around' blew the Lennon/ McCartney-penned 'World Without Love' by Peter & Gordon off the charts and paved the way for The Beach Boys' former crosstown rivals, The Four Seasons, to chart their first number-one hit of 1964.[1] As 'I Get Around' began its gradual descent down the charts, The Beach Boys released *All Summer Long*, which would peak at number four on the *Billboard* album charts in the summer of 1964.

The message was clear: the beach was back. Celebrating the good old American pursuits of skirt-chasing, fast cars, drive-in movies, motorcycles, and even chili dogs, The Beach Boys reaffirmed their position as America's rock'n'roll band with *All Summer Long*. The album encapsulated all of The Beach Boys themes up to that point, even to the album cover, where Murry, still involved with the band, insisted that models be substituted for The

Beach Boys' wives and girlfriends (save for Al and Lynda Jardine, who were photographed later). Murry didn't think they looked enough like "beach girls." The band members threw footballs, built a beach bonfire, and actually buried Carl in the sand for the photographer.[2]

"It does speak to who they were, young men in their early twenties writing about and singing about their lives," Beard added. "To me, it is the consummate summer album."[3]

As usual, Carl gets a solo guitar workout with 'Carl's Big Chance.' Despite its extra-long intro, this is a 12-bar blues instrumental with honky tonk overtones. He also gets a special shout out during their sonic montage of humorous studio moments, 'Our Favorite Recording Sessions,' when Brian calls out, "We're flying over Carl Wilson, who's going to jump 600 feet into a two-foot cup."

But *All Summer Long* also featured a couple of harbingers of the future. 'Don't Back Down' would be The Beach Boys' last song about surfing until 1968's 'Do It Again.' More importantly, during the recording of 'Little Honda' (which would later be a hit for The Hondells), Brian urged Carl to crank his amp up until it distorted. Carl demurred, saying it sounded "like shit."

"Just do it," Brian insisted.[4] So Carl did it.

Had they released 'Little Honda' as a single, as was intended, it might be considered today as one of the first 60s hits to feature a distorted guitar.

* * *

For most Beach Boys fans and historians, the 1965 one-two punch of *The Beach Boys Today!* and *Summer Days (And Summer Nights!!)* occupies the same place in the Beach Boys canon as do *Rubber Soul* (1965) and *Revolver* (1966) for The Beatles; they are preludes to a paradigm shift.

In retrospect, while those two albums are essential to fully appreciating Brian Wilson, both as a composer and producer, they also mark the point where The Beach Boys' myth begins: the idea of Brian as the great genius who recorded his songs with the best and brightest triple-scale musicians in the business, then made his little surf band of brothers learn their parts off the records before sending them out to take his message to the masses. This idea that they 'didn't play their own songs' served both to diminish the band in the eyes of those who didn't like them and established the narrative that Brian was the great damaged genius surrounded by, and often hamstrung by, lesser mortals.

Repetition is the essence of memory, and over subsequent decades rehashing that story served to superfluously inflate Brian's reputation while simultaneously eroding the legacies of the other Beach Boys—particularly Carl. Much of the problem began with the paper trails that followed the recordings of demos, singles, and long players. In Los Angeles, the American Federation of Musicians (AFM) Local 47 had strict rules protecting its members, and rates varied according to the intended outcome of the sessions, so session logs were often 'massaged' by producers to squeeze a few extra dollars out of record companies or provide an occasional bonus to the engineers. In the 80s and 90s, these records would become highly prized by historians and collectors, and even identity thieves, as they contained musicians' signatures, social security numbers, and essential information about session players who went on to individual fame and fortune.

Gold Star Studios offered its 'Glamor Demo'—a fully realized demonstration record using multi-tracked multi-instrumentalists and singers like Don Ralke or Ray Pohlman—in place of a simple instrument-and-voice demo. Although they were designed to put the songwriter's best foot forward when pitching a song to a record company, these demos were often released by record companies as the master. When that happened, the producer merely went back and refiled the session forms and submitted a bill for the higher rates of a master, rather than demo, recording. However, the paper trail for that particular song ended up reflecting only the business, not the history. Few realized then that the pop records bursting from Southern California recording studios would be remembered far beyond the time of their creation.

As Stan Ross frequently observed, "in those days, it wasn't history—it was geography." Studios and session players were not concerned with the future: they just worried about competition from elsewhere.[5] Yet, the music not only survived, it prevailed, and over the years the media carrying that music changed: from vinyl records to tape cassettes to compact discs to digital downloads. And with each new step, each repackaging of the music handed down the mistakes as well as the history.

The narrative that Brian recorded the songs with the Wrecking Crew and merely sent his messengers out on the road to perform them for the crowds proved an easy sell for Beach Boys admirers and detractors alike. Yet the saga of Brian and the Wrecking Crew is more complicated than is usually described in the dozens of books and documentaries chronicling his life and work. Utilizing professional session players was an old story in Hollywood, even for the surf bands of the early 60s. The Challengers' leader and drummer Richard Delvy found it easier to produce his band's records with a session drummer (and an occasional guitarist like a young Larry Carlton) while he supervised from the booth. The Righteous Brothers, aware that they were breaking new ground with their 'blue-eyed soul' approach, often imported the young rhythm & blues and surf musicians performing at the Rendezvous to capture the necessary youthful energy. For his classic 'Miserlou,' Dick Dale brought in jazz guitarist and bassist Rene Hall for support, and Jan Berry recorded many of Jan & Dean's classics using two of Hollywood's top flight drummers, Hal Blaine and Earl Palmer. In the Hollywood music scene of the late 50s and early 60s, the issue facing record producers wasn't quality so much as meeting deadlines.

For Brian, the impetus to use session talent had much to do with the logistics of his independent productions at a time of increasing demand for The Beach Boys as performers. In the four years since they first picked up their instruments in their Hawthorne living room, the musical abilities of The Beach Boys had grown in step with Brian's songwriting and arranging sophistication. Now, however, increasing sophistication of his productions required his supplementing The Beach Boys with additional musicians rather than replacing them.

Of the five original members, Dennis and Mike were the last to learn their instruments, and Mike's saxophone—like virtually all the saxophones in the original surf bands, as guitar technology became more sophisticated—became the earliest casualty. There were two accomplished guitar players in the band, so Brian added mastery of the electric bass to his keyboard playing. He was helped by the fact that in those early surf days, bass players were required to focus only on picking out the notes in the chords. However, with Dennis literally learning his drums on the job, and Brian becoming fascinated with Jan Berry and Phil Spector's percussion-heavy production styles, importing a session musician to augment Dennis became the first order of business for Brian.

The Wrecking Crew began as the Clique—the top 200 or so members of Local 47 of the American Federation of Musicians, who frequently encountered one another on Hollywood recording sessions.[6] Over time, relationships developed among the members, and when producers booked a session they would simply ask engineers to bring in a certain number and type of instrument. The engineer would call a key musician to contract the others. Some producers developed relationships with the musicians as well.

In the early days of the Hollywood scene, most of the demand for session musicians was for film, live radio and television, and orchestras and big bands. Trained musicians who could sight-read were essential to efficient recording sessions. However, with the rock'n'roll era, producers and composers demanded musicians with the ability to improvise and who were familiar with rhythm & blues and blues. While trained jazz musicians like Hal Blaine or Carol Kaye could sight-read a written chart, untrained musicians like Glen Campbell or Jerry Cole would draw on a huge repertoire of stage-tested licks and techniques. This new mix of trained jazz musicians and others more used to life "in the trenches," explained Hal Blaine, became known as the Wrecking Crew when staid older musicians said they were "wrecking the business."

Being a professional session musician required two things: an ability to play to the highest level demanded by the producer, and an ability to get along with fellow musicians. Few could do both as well as Blaine, who, in addition to being one of the most accomplished jazz drummers of the day, had also earned his performance stripes playing in small clubs and bars where performers were expected to entertain as well as play music. Blaine was able to write a drum chart to the producer's satisfaction before tape was rolled, perform flawlessly, and then entertain the musicians and engineers during downtime. For Brian, Hal was one of the two voices he needed to approve a piece of music before it went public. The other was Carl.

Carl, said Blaine, "was a very nice kid. I don't think he felt intimidated by the Wrecking Crew at all. Remember, Brian brought in some great players." These were either already legends, like jazz guitarists Barney Kessell, Tommy Tedesco, and Howard Roberts, or they were on their way to becoming legends, like Glen Campbell and Leon Russell.

Even as a teenager surrounded by seasoned session pros, Carl "played great," recalled Blaine. "He fit right in with everybody and he knew what he was doing and he had great chops. He was a real gentleman. As far as I know, Brian always told him what to play, although when suggestions were offered, Brian's response was usually 'by all means—do it.' And Al Jardine was one of the great guitar players. They were both great." Blaine also bonded with Dennis, whom he recalled as "a good guy who was always getting banged up or showing up in a cast."[7]

On The Beach Boys' principal studio outing of 1964, *All Summer Long*, they had recorded 'Don't Back Down,' their last song with surfing lyrics, while invoking the memories of their musical heroes with 'Do You Remember.' Across the pond, their rivals The Beatles were starting to address more adult concerns in their lyrics, while Bob Dylan brought in the original 'Mr Tambourine Man'—session percussionist and guitarist Bruce Langhorne—to kick off his *Bringing It All Back Home* with a jolt of electric guitar in March of 1965.

In 1964, Sinatra and other singers of his ilk still stood as the gold standard, and even Paul McCartney shuddered when he admitted he couldn't envision himself playing songs like 'I Want To Hold Your Hand' when he was 35. For the few pop critics who took pop music seriously in the early 60s, it often revealed less of a knowledgeable appreciation of this new music than a desire to be viewed as more 'with it' than their peers, in the lexicon of the times. For songwriters, pop music still served as a musical boot camp for writers who hoped one day to hear their songs performed in lounges by tuxedo-clad crooners or middle-aged women in sparkly dresses who closed their sets with 'Born Free' or 'Climb Every Mountain.'

In his in-depth analysis of The Beach Boys' recordings, original session tapes, and data, music historian Craig Slowinski writes that *The Beach Boys Today!* "marked a turning point in the career of Brian Wilson and The Beach Boys, and proved to be the opening salvo of a triumvirate of long-players (excluding *Party)* that defined their status as premier pop artists on a level with The Beatles."[8]

For Brian, *The Beach Boys Today!* marked the first time Capitol Records singled him out and promoted him as a composer and a producer, while the rest of The Beach Boys merely appeared on the cover, making public the narrative that The Beach Boys were simply, in Dennis's words, "Brian's messengers." It also marked the period where Brian announced to the group that he would no longer be a member of the performing band and would stay home and focus on writing and producing.

According to Slowinski, Carl, who had just turned 18 in December, "had developed as a musician sufficiently to play alongside the horde of high-dollar session pros that big brother was now bringing into the studio. Carl's guitar playing on this album is a key ingredient, and in fact this is the most 'guitar heavy' of the Boys' post-surf-era albums."[9]

If 1963 was the summer of surf, and the British Invasion owned 1964, 1965 served as the year that American artists began reclaiming the pop charts: in the course of the year bands and labels such as Motown released some of the most pivotal recordings of the 60s. Bob Dylan's six-minute 'Like A Rolling Stone' still stands as one of the greatest and most groundbreaking singles of the era, while 'Mr Tambourine Man' introduced a new term: folk-rock.

Most surf music historians consider the period between 1961 and 1965 as the first wave of surf music. By 1964, vocals ruled and surf guitar had rapidly transformed over the course of a year from an entry-level guitar style to the most technique- and technology-intensive style to emerge since the early days of solo jazz guitar. In Los Angeles, the band that barely elicited shrugs at the birthplace of surf music in Balboa now headed a dynasty. The Beach Boys, rather than Dick Dale or The Bel Airs, were viewed as the godfathers of surf music, and the definition of surf ceased being the lead-guitar-heavy 'instro' instrumental. Thanks to The Beach Boys, listeners now viewed surf as sophisticated pop music wrapped in youthful harmonies that sent unexpected shivers up their spines.

Music technology, too, was changing. The British Invasion bands brought with them new British amp designs from makers such as Vox, favored by The Beatles, which offered Fender a formidable rival throughout 1964. Yet in England, Vox faced a challenge from music store owner Jim Marshall, who had begun building amps in the early 60s. Marshall hoped to merge the beauty and clarity of the old tweed Fender Bassman with the power of the Fender Showman amps in what became the forerunner of the Marshall stack, intended to be "like a Fender, but more so."[10]

The year 1965 would see a guitar renaissance and that put The Beach Boys' competition back on a level playing field with the band. The end of 1964 had seen The Beatles offer up a feedback intro on 'I Feel Fine.' In February 1965, singer Jewel Akens soared up the charts with 'The Birds And The Bees,' featuring a lead guitar plugged into a Leslie rotating organ speaker. Then Bruce Johnston's songwriting partner Terry Melcher discovered that plugging a 12-string guitar into a compressor produced the shimmering, jangling effect that would define The Byrds' folk rock sound.

The Beach Boys' 'Dance, Dance, Dance,' released as a single in October 1964, is an example of a type of music that helped lay the groundwork for future guitar styles. The bulk of the song is built on a guitar riff, created by Carl. The Kinks did something similar in 'All Day And All Of The Night,' as did The Rolling Stones with 'Satisfaction.' But it was still a rarity in an era when the vast majority of songs were constructed on a keyboard.

Even Phil Spector realized the times were changing and began seeking out guitar bands to mount the folk-rock bandwagon that The Byrds kicked off in April 1965. He began developing a relationship with singer-songwriter Bobby Fuller and often sat in with his band, The Bobby Fuller Four.[11] When the Modern Folk Quartet (MFQ) considered moving into folk rock, Spector herded them into the studio to record 'This Could Be The Night,' written by Harry Nilsson. MFQ member Henry Diltz, later to become a renowned photojournalist, remembered Brian rushing down to Gold Star in his bathrobe to witness the recording sessions for 'This Could Be The Night,' a song Brian loved so much that he recorded an accurate recreation of the song for a 1995 tribute album to Nilsson.[12]

In late 1965, Spector suffered both an insult and injury when his production of The Righteous Brothers' 'Hung On You' stiffed and disc jockeys began flipping the record over to make the Bill Medley-produced B-side 'Unchained Melody' a hit. However, since Spector was technically the executive producer of the session that yielded the hit, he added his name as producer on subsequent pressings. To exacerbate matters, Spector then had to emulate Medley's production on the follow-up, with 'Ebb Tide.' The next big Wall of Sound Righteous Brothers hit, after they'd left to join the Verve label, would be entirely produced by Medley.

The Beach Boys started 1965 auspiciously enough. Co-written by Carl, Brian, and Mike, 'Dance, Dance, Dance' had peaked at number eight in October 1964. It was followed by the band's second most popular Christmas single, 'The Man With All The Toys,' which hit number three in time for the holiday. 'Dance, Dance, Dance' reveals a producer who is now confident in the studio and a lead guitarist who has been listening to The Beatles. The song features three guitars: Carl on electric 12-string, session guitarist Glen Campbell on acoustic six-string, and Al on electric six-string guitar. Brian plays bass, in conjunction with Ray Pohlman on six-string electric bass. Dennis plays drums and Carl Fortina plays accordion—the closest thing to a keyboard on the track.

Typically of The Beach Boys' recordings of the time, Brian had the band play the core instruments while importing session musicians to play incidental percussion. Hal Blaine played sleigh bell, triangle, tambourine, and castanets. Saxophonists Steve Douglas and Jay Migliori pushed unobtrusive intervals to buttress the choruses. Carl played his guitar solo live (with the band) on the takes rather than overdubbing it later.[13]

The first major change in The Beach Boys' sound came about after *Surfin' Safari*, when Carl began running a Fender solidbody guitar through a Showman amp and a Fender Reverb. It would be Carl again who transformed the band's sound in 1964 when he switched from the clean, sharp tone of his six-string Fender Jaguar to the richer, more diffuse sound of the Rickenbacker 12-string—a sound he tried to emulate on synthesizers when he recorded 'Feel Flows' for the *Surf's Up* album of 1971.

Where many 60s artists resorted to studio technology such as compressors to wring out and equalize all of the distinctive tones of the 12-string, Carl kept his sound clean, unencumbered, and understated. On songs like 'Let Him Run Wild' and 'That's Not Me,' he kept his tones so pure that they could be mistaken for a six-string guitar playing octaves. The sound of the 12-string distinguished most of the key hits of The Beach Boys between 'Dance, Dance, Dance' and 'Wouldn't It Be Nice,' just as the sound of the Jaguar characterized the post-*Surfin' Safari* hits. "It changed their texture when you hear a 12-string in their songs," said Jon Stebbins.[14]

More importantly, the new richer Beach Boys sound helped usher the band from the surfing, cars, and girls themes to the more mature romantic themes and dance music Brian began exploring as 1964 gave way 1965. The physical differences between a 12-string guitar and a six-string, however, didn't encourage single note picking as much as playing chords and intervals. It was the choice of a 12-string, and the direction it took both his playing and Brian's productions, that cost Carl respect as a guitarist, while his peers were lavished with praise for playing far less challenging chord forms and arrangements.

"Remember that the first string you strike on a downward picking stroke is the octave string on all 12-strings except for the Rickenbacker;

those 12-strings reversed the order of the octave and natural string pairs," said author and guitarist John Blair. "The other popular electric 12-strings of that time, the Gibson ES 335-12 and the Fender Electric XII, both had a 7.25-inch neck radius, the same as the Fender Jazzmaster at that time. The necks were a lot easier to chord on those [Rickenbacker] guitars."[15]

Yet, the biggest impact the switch to the 12-string had for Carl was when they moved from the old surf sound of heavy flatwound strings to the lighter roundwound strings favored by guitarists in the mid 60s. Carl now faced a new issue: string breakage. Heavy- or medium-gauge flatwound strings withstood the strongest assaults, whereas roundwound strings and lighter gauges tended to wear more rapidly and break, especially when notes are bent. The tale goes that Eric Clapton acquired the nickname 'Slowhand' when his strings broke onstage and the show would stop as he restrung his guitar. As the audience grew restive, they would try to accelerate Clapton's onstage repair job with a slow applause—or 'slow hand.'

Lighter gauge strings and new guitar styles that emphasized bends or slurs brought about the need for backup guitars onstage. Carl soon abandoned the surf sound of the Jaguar for a collection of guitars that ran from Telecasters to semi-hollowbody guitars, both six- and 12-string models.

One of Carl's longest musical partnerships began in 1965 when the original teen idols—Dino, Desi & Billy—opened up for The Beach Boys at a show in Bakersfield, featuring singer Donna Loren and The Byrds. Dino, Desi & Billy were made up of Dean 'Dino' Martin, son of lounge singer Dean Martin; Desi Arnaz Jr, son of Desi Arnaz and Lucille Ball; and their friend Billy Hinsche. Over time, two of these would become Carl's brothers-in-law when he married Billy's sister Annie Hinsche and later married Dino's sister, Gina Martin.

"We were like so many other garage bands," Hinsche said. "The only difference was that we practiced in Lucille Ball's garage." As a guitarist who had grown up in a musical family and studied stringed instruments from violins to ukuleles before tackling the guitar, Hinsche immediately bonded with Carl, who was only a few years older.

Hinsche found that Carl "was always mature for his age—always thoughtful and serious and handled everything in a very mature way." Carl's maturity impressed Hinsche in a big way, as they both became rock stars while still in high school. "When you're young and dumb and you don't know better, you think you're more mature than you actually are."

The show in Bakersfield "was a hell of a show for two dollars and sixty cents. The Beach Boys took us under their wing. The Byrds were not happy that they preceded us in the running order." Dino, Desi & Billy later opened up for The Beach Boys in Hawaii. "I think they took us to Hawaii to make up for taking us to Bakersfield," Hinsche added. "We had so much fun with those guys in Hawaii."

As guitarists are wont to do, Carl spent considerable time on the tour imparting his knowledge and experience to Hinsche, who was five years younger. Billy went on to apply his learning as both a touring Beach Boy and a member of Carl's band in the early 80s.

Carl, said Hinsche, "didn't have to be the lead guitar on everything. That wasn't his style. He was more of a rock'n'roll Chuck Berry soloist than a Buddy Guy soloist and he developed his own solo style. He was more into the subtleties of putting an inverted bass into a chord. *Pet Sounds* is full of inverted bass notes: 'God Only Knows' is a prime example."

Most importantly, Hinsche said, Carl taught him that an instrument was a means to an end, not the end itself. "His family time was his down time. He didn't want to spend hours jamming the blues."[16]

As historian Jon Stebbins has pointed out, for the first years of The Beach Boys' existence, Carl viewed himself as a lead guitarist who sang, rather than a singer who accompanied himself on guitar.[17] Blessed, like Brian, with perfect pitch, Carl supplied vocals that were the lynchpin of the Beach Boys harmonies. In the backgrounds his seamless intervals with Marks and later Jardine provided a perfect tonal center for Brian's signature falsetto and Mike's distinctive bass. Oddly enough, considering he eventually rivaled Mike and Brian as the lead singer on the key songs, Carl allowed Mike, Brian, Dennis, and later Al to carry the bulk of the lead singing until *Summer Days (And Summer Nights!!)*, where he was persuaded to take on 'Girl Don't Tell Me.'

As engineer Stephen Desper noted, Carl always took immaculate care with his guitars, and when The Beach Boys' road crew was busy would carefully wipe down his guitars' strings and finish after each performance. He was also generous with his guitars. The guitarists who later became part of the touring band often availed themselves of Carl's collection. Al, who showed a preference for Stratocasters and later Gibson Les Pauls, is often seen playing Carl's Jaguar, such as in the 1964 *T.A.M.I. Show* (*Teen Age Music International*) appearance or their first *Ready, Steady, Go* appearance, where Carl's Rickenbacker provided a reasonable substitute for the harpsichord Brian used on 'When I Grow Up To Be A Man.'[18]

When John Daly became Carl's lead guitarist during Carl's solo career in the early 80s, he found Carl a far different guitarist than most guitar players. "Most musicians will not allow you to use their instruments under any circumstances," said Daly. "From the first day, he gave me an Epiphone six-string and a 12-string." When they went onstage, Carl motioned to his guitar quiver. "He said 'These are yours to use.' Some of these guitars were made for him."[19]

When Carl became the most successful of the surf guitarists, he more than any other musician sold the sound of surf to the listening public living beyond Southern California. Now, equipped with the first of many 12-string guitars, he would define the guitar sound of The Beach Boys during the most important years of their career.

CHAPTER TEN

Bright Lights

For The Beach Boys, 1965 was the best of times and the worst of times. In the waning days of 1964, Brian suffered his first nervous breakdown, on the plane to an appearance in Houston, and flew back to Los Angeles, where he determined he could no longer be "Mr Everything," as he told The Beach Boys' publicist, Earl Leaf.

"I was very close to Brian," Carl later recalled. "I was with him the day he couldn't continue any longer. I was with him in the morning and I knew that it wasn't just that he was copping out—he couldn't take it any longer."[1]

Session guitarist and folk singer Glen Campbell quickly replaced Brian onstage, playing bass rather than his usual guitar. Although Brian briefly rejoined the band in Glen's absence in February, he made it clear that his role in The Beach Boys would be strictly that of songwriter and producer. At the meeting where he announced the brave new world The Beach Boys would inhabit, band members reacted with dismay (with Al in tears and Dennis reportedly threatening to bash somebody with an ashtray). It would be left to 'good old Carl' to quietly calm everybody's fears, setting out how things would work from there on.[2]

Onstage, The Beach Boys were unstoppable, performing for thousands of screaming fans throughout 1965. Even though Campbell admitted to making about "two million mistakes" during his first performance with the band, he said nobody heard them over the screaming. While Carl never had a formal endorsement deal with Fender Musical Instruments, they often brought him prototype guitars to test-drive. In early 1965, he switched from his Rickenbacker to a Fender XII 12-string guitar, before working his way back to the Rickenbacker and a growing selection of Gibsons and Epiphones.

With The Beach Boys touring constantly, Brian enjoyed the luxury of being able to write and produce at a far more leisurely pace than he had as a member of the band. He began recording *The Beach Boys Today!*, the first of The Beach Boys' 1965 albums, relying more on session players than he had in the past and producing songs and arrangements that would earn him what writer Jules Siegel in his article 'Goodbye Surfing, Hello God' would call the status of a "big G genius" in the music industry.[3] Brian depended less and less on the other Beach Boys to play their instruments in the studio (and they seldom argued because, as Al Jardine noted "we were glad to not be there for all of that hard work").[4]

Nonetheless, Brian still looked to Carl's guitar and "supersensitive" ear to help him in the studio for both his Beach Boys work and independent productions such as 'Guess I'm Dumb,' the single he wrote for Glen Campbell. "When I sit down at the piano and play a new song, the others can visualize the whole arrangement right away," said Brian in 1965. "We take the melody apart and work it out phrase by phrase. If they don't like my approach, they suggest another. If Carl doesn't dig my idea, I'll change it immediately, because Carl has exquisite musical taste. I trust it completely."[5]

With the exception of their 1963 album *Little Deuce Coupe*, The Beach Boys' musical sophistication rose in a steady arc, and with *The Beach Boys Today!*, released in March 1965, the arc rose more steeply. With Murry no longer a part of the organization, and his involvement now on an invitation-only basis, Brian experienced a creative freedom in the studio known by few other producers.

However, firing Murry didn't resolve the problem of Murry. *The Beach Boys Today!* featured the original version of 'Help Me, Ronda,' which would be reworked and renamed as 'Help Me, Rhonda,' to become their second number one. For 'Help Me, Ronda,' Brian surrounded Carl—the only Beach Boy to perform on the rhythm track—with members of the Wrecking Crew, including Glen Campbell, Leon Russell, Hal Blaine, Ray Pohlman,

Billy Strange on ukulele, and Billy Riley on double-reed harmonica, among others. The remaining Beach Boys formed a handclap chorus.

When Brian attempted a leaner, more AM radio-friendly version for a single release, he made the mistake of inviting Murry to the session. The results of that decision are now known among Beach Boys enthusiasts as the 'I'm a genius, too,' session, after a clearly inebriated Murry managed to sabotage the session under the guise of being supportive.

The original tape of the session, from February 24, runs for nearly three-quarters of an hour, and while Murry compliments both Al and Mike, he accuses Carl of "loafing." He admits to being drunk and requests the guys sing "a chord … like we used to do when you used to make clear records." As his halting diatribe continues—"I've got 3,000 words to say"—he begins slurring his words.

A calm Brian stands up to his father and says, "We would like to record in an atmosphere of calmness." Murry makes the remark that will haunt what is left of his reputation for years when he attempts to dress down Brian: "I'm a genius, too." With Audree's encouragement, Murry finally leaves and the session is aborted.[6] Nonetheless, like 'Fun, Fun, Fun,' the new single, sung by Al, reached number one, vindicating Brian once again.

The affair didn't end there. In May, Murry sent Brian a rambling and sometimes barely coherent nine-page letter on the letterhead of Sea Of Tunes, the publishing company he had set up in 1962 to manage The Beach Boys' songwriting. In it, he attempts to exculpate himself of any wrongdoing and lay blame for his sins and misfortunes on pretty much everybody but himself. He indicts Audree, Mike Love, Jan Berry, Hollywood "phonies," and even David Marks's mother, among others, for turning The Beach Boys against him. At one point, he suggests that The Beach Boys break up because of the many sins they have committed: "lascivious conduct on the part of one of the members, which I can prove, along with one or two more violations of the law which could be construed as felonies by a judge in a court of law."

In the letter, Murry strikes back like a wounded beast, regurgitating every slight, real or imagined, while ladling on the guilt. It is not the letter of an angry parent, or a loving, but disappointed parent, but somebody who needs professional help—but doesn't get any.

After accusing Audree of a lifetime of undermining her son's confidence in their father, Murry portrays himself as a victim: "Maybe now you can begin to understand that the last seven years has been almost a living hell for me and although I have wanted to give up completely on two separate occasions, something told me to hang on and keep trying because I felt my sons were worth it. ... I could no longer reach you, and your natural resentment against me which had been building up through things mentioned before in this letter, became magnified to the point where you acted like you hated me on many occasions."[7]

The letter clearly devastated Brian, yet, in true Wilson fashion, he soldiered on. Now freed from the bonds of family on the road and in the control booth, Brian wrote the songs that inspired legions of followers and kept The Beatles on their toes: 'She Knows Me Too Well,' 'Kiss Me, Baby,' 'In The Back Of My Mind,' and others.

With Brian anchoring the studio, the musical leadership that had shifted so often before in the touring band fell permanently to Carl and Mike, while in the studio Carl would be Brian's first call. He would also keep the band informed of what was going on in the studio while they slugged it out on the road before ever-growing legions of screaming fans.

With Murry busy with The Sunrays, Brian found time to explore new horizons. While Brian and the others had experimented with marijuana and drunk alcohol on the road, a friend now suggested he try a new drug: LSD. After hours of tripping, Brian found his way to a piano at about 2:30 in the morning and became mesmerized by a phrase that reminded him of an old western movie. It would be the start of 'California Girls.'

* * *

In late 1964, Lyndon Johnson defeated Senator Barry Goldwater in a landslide victory to become president. The conflict in Vietnam was escalating, and young Americans were being sent abroad to fight. Carl had no infirmities that would land him the coveted 4-F status that would exempt him from military service under the United States Selective Service System, commonly known as the Draft.

With two older brothers exempt (Brian had hearing loss and Dennis claimed he had told his local draft board he was gay, gays being automatically exempt in the 60s), and because he was not attending college, Carl would become a prime target for the draft. Healthy, heterosexual 19-to-21-year-old single males, neither in college nor working in the defense industry, were the preferred demographic for selection. And, with his two older brothers exempt, he was not his parents' 'only living son,' which would be a major issue, were he killed in conflict.

In real life, Carl was one of the most valued members of the biggest band in America and a beloved musician who had performed in front of hundreds of fans, made movies like *The Monkey's Uncle* and *The Girls On The Beach*, and recorded television theme songs like 'Karen,' from the short-lived series *90 Bristol Court*. To his local draft board, Carl was merely an uneducated young single man healthy enough to carry a rifle and fight and die for his country.

Debate rages to this day about the degree to which the famous Gulf of Tonkin incident constituted a 'false flag' event—an event fabricated or exaggerated to bring America into the growing Vietnam conflict in Southeast Asia. On August 2, 1964, an American destroyer, the USS Maddox, reported being attacked by three North Vietnamese torpedo boats, and conflict ensued. President Johnson used the incident to request Congress's support to take action against North Vietnam without securing a formal declaration of war. The first American ground troops (besides military advisors) arrived in March 1965.

Most of Carl's contemporaries in 1965 were far enough past their late teens/early 20s that the draft ceased to be of concern. Johnson intimated during his campaign that he didn't want to preside over American boys dying in an Asian war. Yet, for the next two years, in the eyes of the Selective Service System, Carl Wilson was a moving target.

Meanwhile, Brian proceeded with 'California Girls' and Glen Campbell donned Brian's candy-striped shirt and Olympic white bass. The Beach Boys were now on the road, constructing their set lists from an ever-growing selection of hits and album favorites for ever-growing audiences.

On the pop charts, hits by harder-edged blues-based bands from the UK such as The Kinks, The Yardbirds, and The Rolling Stones squeezed out the poppier hits by charming British Invasion bands such as Herman's Hermits and Freddie & The Dreamers.

Newer surf bands along the California coast, such as The Sandals, progressed from the old Dick Dale-style driving lead guitars to the fatter sounds of semi-hollow and acoustic guitars and exotic European instruments. They used them to back the surfing footage that became Bruce Brown's critically acclaimed feature film *Endless Summer*. Between The Beatles' impact and the massive success of three years of Beach Boys hits, the old surf bands found themselves—in modern terms—'repurposed' either to sound English or to mimic the harmonies of The Beach Boys.

In 1965, the competition grew fiercer. Every day a new generation of record buyers swelled the ranks while a new generation of folk music refugees such as Bob Dylan, Roger McGuinn, David Crosby, Neil Young, and Stephen Stills abandoned the folk scene in favor of Beatles-inspired electric rock. Listeners from earlier generations—particularly America's literati on the East Coast, who recoiled at The Beach Boys' simple sun-and-fun lyrical themes—now embraced the burgeoning lyrical complexity of the new music emerging in 1965. The old order had fallen and a new one begun, and those who couldn't keep up would be consigned to small-town dance halls and county fairs and then oblivion.

Thanks to the influence of folk music, lyrics became increasingly important in what was once seen as mindless teenage entertainment. Bob Dylan now stood as the intellectual gold standard when his six-minute opus 'Like A Rolling Stone' finally broke the unwritten three-minutes-or-less single rule (although Phil Spector inflicted the first cut with The Righteous Brothers' 1964 hit 'You've Lost That Lovin' Feelin',' which came in at 3:55).

A new generation of folk singers such as Phil Ochs, Donovan, and even former New Christy Minstrels singer Barry McGuire now had, in Ochs's phrase, "something to say, sir, and I'm going to say it now."[8] For many, the carefree sunshine-filled lyrics of The Beach Boys were an important tonic for a world consumed by the Cold War, the escalating Vietnam conflict, and the racial tensions revealed by the civil rights movement. However, others began to view the band as an anachronism, mere vestiges of a simpler time now overtaken by grim events.

Context is critical when assessing this period of The Beach Boys' music. They had survived the British Invasion with 'the formula,' a much-maligned Mike Love term to describe music that entertained and made people happy. To use his other favorite term, it was 'positivity' with a great beat, and you could dance to it. While Brian made the rounds in Los Angeles, recording at his favorite studios surrounded by Hollywood's rock'n'roll aristocracy and spending his days in the studios with the cutting edge producers of modern pop such as Phil Spector, The Beach Boys were on the road selling songs that had been recorded months or years before. While Brian witnessed and pursued the future in Los Angeles, The Beach Boys personally witnessed the impact of their music on the audiences from a matter of yards.

However, while waves of applause washed over the band on tour, Brian still felt the pressure at home. In music as in movies, one is only as good as one's last hit. The first thing songwriters learn is that, while record companies will pressure them to produce a new and improved version of their last hit, they can only produce so many similar-sounding songs before they start running out of viable melodies and risk repeating themselves.

Comebacks in the mid 60s were few and far between. The first generation of 50s rockers gradually receded back into the roots music, such as country and rhythm & blues, that had spawned rock'n'roll. In the early 60s, most singers, such as Elvis or Bobby Darin, saw the path of superstardom as leading from records to movies, movies to trendy nightclubs, and then on to the entertainment industry's elephant's graveyard known as Las Vegas.

But the audiences of 1965 changed all of that. In Hollywood, older clubs, such as Ciro's, which once catered to the mink coat and dinner jacket crowd, turned from older 'showbiz' types of acts to newer acts like The Byrds to attract younger audiences. They saw it as simple arithmetic: bands drew girls, girls attracted guys, guys bought drinks. Rock'n'roll was as much a mating ritual as a style of music. Clubs were no longer the refuge of artists with a solid canon of hits and a devout fan base; they became launching pads for acts who would move up the street to larger venues and sign lucrative record contracts.

The Beach Boys were born of technology when Carl plugged his Stratocaster into a Showman and transformed a singing group into a surf band. Brian's songs, recorded in a selection of state-of-the-art recording studios, broke the British occupation of American radio playlists. The Beach Boys anchored the West Coast sound. They were the first band to self-produce, self-publish, and take on their own management. Now, they established another 'first' by acquiring the first custom-designed public address (PA) system.

In the 50s and early 60s, bands were at the mercy of concert promoters when it came to public address systems. For The Beach Boys, whose livelihoods depended on their harmonies, using other people's PA systems proved to be too much of a risk, so they contacted Conrad Sundholm, co-founder of the Sunn Musical Equipment Company. It was, he said, "a custom-built system, better than anything else out there.

"It was first called the Beach Boys PA and it had a four-channel passive mixer in a box with a Mark III amplifier. That was the head, with the four-channel Switchcraft mixer. We built it, checked it out, and within a couple of hours I was on a plane to Salt Lake City. They were performing at the Lagoon Amusement Park and I had trouble finding someone to cart the stuff out there. The band was waiting to perform, but we got there and got set up and they ended up buying it; took it with them."[9]

In an ironic twist, even though The Beach Boys would drop out of the 1967 Monterey Pop Festival, they had contracted out their system, commanded by Beach Boys engineer Stephen Desper to supply live sound for the event. When Jimi Hendrix burned his Stratocaster onstage, it was only a few feet in front of Desper running the sound.[10]

Like its predecessors. *The Beach Boys Today!* shot up the charts and peaked at number four. The reworked 'Help Me, Rhonda' gave The Beach Boys their second number one single. Glen Campbell turned in his resignation to return to his lucrative session work and burgeoning solo career. As a thank you, Brian and Carl went into the studio to deliver a Burt Bacharachesque single, 'Guess I'm Dumb.' (At a 1971 concert at the Santa Monica Civic auditorium, Mike joked that Campbell left because he caught Dennis "cheating at poker."[11])

Mike made a frantic call to classically trained pianist and songwriter Bruce Johnston, a long-time veteran of the Los Angeles music scene, to help them find a bassist to fill in during their April/May tour of the South and East Coast. When Johnston couldn't find a suitable replacement, he volunteered himself and learned enough basslines to make the first show on April 9 in Louisiana. Like Carl, Johnston had begun in the music business as a teenager and played in a band with Ritchie Valens but was too young to go on tour. He played briefly with The Gamblers (and performed on their record 'Moon Dawg'), and recorded a seminal 'surf' album for Del-Fi Records, before scoring hits with his songwriting partner Terry Melcher as Bruce & Terry and with The Rip Chords' hit 'Hey Little Cobra.'

In 1958, Johnston had witnessed the murder of one of the most important figures on the early Los Angeles music scene, producer John Dolphin, founder of the Dolphin's of Hollywood record store. An irate songwriter had barreled into the office with a gun and pumped rounds into the startled Dolphin. A shocked Johnston, who had just been speaking to Dolphin, managed to calm the shooter and convince him to put down the gun.

Not only did Johnston's newly found bass skills pass muster, after instruction by Carl and Al, the band's original bass player, but he provided an excellent substitute for Brian's vocal parts. He also gave the touring Beach Boys a majority of actual surfers for the first time in their career.

* * *

When The Beach Boys returned from touring, they found waiting for them what would be their next hit single, 'California Girls.' True to the formula,

'California Girls' loped along on a rolling bassline that could have come from Aaron Copland or a western movie. Yet, while Mike scribbled out lyrics for the song—a celebration of girls all over the world, but mostly California—Brian threw the band a curve. The song began with what could be called more of a prelude than an intro. It is built on Carl's 12-string guitar, supporting swelling horns and punctuated by delicate percussion, before launching into what Brian called "a traditional country & western left hand piano riff, like an old country song from the early 50s. I wanted to get something that had kind of a jumpy feeling to it in the verses."[12]

"We got a very special sound [for 'California Girls'] by isolating Carl from the band," Al Jardine told David Beard. "I used the same technique in 1979 for the intro for 'Lady Lynda.'"[13]

Released in July of 1965, *Summer Days (And Summer Nights!!)* served as Brian Wilson's musical state-of-the-union address. In true competitive Beach Boys spirit, the band took on all comers. 'California Girls,' 'Salt Lake City,' and 'Amusement Parks USA' distilled The Beach Boys' essence of rollicking, harmony-laden rock'n'roll. Carl's first vocal solo since *Shut Down Volume 2* on 'Girl Don't Tell Me' took on The Beatles on their own musical turf. In it, he first exhibits his ballad voice, somewhere between John Lennon's and Paul McCartney's, foreshadowing the sound and mood he would bring to perfection on 'God Only Knows.' Just as Carl would 'shadow' Brian's vocals later, during the reconstruction of *SMiLE* tracks in the *20/20* and *Sunflower* eras, on 'Girl Don't Tell Me' he shadows the two Beatles' vocals without directly imitating either of them. And here he shows a real feeling for the lyrics, too: the protagonist has moved beyond heartbreak into healing and just wants to close out the affair. Carl sings with the voice of a man whose heartache is still real, but recognises there is no future in the relationship. In his liner note, Brian wryly remarked, "I'm glad I finally wrote a song Carl dug singin'."[14]

Meanwhile, 'You're So Good To Me' showed the band could deliver the dance beat popular on Stax/Volt and Motown records. The chorus nearly incapacitated the exhausted band during the recording. "I remember how hilarious that session was," Jardine later recalled. "Brian would have us in the studio as soon as we returned from the road, because he was so impatient to get us back in the studio. We started laughing around the microphone so hard that I couldn't stop laughing. The actual muscular requirement to sing the 'la la la la la la las' made my tongue start to freeze up—literally—from the exertion after being on the road for so many months. I completely lost control of myself and fell on the floor laughing."[15]

'Let Him Run Wild,' seen by most music historians as a prelude to *Pet Sounds*, perfectly captured the dynamics, gorgeous melodies, and shifting tempos of a Bacharach/David hit, while 'The Girl From New York City' threw a sunburn on The Ad Libs' monster hit 'The Boy From New York City.' As always, Brian honored Phil Spector, in this case with a reworking of his hit for The Crystals, 'Then I Kissed Him,' with the genders switched to 'Then I Kissed Her.'

For this album, there would be no rock'n'roll guitar instrumental workouts, but instead a lovely orchestrated instrumental interlude, with a jazzy tremolo-laden guitar, called 'Summer Means New Love.'

According to legend, Dennis Wilson either passed out or overslept in his trailer for the requisite Beach Boys 'humor' track: a barely disguised dig at Murry called 'I'm Bugged At My Old Man,' where Brian (billed as 'Too embarrassed' on the jacket) burlesques Elvis yet still manages to wail on the high notes. They end with what would be for Murry the unkindest cut of all: "And he doesn't even know where it's at." The final track, 'And Your Dream Comes True,' was a gentle reminder to the world that, when it came to sophisticated harmonies, The Beach Boys were still the best.

Carl saw *Summer Days (And Summer Nights!!)* as a "turning point" in the way that it showed "Brian really getting into a very expansive stream of energy. We could see that he was opening up and making very serious music, and it was serious rock'n'roll music, which made it complete."[16]

As printers and pressing plants prepared the one-two punch of *Summer Days (And Summer Nights!!)* and 'California Girls,' The Beach Boys prepared for another summer of incessant touring. Brian rejoined the group just long enough to make their first hometown performance at the Hollywood Bowl on July 3, in front of 14,000 fans, where they headlined over a variety of major acts including Dino, Desi & Billy. The next day, a badly promoted Fourth of July show in San Francisco drew only 3,500 people for a performance on a hot, muggy afternoon. After the promoters were unable to pay one of the support acts, The Kinks, they simply waved to the audience and walked offstage.

Bruce had now become an official member—but not a corporate member—of The Beach Boys, and within months, *Summer Days (And Summer Nights!!)* would reach number two on the album charts while 'California Girls' peaked at number two on the singles charts, up against some of the stiffest competition of their career, coming from Detroit, England, the East Coast, and even their own Hollywood backyard. Yet in the summer of 1965, The Beach Boys were making more than hits. They were making history on the road and in the studio. All that was left for them to do was to produce the greatest American musical statement of the 60s.

Hurry Love

For budding guitarists in America's heartland or the United Kingdom, radio didn't always offer the diversity available to musicians raised along the southern third of California's nearly 3,500 miles of coastline. Los Angeles not only featured dozens of radio stations, it had the distinction of offering KGFJ, which in 1927 had become the first radio station in the United States to broadcast 24 hours a day. Added to which, on clear nights, wisps of country radio from Bakersfield or rhythm & blues from Mexican border stations might drift into Los Angeles's airspace. "Listening to the radio when we were growing up was such a big part of life," said Carl.[1]

One of the most important stations in pop music history, KRKD, broadcast from the 24-hour music store Dolphin's of Hollywood, founded by John Dolphin, which specialized in African-American music. Dolphin's store was located in the South Central section of Los Angeles district near the intersection of Vernon Avenue and Central Avenue. He added 'of Hollywood' when he was unable to open there, and announced that if he couldn't bring African-Americans to Hollywood, he would bring Hollywood to them.

Record buyers could watch disc jockeys such as Hunter Hancock and Dick 'Huggy Boy' Hugg spin platters while they perused the racks into the small hours of the morning. When producers had new records to spin, a pitch to Dolphin was their first stop. Hugg even debuted the record that today is defined as the first soul record, combining pop sensibilities with pure gospel emotion and singing techniques: 'You Send Me' by Sam Cooke.

The Beach Boys reaped the musical rewards of growing up in a major metropolis in the increasingly technological post-war years. The radio had once been the center of family life, where the whole family would gather around to listen to programs like *The Lone Ranger*, or live broadcasts of music. Now transistor radios meant that young people were privately connected to worlds parents or siblings would neither endure nor request.

While the history of rock'n'roll has been generally accepted as a black-and-white paradigm in most major cities, California's south west coast offered a far more diverse mosaic of musical influences. Carl Wilson grew up in the narrow timeframe between radio-as-family-activity and the beginnings of the 'Boss Radio' or 'Top 40' formula, where disc jockeys yielded up their power to program directors, playlists were limited to repeating the most popular songs in the upper reaches of the charts, and strict formats were imposed to limit what radio stations called 'tune-out' factors such as talk and news breaks.

After years of scoring hit after hit, the number of cover tunes The Beach Boys performed dwindled. With ten chart-topping albums and nearly twenty Top 40 singles released over the course of the preceding three years, their set lists were filled with Beach Boys' originals, while covers like 'Riot In Cell Block Nine,' 'The Wanderer,' 'Let's Go Trippin',' and 'Monster Mash' gradually receded into memory.

Cover tunes perform a double-edged function for live acts. Recent hits serve as crowd pleasers to keep audiences attentive while they're trying to digest newer music. And classics like Chuck Berry's 'Johnny B. Goode' (which The Beach Boys retained in their set for decades) make and retain connections with their audience by showing the context from which an artist has emerged.

With *Summer Days (And Summer Nights!!)*, released in July 1965, with its wide range of styles and influences, from Motown to Mancini, Brian had made it clear that he was listening to—and learning from—the radio. The Beach Boys' next album would be another innovation: *Beach Boys' Party!*, a live album that wasn't a concert album. Often dismissed as a simple stopgap measure for Brian to marshal the necessary resources for what would become *Pet Sounds*, *Beach Boys' Party!* served two purposes: offering their fans interpretations of songs by The Beach Boys' influences, and revealing the individual members and the music they listened to. For example, 'I

Should Have Known Better,' the flip side of The Beatles' American single of 'A Hard Day's Night,' was Carl's favorite Beatles song, according to Brian. He sang it here, along with Al, and they also shared the lead on another Beatles song, 'Tell Me Why.'

Beach Boys' Party! began when Capitol notified Brian that he should have an album ready for release for the Christmas buying season. Creatively drained after releasing two hit albums and four Top Ten singles in less than a year, Brian scoured his brain for an idea that would please record company and fans alike. In September, Brian herded The Beach Boys and their wives, significant others, and friends back into the studio for a very different album than they had produced before. Carl arrived with both his fiancée Annie Hinsche and her brother Billy. With Hal Blaine on hand to play bongos and incidental percussion, they recreated the informal jams that harked back to the old Hawthorne living room days. As Brian later wrote, "The way that the conversation kept goin' between songs was exciting. We were cookin'. Our friends were all smiles throughout the whole recording. The mood was up and we were on our way."[2]

To most, *Pet Sounds* rightly stands as the apotheosis of The Beach Boys' art, with *Today!* and *Summer Days (And Summer Nights!!)* coming in right behind. *Sunflower*, *Surf's Up*, and *Holland* are often considered in the same breath as *Pet Sounds*, but are qualified with an asterisk as they were produced by The Beach Boys and not Brian. Some are controversial, such as *The Beach Boys Love You*, and many fall into the 'love 'em or hate 'em' category, such as *Smiley Smile*, *M.I.U. Album*, and *Carl And The Passions "So Tough"*.

Many of The Beach Boys' albums are seen as mere historical milestones on the road to worthier works, and these are considered the orphans of the canon. *Surfin' Safari*, *Surfin' USA*, and *The Beach Boys* (1985) suffer in the historical assessment of their work because the production credits list a producer other than Brian Wilson or all of The Beach Boys.

The importance of *Beach Boys' Party!* is that, by 1965, it was becoming common knowledge that Brian imported session musicians to augment the band. Yet *Party!* offers an important snapshot of the most important American band of the 60s, showing them to be excellent singers and musicians, playing songs they loved. It showed they could match their rivals in contemporary folk- and country-based pop, with songs such as Johnny Rivers's version of 'Mountain Of Love' and The Beatles' 'You've Got To Hide Your Love Away,' sung by Dennis, as well as in hometown rhythm & blues and the jazz-flavored Spectoresque pop in which they'd trafficked since the beginning.

The album also illustrated the importance of Al Jardine's replacing David Marks on rhythm guitar and vocals. David and Carl were musical soul brothers, anointed by John Maus's teachings and immersed in the heavier guitar styles of Dick Dale, Duane Eddy, and Chuck Berry. Al brought a folk sensibility that became more important after folk music began winding its way through The Beatles' repertoire, reaching its apex with the folk- and country-based songs that would be included on the American version of *Rubber Soul*, on Capitol, rather than the English version on Parlophone. Marks's knowledge of rock'n'roll and blues styles perfectly complemented Carl's rhythm & blues and surf background, but Jardine introduced the strumming and picking techniques that propelled folk, topical, and protest songs. These included 'Carter picking' (named for Carter Family guitarist June Carter) in which the player alternates between single-note runs and fully strummed chords, weaving elements of melody into the overall rhythm picture, best exemplified by the introduction to Donovan's hit 'Catch The Wind.'

As an added treat for listeners, The Beach Boys burlesqued themselves with rocking parodies of their own 'I Get Around' and 'Little Deuce Coupe.' On 'Little Deuce Coupe,' Mike sings, "We always take my car even though it's a heap." Carl throws in a few jazz changes on his 12-string to turn 'Little Deuce Coupe' into a parody of lounge singing styles.

For Bob Dylan's 'The Times They Are A-Changing,' a fine and very serious effort by Al quickly succumbs to the raucous party atmosphere, with the band shouting "Right!" at intervals. But Al prevails and recovers the song's sanctity at the end. Dennis reveals his love for The Beatles with 'You've Got To Hide Your Love Away.' Meanwhile, Jan & Dean's Dean Torrence wanders into the studio, and his entrance is heralded by a piano playing Jan & Dean's hit 'Heart

And Soul.' Then the room erupts in a hysterical satire of 'Baa Baa Black Sheep' before Mike opens up with the introduction to The Regents' 'Barbara Ann.'

Released in November of 1965 with a special photo insert and another gatefold cover, *Beach Boys' Party!* promptly charted in the Top Ten in the USA and the UK. When The Beach Boys' studio single, 'The Little Girl I Once Knew,' stalled at number 20 (disc jockeys balked at the song's unusual two-bar rest before the verses, which they saw as dead air), Capitol quickly rushed out a truncated version of 'Barbara Ann' backed with Carl's recent vocal outing on 'Girl Don't Tell Me.' Released in December, it promptly recovered the band's momentum when it shot to number two.

In November, The Beach Boys had returned to touring and performed at a special benefit at the University of Massachusetts to raise money for a library honoring the late President John F. Kennedy. The concert marked the first time The Beach Boys performed for what was primarily a college-age crowd, and they were surprised at how well they were accepted. Playing to a crowd that listened, rather than the customary screaming teenagers, Carl later remarked that college audiences "can be so wonderful—so quiet. If it's quiet at a regular date, it's a disaster."[3]

The next night, they returned to their usual diet of screaming fans rushing the stage.

* * *

Two long playing records released in the 13-month span between May 1966 and June 1967 changed the course of modern music for ever: The Beach Boys' *Pet Sounds* and The Beatles' *Sgt Pepper's Lonely Hearts Club Band.* Today they are viewed as the point at which modern music matured into a serious form; coincidentally, both album projects began with songs about childhood.

In November 1965, long before John Lennon's 'Strawberry Fields Forever' and Paul McCartney's 'Penny Lane' began taking shape as the intended opening tracks of what became *Sgt Pepper*, Brian brought a winsome song called 'In My Childhood' into Western Studios in Hollywood, complete with bicycle horns and bells as instruments. Despite his undying admiration for Phil Spector, who recorded at Gold Star, Western was Brian's first choice of studio. Gold Star engineer Larry Levine said it was "perfect for surf music—it had a good, lightweight sound."[4] Carl appreciated Western's spaciousness, he said, because "they could get all kinds of guitar sounds there, because the studio players would just bring in real small amplifiers so they could drive them a little bit and get a real biting, full sound."[5]

Brian followed the initial recording of 'In My Childhood' with a guitar instrumental he had originally intended as a possible theme for a spy movie or even a James Bond film. He first called it 'Run James Run.' It eventually provided the title track for the album he would call *Pet Sounds*.

In the days of magnetic tape, using session musicians like Hal Blaine proved a necessity for record producers, because record companies were often footing the bill and wanted deadlines met. Time was of the essence in recording studios of the 60s, when even making simple edits involved slow manual labor with razor blades and adhesive tape. Engineers made subtle changes in pitch by painstakingly wrapping a small strip of masking tape over the tape machine's capstan to raise the pitch of a singer's voice. The early days of recording are rife with tales of musicians who arrived for their first recording sessions only to be informed that they could sit and watch while paid professional musicians played their parts. During the sessions that yielded Dino, Desi & Billy's first hits, Billy Hinsche gasped when he found that, to perform them live, "I've got to learn the guitar solo that James Burton did."[6]

With The Beach Boys touring constantly, Brian faced a tight deadline for the next album and, as he had done on occasion before, for his new album he would import session players and record while The Beach Boys conquered the world from the stage.

The Beach Boys had often played their own parts on their records. Prior to *Summer Days (And Summer Nights!!)*, Brian utilized session players to augment the band's instruments to produce fuller sounds, as with the guitar intro on 'Dance, Dance, Dance' (where Glen Campbell made a mistake on one of the notes and Brian liked it enough to keep it). The new approach would save time but offer a dilemma: instead of developing their own parts

LEFT Carl Wilson as a student at York
Elementary School in Hawthorne.
BELOW The first known picture of The Beach
Boys performing, with Carl playing his first
Stratocaster through his Fender Showman
amplifier. LEFT TO RIGHT Carl, Dennis, Mike,
David Marks, and Brian.

ABOVE The iconic cover of *Surfer Girl*.
BELOW Carl and Mike adjust the
custom ribbon-controlled synthesizer
The Beach Boys used onstage to
mimic the theremin for songs like
'Good Vibrations' and 'Wild Honey.'
RIGHT Recording *Beach Boys' Party!*

LEFT As The Beach Boys music moved away from the surf guitar to more complex music, Carl began favoring semi-hollow or 'thinline' guitars. ABOVE Carl and wife Annie Hinsche Wilson pose for photographers.

Carl listens to a playback with an unidentified engineer in a London recording studio in the early 70s. He would be credited with producing some of the most notable Beach Boys recordings of the era, including 'I Can Hear Music,' 'This Whole World,' and 'Marcella.'

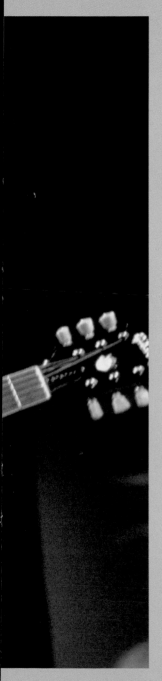

LEFT Carl plays one of his favorite Gibson thinline guitars on *Top Of The Pops*, 1970. ABOVE The title of *Carl And The Passions "So Tough"* aimed to acknowledge Carl's growing role as The Beach Boys' producer and leader. Carl also came up with the cover-art concept for *Sunflower*.

ABOVE Carl stayed close to a
telephone during sessions for
Surf's Up as Brian's bedroom
was just above the studio and
he would often call downstairs
with suggestions. LEFT For years,
Holland held the distinction
of being one of the most
expensive albums in history
as the band relocated their
families, crew, and studio to the
Netherlands to create it.

CARL WILSON

LEFT The Beach Boys' 1976 album *15 Big Ones*, and a promotional portrait from the period.
BELOW The Beach Boys were probably Fender's longest-lived and most effective musical ambassadors. Here, the *Passions*-era band—Ricky Fataar, Blondie Chaplin, Al Jardine, Mike Love, and Carl—try out some new Fender amplifier and instrument designs.

LEFT Carl's second solo album, 1982's Youngblood. BELOW The Carl Wilson Band in 1981: Billy Hinsche, Myrna Smith-Schilling, Carl, Alan Krigger on drums, John Daly on guitar, and Gerald Johnson on bass. RIGHT Carl pictured in 1983 with Gina Martin, whom he married in 1987, and her father, Dean Martin.

in the studio, they would be expected to learn parts developed by others. And they'd be playing more complex music than they—or any other rock band—had tackled before.

Brian brought in musicians in sections and went over the song to help them develop their own parts. The songs were growing more sophisticated and more complex. Long-time Beach Boys stage band member Chris Farmer recalled that, after hearing some of the songs Brian intended for the upcoming album, "Carl turned to Bruce and asked 'How we going to perform this when we're a little surf band?'"[7]

Bruce found the solution, revealing he still harbored concerns about simultaneously singing and playing bass. After the recording of *Summer Days (And Summer Nights!!)*, he told Carl he wanted to start supplementing the stage band with additional musicians. Carl agreed. The decision meant that his role in the band greatly increased. Always Brian's 'ear' in the studio, where his opinion could make or break a song, Carl would now have to make his suggestions before Brian went into the studio with the Wrecking Crew.

Onstage, Carl would now have to interpret the parts written by other players or dictated by Brian to the rest of the band. Seasoned by years of live performance for some of the toughest audiences—particularly the lukewarm surfers and racially mixed audiences of the rougher neighborhoods of Los Angeles County—The Beach Boys would have to supplement their stage lineup with musicians as good as those Brian was using in the studio. They would include Ed Carter (bass), Daryl Dragon (keyboards), Mike Kowalski (drums), Bobby Figueroa (drums/percussion), and Billy Hinsche (guitar). Even Bruce Johnston played some sessions before he joined the band.

The new approach worked by Carl's playing to his own strengths. While his relentless calm and imperturbability may have masked turmoil boiling underneath, he found his warmth, sweetness, and gentleness to be an extremely effective management tool when The Beach Boys began importing touring musicians, many of them as highly trained as the Wrecking Crew. Later, as happened with Jeffrey Foskett, Carl found himself in the position of orienting musicians who had learned their craft listening to Carl Wilson.

Chris Farmer, a classically trained pianist who also played bass, toured with The Beach Boys in the 80s and then again in the 90s and found that Carl led from the front by inspiring—rather than simply demanding—excellence. "Anyone who worked with him or for him wanted to do the best job he could," he said. "He was that kind of musical director. He didn't need to crack the whip. He was such a nice guy."[8]

Much of Carl's authority came from being one of the best guitarists in the business, but with a style that supported the overall performance rather than calling attention to itself as did the playing of the reigning guitar gods of the era. "It's just a real simple style," Carl later explained to Billy Hinsche. "It's not a very elaborate or fancy way of playing—not a lot of notes. I like to get a little more mileage out of each note."[9]

Every good jazz musician learns that the notes one does not play are as important as the ones that are played, and Carl learned early on how to subtly embellish rather than overtake or overcomplicate an arrangement. His approach resonated with musicians, whether classically trained or self-taught players marinated for years in The Beach Boys' music. Carl's style, said Farmer, "is similar to Pete Townshend's, who gets accolades for his techniques and figures rather than his solos."

The hired guns who became onstage Beach Boys learned why Brian depended so much on Carl's ears. "Carl would start a song, as he always did—he was the one who always counted them off—and he would keep that beat and pocket right where he wanted it," said Farmer. "All eyes were on Carl Wilson mainly because you knew he was listening to everybody."[10]

As the mid 60s became the late 60s, the occasional onstage screaming match or fistfight between band members was not uncommon. Being a bandleader often meant having the shortest fuse, the loudest voice, or the fastest fists. At one Buffalo Springfield club performance, seeking to get his bass player Bruce Palmer to turn down, Stephen Stills eventually tired of shouting and merely punched Palmer in front of the audience.[11] When Mike Bloomfield first saw his future Electric Flag drummer Buddy Miles performing with Wilson Pickett, he was surprised to see that, in the course of a song, Pickett would occasionally spin around and shout a number at Miles. He discovered later that Pickett was fining Miles for mistakes.

While Mike Love entertained the crowd from the front, Carl developed a system of maintaining order and excellence onstage with a pair of silent facial expressions that usually resolved the problems with no interruptions in the performance. The first—and worst—was what became known as the 'stink eye,' a visible grimace that let the player know that something needed to be corrected right away. The second was what Farmer called the 'confused eye'—a quizzical look from Carl meaning something was amiss. Musicians knew all was right with the performance when a contented Carl faced the audience at the microphone with his hips swaying to the music.

Leadership often meant being the best musician in the group and possessing a working knowledge of all of the instruments and their role in a given song. When Farmer joined the band, he found Carl to be a perfectionist who hoped to resolve issues before they became problems onstage. When Farmer first performed 'Darlin'' at a rehearsal, he played the wrong bassline in the opening bars. Carl flashed his stink eye and stopped the song. "Farmer," Carl asked, "what are you playing?"

"You could hear a pin drop," Farmer said. Carl then proceeded to play the whole part on his guitar: "Not just the verses, but the chorus, the middle part—the whole song. He was always so nice, but if it was business, boom! Carl was *business*."[12]

And with The Beach Boys now supporting road crews, a state-of-the-art sound system, triple-scale session players, wives, ex-wives, a growing brood of children, and the infrastructure of a major rock band such as lawyers, accountants, managers, a publishing company, and publicists, it was a big business. And most of the burden of running the business now fell on the shoulders of a musician who wasn't old enough to vote.

* * *

With 'Barbara Ann' and *Beach Boys' Party!* tearing up the pop charts at the end of 1965, The Beach Boys enjoyed some well-deserved time off before commencing their first Japanese tour in the first week of January. The holiday season brought a new challenge to Brian, however. In December, Capitol Records released the American version of The Beatles' *Rubber Soul*. The albums released by Capitol in the United States and Parlophone in England (both labels being owned by the British company EMI) amounted to essentially two different albums sharing some similar tracks. The Parlophone version—now the accepted version—featured 14 new Beatles songs. American albums generally featured between 10 and 12 tracks and included the hits, which British albums often omitted. With *Rubber Soul*, Capitol sought to take songs from The Beatles' newest effort and mix them with tracks left over from their 1965 *Help!* album; the Capitol version featured only seven Beatles songs, interspersed with segments of film music. This deconstructing and reconstructing process also ensured that Capitol would have another album ready to go in the spring before The Beatles released *Revolver* in the late summer.

Hoping that they could construct a version of *Rubber Soul* to capitalize on the folk-rock craze that had exploded in the United States over the summer, executives at Capitol eschewed the usual American album format, which Phil Spector scorned as "two hits and ten pieces of crap," and built an American version of *Rubber Soul* without any hit singles to drive it. Instead, they used songs from the Parlophone version of *Help!*, including the acoustically based 'I've Just Seen A Face' and 'It's Only Love.'

The result was that the Capitol version of *Rubber Soul*, released on December 6, 1965, featured a seamless, balanced selection of understated songs of equal quality rather than the jarring rocker-followed-by-ballad format heard on most American albums of the time. It was, Brian later stated, "like a folk album."

"When I first heard it, I flipped," he said. "I said, 'I want to make an album like that: a whole album with all good stuff.' I really wasn't quite ready for the unity. It felt like it all belonged together. *Rubber Soul* was a collection of songs ... that somehow went together like no album ever made before, and I was very impressed."[13]

Brian informed Marilyn he was embarking on the greatest rock album ever. However, the pressure was on for a new single, and three days before Christmas 1965, Brian had folk-rock on his mind. He brought The Beach Boys into the studio to record an old song that Al had suggested earlier in the summer, a traditional West Indian tune that had been a staple of both the old 'hootenanny' folk groups like his heroes, The Kingston Trio, and the early surf bands: 'Sloop John B.' In the early 70s, Mike Love addressed the criticisms of Beach Boys lyrics by introducing the song onstage as having lyrics by the great American poet and author Carl Sandburg, who collected the song and published it in 1927.

Because The Beach Boys were on tour at the time, Brian had to replace Carl in the studio with three session players. To keep the now-signature Beach Boys sound, Brian bought session guitarist Billy Strange his first 12-string guitar to record the song.

Meanwhile, as The Beach Boys prepared for their first Japanese tour, Brian began looking for lyrical help for what would become *Pet Sounds*. Before the year was out, he partnered with a young advertising copywriter named Tony Asher rather than dipping into his usual pool of co-writers from The Beach Boys' inner circle. The next album would be like no other Beach Boys album before it.

Asher first met Brian at a session for a commercial jingle Asher had written for his advertising firm. "Brian was doing some demos of something or other. We ran into each other in the hall. We started chatting, and he asked me to take a listen to what he had been doing. He then went into the studio to play something for me on the piano. I played a couple of things for him, and that was pretty much it," Asher later recalled. "Frankly, I never expected to hear from him again."

A few weeks later, however, Brian called Asher and said he had an album that was overdue and asked him to provide lyrics for it. "I thought it was somebody in the office playing a joke on me," Asher said, then realized Brian wasn't kidding. His first assignment was to transform the finished track of 'In My Childhood,' replete with childhood sound effects, into the romantic ballad 'You Still Believe In Me.' Other tracks followed, with Asher and Brian working together at the piano during the day and Asher returning home at night to polish the lyrics.[14]

When The Beach Boys returned from their wildly successful performances in Hawaii and Japan, at the end of January 1966, Al Jardine recalled, "There was this masterpiece sitting there, kind of an uncut gem. And we're going, 'Wow, hmm, what's up, Brian?'" The tracks The Beach Boys heard upon their return offered "a whole new horizon for us. We were a surfing group when we left the country, and now basically we came back to this new music … and it took some getting used to."[15]

Asher later described the group's response as "less than enthusiastic," but while Carl and especially Dennis privately admitted they were thrilled with the new sounds, they both expressed serious concerns about their ability to perform this new music onstage.

Carl was also worried about Capitol Records' similarly lukewarm response. "I think they were a little bit afraid of it. They probably thought they would lose a market or a segment of people. … It certainly was a groundbreaking album. It was just so much more than a record; it had such a spiritual quality. It wasn't going in and doing another Top Ten record. It had so much more meaning than that."[16]

However, in January, *Pet Sounds* was nowhere near finished. Brian returned to the studio a few weeks later with Carl, Dennis, Bruce, and Terry Melcher to cut one of the standout tracks on the album, the only one on which Carl, Dennis, and Brian play: 'That's Not Me.'

Session tapes unearthed years later for the *Pet Sounds Sessions* boxed set, released in 1997, reveal one of the musicians (probably Melcher) needling Carl as he warms up: "Haven't you read your own guitar book, Carl?" He was referring to Carl's recently released songbook, *Guitar Sounds Of The Beach Boys, Featuring Carl Wilson*.[17] But Carl had other things on his mind. On February 3, 1966, he became the last Beach Boy to tie the knot when he married a dark-eyed German/Filipino beauty named Annie Hinsche.

CHAPTER TWELVE

Like A Brother

Like Carl, Annie Hinsche grew up in a musical family, where she and younger brother Billy were raised on a variety of instruments such as piano and violin. Their father, Otto, frequently recorded his children singing nursery rhymes on acetates. "I've been recording since I was three," Hinsche said.[1]

Born in Frank Sinatra's hometown of Hoboken, New Jersey, Otto Hinsche moved to Manila in the Philippines to start a supper club and casino with his American partners. After the Japanese occupation in 1941, Otto was rounded up with other civilians and herded into a prisoner of war camp. Upon his release, after the liberation of the Philippines, he opened another club on Manila Bay and married a young Filipina named Celia Bautista.[2] Otto moved his family to Los Angeles, and later Beverly Hills, where his son Billy attended Beverly Hills Catholic School with Dean Paul 'Dino' Martin and Lucie and Desi Arnaz Jr.

"Dino and I became the very best of friends at age seven, and we both befriended Desi a few years later when we asked him to join us to form our band," said Billy.

Dino, Desi & Billy commenced rehearsals. One afternoon in late 1964, Dino's mother suggested that family friend Frank Sinatra come over and give the teenagers a listen. In rapid succession, the boys were signed to Sinatra's fledgling Reprise Records label and began appearances on variety shows such as *The Hollywood Palace*.[3] Celebrity children performing in bands in the early 60s wasn't unusual. Some star scions like Jerry Lewis's son Gary succeeded, while others, like Peter Lewis of Moby Grape, made it without making an issue of his being the son of popular film and television star Loretta Young. However, unlike many celebrity offspring, Dino, Desi

& Billy could deliver. They scored a pair of bona fide hits with 'I'm A Fool' and 'Not The Lovin' Kind.'

In July 1965, the group scored a plum spot on the lineup for a Fourth of July concert, headlined by The Beach Boys and featuring Sonny & Cher, The Byrds, The Righteous Brothers, and The Kinks. At a soundcheck two days before, Billy met Carl, his future brother-in-law. After the performance, The Beach Boys invited Dino, Desi & Billy to open for them in Bakersfield, and Billy found himself the beneficiary of sage advice from another teenage rockstar. A musical partnership was born.

"After our show in Bakersfield, I went to visit Carl in his hotel room," Hinsche recalled. "His door was wide open and the room was full of friends and well-wishers. He was sitting on the edge of his bed, holding a brand new guitar in his hands, inspecting it carefully and strumming it casually. I'd never seen a guitar like this before. It looked like a goofy-footed Stratocaster to me. It was a Mosrite and the local dealer was trying to get Carl to accept one, at no charge, in return for an endorsement. After the somewhat high pressure sales pitch had concluded, Carl thanked the guitar rep for the offer and politely told him he wasn't interested, returning the guitar to its case to emphasize the finality of his decision. I couldn't believe it. Carl turned down a chance to get a free guitar. It was the first of many lessons I learned from Carl and speaks to his lifetime of integrity."[4]

The two bonded, and Carl quickly met and fell hard for Billy's older sister Annie. A love-struck Carl had a gardenia delivered to her home every day while he was on tour. "They were very young and very much in love," said Annie's friend Greer Upton.[5] On February 3, 1966, with Murry and Audree in attendance, Carl married Annie in a quiet civil ceremony. Little over a week later, Carl joined The Beach Boys for a photo session at the petting zoo at San Diego Zoo for the upcoming *Pet Sounds* album. There is no agreement as to who originally came up with the title: Brian always credited Carl, although Carl himself credited Brian. (Mike also claimed to have come up with it.)

"The idea he [Brian] had was that everybody has these sounds that they love, and that this was a collection of his 'pet sounds,'" Carl said. "It was hard to think of a name for the album, because you sure couldn't call it *Shut Down Volume 3*."[6]

Two weeks later, Brian sent Capitol Records a list of ten tracks planned to appear on the new album, including 'Hang On To Your Ego' (later changed to 'I Know There's An Answer' after Mike complained about a possible LSD connection) and 'Good Vibrations.' The list also named The Beach Boys' next single, 'Sloop John B,' although there is some dispute about whether Brian intended it to appear on the album or whether Capitol forced its inclusion after it became a Top Ten hit.

In the succeeding weeks, Brian dropped 'Good Vibrations' from the album's lineup. "At the time, we all had assumed that 'Good Vibrations' was going to be on the album," Al said later, "but Brian decided to hold it out. It was a judgment call on his part. We felt otherwise but left the ultimate decision up to him."[7]

In early March, The Beach Boys returned to the road for a brief college tour of three Oregon universities with *Los Angeles Times* reporter Art Seidenbaum in tow, covering the tour for a series in his paper. Dodging fan riots where "little girls hurled themselves at police lines as if they were rabid dogs," Seidenbaum found himself impressed with Carl's maturity, especially since he had only turned 19 a couple of months before. He called him "the anchor on road trips around which the others can rally."[8]

After a show in Cleveland, The Beach Boys proceeded to tour the East Coast and later Texas, where The Lovin' Spoonful and Chad & Jeremy opened for them. Annie joined Carl on the Texas leg of the tour, and Dennis struck up a friendship with Chad & Jeremy guitarist William James Guercio, a relationship that would prove beneficial during The Beach Boys' comeback in the 70s.

As applause from screaming fans washed over the band, Brian decided that one of the songs for the album needed something different. Recorded on March 10, with Carl playing guitar, and after the two brothers had prayed together, 'God Only Knows' would provide one of the standout tracks on a standout album. Admired by Brian's peers, such as Paul McCartney, it is widely considered one of the most beautiful songs ever written.

Brian wasn't satisfied with his own vocal on the song, however, and pressed Carl into service as a lead singer on the track. Carl's previous vocal efforts had all been rockers such as 'Pom Pom Playgirl,' 'All Dressed Up For School,' or the mid-tempo ballad 'Girl Don't Tell Me.' 'God Only Knows' provided a different challenge. It was a dynamic, beautifully orchestrated piece that could collapse under the weight of anything but an understated vocal—and understatement was Carl's forte. 'God Only Knows,' when released as a single, charted in the Top 20 and inspired Paul McCartney to compose a similar musical prelude to open 'Here, There, And Everywhere,' his classic romantic ballad from *Revolver*. After 'God Only Knows,' Carl would gradually replace Brian as the key ballad singer in the band.

Carl's voice "is probably one of the best voices in rock'n'roll," said Phil Volk of Paul Revere & The Raiders. "I think Carl has found his place in rock'n'roll history. I know that Brian, his brother, has been quoted many times as saying he couldn't have done what he did without Carl at his side."[9]

Years later, Carl revealed his vocal secrets to Chip Rachlin, founder of Rachlin Entertainment Company and one-time Beach Boys agent. "Carl would take me down to the studio and show me how he recorded. 'The only way you can sing the parts I do is when your voice is relaxed,'" Carl explained. Rachlin, granted access to Carl that few Beach Boys insiders could claim, found that, as a vocalist "he was quite a technician."[10]

"Every time I hear his voice, it really truly is the voice of an angel," said Darian Sahanaja of The Wondermints and the Brian Wilson band. "He taught me so much about phrasing, about easing into notes, laying back— he just had so much soul. I think the way people feel music is where they hit the notes ... I loved the way Carl always eased in and laid back. It was so much a part of The Beach Boys' sound."[11]

One of the best descriptions of Carl's vocal style came from Steve Kalinich, the poet and lyricist for whom Carl produced some solo recordings in the mid 60s. "Carl would teach me—I'm not the greatest singer, I'm more of a spoken kind of artist—but he said, 'When you do sing … whisper, whisper and then add volume.'"[12]

In April, The Beach Boys returned to the road to be met by enthusiasm bordering on pandemonium. In Scranton, Pennsylvania, on May 4, promoters provided a fraction of the police officers promised, and The Beach Boys' road manager Dick Duryea canceled the show, saying, "We simply could not let the boys go on stage without proper policing."[13]

However, in one of their last performances before the release of *Pet Sounds*, The Beach Boys' past had already started dogging their present. Concert tours in the 60s were designed to promote new singles and albums, and while The Beach Boys had been around longer than most of their support acts, their past hits were considered just that: blasts from the past.

On May 14 in Milwaukee, in front of 5,000 fans, with The Sir Douglas Quintet as one of the opening acts, The Beach Boys performed a solid selection of their most recent hits, such as 'Sloop John B' and 'Barbara Ann.' Yet toward the end of the show, they trotted out some of their earlier favorites, such as 'Surfin' USA,' 'The Little Old Lady From Pasadena,' and 'Papa-Oom-Mow-Mow.' These, reported Peggy Murrells of the *Milwaukee Journal*, received the "biggest ovations."[14]

* * *

Two days later, on May 16, 1966, with little fanfare or marketing muscle behind it, The Beach Boys' *Pet Sounds* seemed miraculously to appear in record stores. (It appeared six weeks later in England.) Capitol released the album in two audio formats: monaural and a faux stereo called 'Duophonic,' in which the lower registers of a monaural recording were emphasized on one channel while the higher registers were emphasized on the other. When the listeners sat between the two speakers, they got an impression of a stereo recording, but stereos then still had mono switches and most listeners simply listened to it as a mono experience. Because of the 90 percent hearing loss in Brian's right ear, a genuine stereo master of *Pet Sounds* wasn't released until 1997.

Much has been made of The Beach Boys' resistance to *Pet Sounds*, and that resistance fueled antagonisms that exist to this day. Some of the band felt they were witnessing Brian working toward a solo career, especially since he had, in March, released 'Caroline, No' as a single under his own name. Secondly, *Pet Sounds* marked the first full album where The Beach Boys' participation and input was limited almost exclusively to recording vocals; even the most sophisticated arrangements on earlier albums often featured the band's members, often with Al playing bass rather than guitar.[15] Prior to *Pet Sounds*, The Beach Boys were partners in Brian's productions. With *Pet Sounds*, they saw themselves simply as singers.

Carl was *Pet Sounds'* biggest supporter from the start. "Very early on in the recording of *Pet Sounds* I got what it was about musically," Bruce Johnston told *Rockcellar* writer Ken Sharp. "Carl was excitedly telling me, 'You've got to come to some of the sessions. I've been there and you should hear what [Brian's] doing!'"[16]

Yet when The Beach Boys came off the road and into the studio to sing, they found much of the experience more exhausting than exhilarating. "We spent so much time perfecting the vocals that I think I got turned off of the album just by the sheer volume of work we did on it," Al Jardine said later.[17]

"We worked and worked on the harmonies, and if there was the slightest little hint of a sharp or a flat, it wouldn't go on. We would do it over again until it was right," Mike added. "Every voice had to be right, every voice and its resonance and tonality had to be right. The timing had to be right. The timbre of the voices just had to be correct, according to how he felt. And then he might, the next day, completely throw that out and we might have to do it over again."[18]

Brian later admitted that "there was resistance. There was a little bit of intergroup struggle. It was resolved in that they figured it was a showcase for Brian Wilson, but it [still] was The Beach Boys. In other words, they gave in."[19] Carl played a key role in the group's increasingly bitter disputes. "People say he's the one who keeps the group from going at each other's throats," said Brian. "It's true—he can spot a rough situation and avert it before you knew it was there. It makes me rather unhappy that I'm only realizing his worth now. You know how teenage boys treat kid brothers. But now, after all those rough years, I discover how much we have in common and how much I respect him."[20]

As *Pet Sounds* was released, The Beach Boys returned from their tour, having experienced a new phenomenon: the 'fun in the sun' songs from the surfing years of 1961 to 1963 often proved greater crowd pleasers than their most recent material. This would prove problematic in the future.

Because there was a six-week delay in releasing *Pet Sounds* in the United Kingdom, Bruce Johnston took a brief vacation to England to visit Keith Moon and found himself hosting an impromptu *Pet Sounds* party for several important English artists, including John Lennon and Paul McCartney, who, upon listening to the record, insisted he play it a second time. (Producer Lou Adler had reportedly played an acetate of the album to McCartney earlier at the home of Rolling Stones producer Andrew Loog Oldham. Oldham found himself so enthralled with the record that he personally took out advertising in the English press, comparing *Pet Sounds* to Nikolai Rimsky-Korsakov's symphonic poem *Scheherazade*.) Upon its release in the United Kingdom, *Pet Sounds* garnered both supporters and detractors, yet it generated considerably more attention than it had in the USA. But while Paul McCartney and Eric Clapton lavished praise on the album, Pete Townshend of The Who dismissed it.

The album's release, and a lawsuit The Beach Boys initiated a year later, spawned a conundrum about the band that persists to this day. While each preceding Beach Boys album had sailed easily up and off the charts to attain a coveted Recording Industry Association of America Gold Record Award (for sales of 500,000 units) soon after release, it took *Pet Sounds* until February 2000 to finally attain its Gold Record certification.

According to Eric Boehlert, writing in the March 10, 2000 issue of *Rolling Stone* magazine, "the answer to the *Pet Sounds* riddle lies in the certification process. The RIAA only certifies albums when a record company provides, for verification, all the shipping documentation on a specific title.

That means the RIAA only acts when a label makes a formal certification, or re-certification, request."

According to Boehlert, Capitol Records didn't request a certification for *Pet Sounds* until the 90s, and when they did, they "had to withdraw the request when it was unable to uncover the requisite shipping history. The label came back again late last year with sales information, but only covering the last 15 years. It was enough to earn the record gold status, accounting to roughly 670,000 copies sold."[21]

Mike Etchart, who oversaw the certification for *Pet Sounds* and spent three months searching record company vaults in vain for the critical sales figures from 1966 through 1985, guessed that the actual number of units sold was closer to double-platinum at the time. Whether the understatement was incompetence or a reaction to The Beach Boys' legal action against the record company is unclear.

Weeks after *Pet Sounds'* release, The Beach Boys were back on the road. Their tour began in the Midwest and then headed south before returning to California, where a critic from the *Oakland Tribune* complained that he couldn't hear the music over the loud guitars and screaming girls in the audience. In San Diego, another critic complained that the set was too heavy on oldies and featured no songs from *Pet Sounds*, even though 'Sloop John B' had already charted.

On Thursday, July 28 in Massachusetts, The Beach Boys debuted 'God Only Knows' and noticed another phenomenon. The nonstop screams of the past three years now began to subside during the performance of the song and only rise again when Mike introduced the next one. On August 12, they performed at a concert in Springfield, Illinois, where only six police officers were present to control a crowd of 21,000. Afterward, Carl, Bruce, and Mike flew to Chicago to meet The Beatles, who were starting out their final tour.

After a brief tour of Canada, The Beach Boys flew back to Los Angeles, where they helped Brian complete their latest single, 'Good Vibrations,' the second of Brian's masterpieces to be handed to his youngest brother to sing. It is a magnificent performance: ethereal, as suits the subject matter, yet powerful. When the band returned to the road, on October 22, Brian joined them at the University of Michigan to direct the live version of the new single. At the end of the second show, he joined them on bass for a rave-up on their now-standard closer, 'Johnny B. Goode.'

Two days later, with 'Good Vibrations' an instant smash upon release, The Beach Boys—with Murry along for the ride—landed in Paris to conquer Europe. After that they went to Germany and Sweden, before moving on to England where Carl was reunited with John Maus, now John Walker and a star in his own right. After a series of UK shows, The Beach Boys returned to California by way of the East Coast and Canada. The tour wrapped on December 28, 1966.[22] A week later, Carl Wilson awoke to find he was a wanted man.

CHAPTER THIRTEEN

Hold Me

By January of 1967, The Beach Boys were bigger than any band on earth except The Beatles. While *Pet Sounds* hadn't scored the chart success many had hoped for, in an age where hit singles were valued above album sales, The Beach Boys in the opening days of 1967 were more successful than they had ever been in terms of concert grosses and single record sales. And *Pet Sounds* was a critical success, which proved especially important for a band who seldom found themselves or their music taken seriously by the musical cognoscenti of the time.

Meanwhile, Brian had recorded sections of virtually all of the tracks that would compose his "teenage symphony to God," an album he first entitled *Dumb Angel* (a term of endearment for brother Dennis) then changed to *SMiLE*. After the success of 'Good Vibrations,' *SMiLE* became one of the most breathlessly awaited musical events of all time. Anticipating a rousing success, Capitol Records printed 400,000 *SMiLE* covers and booklet inserts, as well as four-color sleeves for the single of 'Heroes And Villains.' The final running order of *SMiLE* would be revealed on the record labels.

All of this transpired against the backdrop of one of the most tumultuous periods of American history. As 1967 dawned, American troop strength in Vietnam reached 385,000, with an additional 60,000 sailors stationed offshore. The American casualty count for 1966 had been 6,000 killed and 30,000 wounded. Estimates placed the Vietcong guerilla forces at over 280,000.

In the years since South Vietnamese President Duong Van Minh surrendered unconditionally to North Vietnam, on April 30, 1975, retellings have condensed the 30-year history of the conflict into a simple case of hawks (supporters of the war) versus doves (opponents). Yet many on both sides of the argument agreed in their opposition to the Selective Service System, known as the draft, which conscripted healthy young men into the military to fight an undeclared war against an army of guerilla fighters rather than an opposing nation. Many saw it as a massive social-engineering experiment to protect those deemed worthier in the population while sending the less privileged to fight.

Cringing at news reports of the extravagant wedding plans of President Richard M. Nixon's daughter Tricia, Creedence Clearwater Revival frontman and Army Reserve veteran John Fogerty angrily scribbled the lyrics to CCR's classic 'Fortunate Son,' a song *Rolling Stone* magazine called "a blast at rich folks who plan wars and then draft poor people to fight them." Watching the Washington elite prepare for the wedding of the year, Fogerty said, "You just had the feeling that none of these people were going to be too involved with the war."[1]

On the other hand, with two 'righteous' wars behind them, many Americans saw refusing induction into the military during wartime, even by members of recognized religions that opposed war, such as Quakers or Mennonites, as little more than government-sanctioned cowardice.

The Academy Award-nominated actor Lew Ayres, who attained stardom in the 1930 anti-war epic *All Quiet On The Western Front* and starred in the successful Dr Kildare franchise, had claimed conscientious objector status after America entered World War II. He had a religious objection to bearing arms, which he said would cause him "to live in a nightmare of hypocrisy." Even though he spent two months in a labor camp, and served honorably in the US Army Medical Corps for three and a half years as a noncombatant (and was awarded three battle stars), Ayres returned home to find his career in tatters. Because exhibitors and theaters often refused to show films he appeared in, it reduced the former A-list star to B-movies for decades.[2]

In 1966, two years after joining the Nation Of Islam and changing his name from Cassius Clay to Muhammad Ali, America's 25-year-old heavyweight boxing champion—guest of The Beach Boys at their 1988 induction into the Rock and Roll Hall of Fame—refused induction, on the grounds that he was a practicing Muslim minister whose religious beliefs prevented him from fighting in the Vietnam conflict. In 1967, draft evasion was a felony. Ali's judge sentenced the champion to five years in prison and fined him $10,000, the maximum penalty.[3] The Boxing Association stripped Ali of his title and handed down a three-year ban to the greatest boxer in history.

Record companies during the Vietnam era were prepared to protect their investment in their artists by finding ways to circumvent the draft. When The Seeds' keyboardist/bassist/composer Daryl Hooper reached draft age, his record company sent him to a doctor, who found a residual hearing impairment from a childhood disease, although Hooper insisted, "I could hear a pin drop."[4]

Artists like songwriter Jesse Winchester, who fled to Canada, or activist David Harris, who chose prison over military service, were regarded as heroes, while the music press and fans scorned musicians like Gary Lewis of Gary Lewis & The Playboys and Jim Pash of The Surfaris who dutifully answered the call and served their country.[5] Despite a string of consecutive *Billboard* Top Ten hits prior to his induction, Lewis reported for duty in early 1966. But he came home to find his career vaporized, despite his previous success and the best efforts of producers and arrangers such as Leon Russell and Snuff Garrett. After a few failed stabs at a comeback, he ended up teaching drums in a neighborhood music store.

While the other Beach Boys were exempt from the draft, on January 3, 1967, Carl Wilson, just turned 20, failed to report for induction into the military. Seventeen days later, he declared himself a conscientious objector before the Gardenia, California, Draft Board.[6] Among The Beach Boys family, most of whom opposed both the war and the draft, there was solid support for Carl. "We totally understood why Carl was a conscientious objector," said Marilyn Wilson Rutherford. "Knowing what a gentle soul he was, there was no way he would harm anyone for any reason or be put in that situation … not Carl."[7]

On April 5, Carl was indicted by a Los Angeles federal grand jury on charges of draft evasion in violation of the Selective Service Act.[8] Three weeks later, he was arrested by FBI agents at a concert in Commack, New York. He was charged with draft evasion, a crime that carried a potential five-year jail sentence. He was released from custody on a $15,000 bond in time to make the performance. But he learned that the Selective Service Board opposed his leaving the country, putting The Beach Boys' upcoming European tour at risk.[9]

* * *

Getting embroiled in a protracted legal battle with the government, and risking spending time in a federal prison, came at a turbulent time for Carl and The Beach Boys. On January 11, 1967, The Beach Boys filed incorporation papers in Los Angeles. On January 15, Brian failed to deliver the *SMiLE* album to Capitol Records as scheduled. On January 28, The Beach Boys sued their record label for unpaid royalties and nearly a quarter of a million dollars owed them due to an archaic 'breakage' clause in their contract.[10] The clause was a relic of the days when 78rpm records were made of a brittle shellac-based compound. The notorious clause enabled record companies to recover from artists the cost of records they claimed had been broken.

Brian was still committed to completing *SMiLE*, the record that was expected to sound like an album's worth of 'Good Vibrations.' The other Beach Boys, meanwhile, prepared to embark on a tour of the Midwest that would consume much of February.

CBS Television was working on *Inside Pop: The Rock Revolution,* a CBS News special presented by the composer and conductor Leonard Bernstein. In it Bernstein would explain the "strange and compelling scene called pop music" to American television viewers.[11] It featured a young Janis Ian and pop icons of the time such as The Byrds' Roger McGuinn, Frank Zappa, Tim Buckley, and Herman's Hermits' lead singer Peter Noone. Its highlight, though, was Brian sitting at the piano, performing one of the new songs from *SMiLE*. Broadcast in April 1967, it would provide the only glimpse of 'Surf's Up' that fans would hear until its official release nearly five years later. For now, it raised expectations for the delayed *SMiLE* album.

As on previous Beach Boys albums, Carl's guitar served as the rhythmic center for many of the songs intended for *SMiLE*, and he still led the band onstage. But to add to the pressure on him, new guitar technology and techniques gave the electric guitar another burst of energy during what is now known as the Summer of Love. By 1967, reverb units had been incorporated into The Beach Boys' preferred Fender Showman and Dual Showman amps. The new design both reduced the old clicks, pops, drizzles, and crashes of the earlier outboard units and considerably reduced the cost of big amps to guitarists. In England, where American guitars and amplifiers were considerably more expensive and harder to acquire, music store owner Jim Marshall began constructing his own amplifiers based on Fender designs: most notably what became the Marshall JTM 45, popularly known as the Marshall stack. It invigorated the English music scene.

New bands burst on the LA scene, often composed of veterans of the early surf bands, including The Mothers Of Invention, The Seeds, The Strawberry Alarm Clock, Blue Cheer, Moby Grape, and Buffalo Springfield. They now added a new effect to their arsenals: distortion pedals or 'fuzz boxes.' With controlled distortion through powerful amps, guitarists could now sustain individual notes to perform more expressive solos—an innovation warmly embraced by users of recreational drugs like marijuana or LSD. The year 1967 was becoming one of the most pivotal in popular music and the development of the electric guitar—and Carl risked missing it all by standing up for what he believed in.

On May 2, 1967, after appearing before a Federal Grand Jury in Los Angeles and being released on $40,000 bail, Carl chartered a plane and flew to join the rest of The Beach Boys in Ireland.[12] They were booked for two shows at the Dublin Adelphi. The first performance, without him, was assailed by critics as "a brave, misguided failure" that "shouldn't have happened." B.P. Fallon of *Melody Maker* magazine wrote, "It was, to be as polite and charitable as possible, a disaster. The audience wanted Carl, but not as much as the four men who were struggling to make do without him.

They seemed at a complete loss, like some amateur group struck with stage fright at a local talent contest."

Boos and shouts of "we want Carl" washed over the band, and some 70 audience members demanded their money back. Backstage, The Beach Boys were debating whether or not to play the second show when they received word that Carl had landed at the local airport and was on his way. When Carl arrived in the middle of the set, he rushed onstage without even changing into his stage clothes and saved the show, to the visible relief of the band and generous applause from the audience.

When Carl's case came up in interviews, he was publicly upbeat about the outcome of the trial. "I am an objector on the grounds of conscience," he told *Melody Maker*, noting that three years in prison was the customary sentence for failure to report. "But I have feelings about these things and I feel absolutely certain that the worst will not happen," he added. "I only hope I'm right."

Carl was famous for keeping his true feelings under wraps and always played the polite, calm diplomat in public. But the stress of his case was blamed for some of Dennis's growing volatility. During a performance three nights earlier he had loaned his drum kit to a local band called The Doughboys for their opening show. The band's drummer kicked over Dennis's kit, Keith Moon style, at the end of the performance. An enraged Dennis rushed onstage and began raining blows on the shocked Doughboys drummer, in full view of the audience. The fracas spread backstage as the stage crew frantically closed the curtains while other band members leaped in and tried to separate the battling drummers.

After the Dublin show, The Beach Boys proceeded to tour Europe, where the mood had soured somewhat from the 'hail the conquering heroes' enthusiasm of their previous tour. Critics compared the live performances unsatisfactorily to their studio versions, and some critics bared their fangs when The Beach Boys edged out The Beatles as the top vocal group of the year in Britain's *New Musical Express* poll. The band actually apologized to Ringo later, saying there was only one top vocal group, and that was The Beatles.[13]

The tour, and its prickly critical reception, only reinforced the fears Carl had voiced about Brian's new material. The Beach Boys were, in Carl's phrase, "just a little surf band" and he wondered how were they going to perform the new music. Brian layered multitudes of instruments on top of each other, and rehearsed and recorded vocals until the band's throats gave out. How were they expected to sing and play these little masterpieces at the same time, with only four instruments and five voices? [14]

* * *

The 1967 Monterey Pop Festival, held on June 16–18, inaugurated the Summer of Love and set the stage for the festival era of rock'n'roll shows. In any retelling of The Beach Boys' story it serves as a coda to the story of *SMiLE* and reveals the first cracks in what would become a great divide between the first and subsequent eras of the band.

The saga of *SMiLE* began at Gold Star with the initial sessions for 'Good Vibrations' on February 17, 1966, and ended with a canceled Gold Star session for 'I Love To Say Da Da' on May 18, 1967. (The band's publicist, Derek Taylor, had announced two weeks earlier that Brian had "scrapped" the album.)

Conventional wisdom has always pointed to the release in June of The Beatles' *Sgt Pepper*, and Brian's opting out of what he deemed a "production race," as the reason for the death of *SMiLE*—a race he felt he was winning just a few months before. But the arrival of *Sgt Pepper* did not catch him by surprise. During a visit to Los Angeles in April 1967, while Al Jardine recorded vocals on the 'Vega-Tables' section of 'The Elements' suite, Paul McCartney stopped by the studio to visit Brian and play him an acetate of *Sgt Pepper*'s centerpiece, 'A Day In The Life.' Brian, in return, played Paul one of the intended *SMiLE* tracks, 'Wonderful.'

At dinner later that night, Paul noted that EMI had scheduled *Sgt Pepper* for a June release, and urged Brian to put out *SMiLE* as soon as possible to avert a possible conflict of sales and airplay. When *Sgt Pepper* arrived in record stores, immediately after the news that Brian scrapped

SMiLE, many concluded that Brian had simply surrendered in a race that only existed in his mind.

Many plausible explanations have been given over the years for the demise of *SMiLE*: drugs; resistance from the band and Capitol Records; Brian's growing, then dwindling, circle of supporters and sycophants; and a music press tired of hearing about Brian's great statement, yet seeing no further evidence for it. The culprit may have been any or all of the above, or something with far deeper roots.

SMiLE, as Carl said later, was written and recorded in segments rather than whole songs. "We did things in sections. There might just be a few bars of music, or a verse, or a particular groove or vamp. They would all fit. You could put them one in front of the other or arrange it in any way you wanted. It was sort of like making films, I think."[15]

Brian later recounted that during his first LSD experience he became fascinated with a simple phrase that he played over and over on the piano. "This remains noteworthy, though, as such repetitive rhythmic figures would later come to define Wilson's approach to songwriting after *Pet Sounds*, from 1966 onward," wrote Stefano Belli. "During this time his behavior became increasingly erratic and his delusions reached a stage where they were interfering with his normal functioning (eg, halting work and destroying music because he believed that it had unnatural power, as he did during the recording of the song 'Fire' in 1967; purposely avoiding people or refusing to leave his room as a coping method for his increasingly severe auditory hallucinations), suggesting that his symptoms were becoming pathological. Around this time, Wilson's auditory hallucinations also started worsening."[16]

The fragmentary nature of the *SMiLE* recordings might indeed be symptomatic of a fragmenting mind, whether caused by Brian's escalating drug use or by a mental illness exacerbated by those drugs. Over the course of its journey from its first tracking session at Gold Star in May of 1966 until its release in July of 1967, one typical track, 'Heroes And Villains,' had undergone dozens of permutations, with sections obsessively rerecorded and others added and removed. With words by Van Dyke Parks, an extravagantly gifted musician and writer, it was intended to be a worthy follow-up to 'Good Vibrations.' Brian described 'Heroes And Villains' as a "three-minute musical comedy" that would explore similar 'Americana' themes to songs such as 'Cabinessence' and 'The Old Master Painter/You Are My Sunshine.' He continued to tinker with it even after *SMiLE* was officially scrapped.

Aside from Brian's personal nightmares, The Beach Boys' problems were mounting up. On top of coughing up back royalties to the band, Capitol Records now had to store a warehouse full of unused *SMiLE* album record covers, booklets, and 'Heroes And Villains' color sleeves. Meanwhile, rock'n'roll had become simply 'rock' and critics were taking it seriously, which was not always good news for The Beach Boys. In February 1966, 17-year-old college student Paul Williams had begun publishing *Crawdaddy!* magazine from his room at Swarthmore College, Pennsylvania. In November 1967, in San Francisco, an aspiring guitarist named Jann Wenner would partner with jazz critic Ralph J. Gleason to create *Rolling Stone* magazine. The two magazines from opposite coasts would take opposite views of the demise of *SMiLE*: Williams offered up a sympathetic postmortem, with an extensive interview with Brother Records head David Anderle that became part of his 1969 book *Outlaw Blues*. In The Beach Boys' home state, Wenner and Gleason shrugged off the loss of *SMiLE*. To Gleason, The Beach Boys' only value was as a cultural relic, celebrating the vapid pursuits of vapid California teenagers with vapid music. Wenner chafed at what he saw as The Beach Boys' attempt to hitch their musical wagon to The Beatles' star and the elevation of Brian—a fine songwriter, Wenner conceded—to the level of a John Lennon or a Bob Dylan.

In the feature-length documentary, *The Beach Boys: An American Band*, Carl tells the camera in a clearly scripted segment that The Beach Boys felt that the world of music had passed them by. It was another Beatlemania moment, in which they suddenly felt, in Brian's term, "unhip."[17]

The 'great Satan' in these retellings of The Beach Boys' travails is Jimi Hendrix, whose performance at Monterey involved him sacrificing his Stratocaster after dousing it with cigarette lighter fluid and setting it ablaze.

On the spoken fadeout on 'Third Stone From The Sun,' from his album *Are You Experienced?*, released in America two months after the festival, he intones, "I'll take you away, and you'll never hear surf music again." It suggested the dawn of a new day in which the harmonies of The Beach Boys were no longer required and a wild new electric music—one in which the words mattered—had claimed dominion over the decade.

* * *

The Beach Boys were certainly under pressure. By the terms of most record contracts of the time, it was extraordinary that the band had gone eight months without releasing a single, and a follow-up album to *Pet Sounds* should have arrived in stores well ahead of the Christmas 1966 buying season. To make matters worse, 'Good Vibrations' had shot to the top of the charts upon its release and critics hailed it immediately as a masterpiece. It would not be easy to follow.

It was on the final leg of the 1967 European tour, serving as the countdown to Monterey, that The Beach Boys first encountered Jimi Hendrix. They joined The Beatles' Ringo Starr and The Rolling Stones' Brian Jones at a May 7 performance by The Jimi Hendrix Experience at London's Saville Theatre. Yet, their paths might easily have crossed before. Jimi had recorded 'My Diary' with Rosa Lee Brooks at Gold Star in 1965, and Jimi and Carl shared Dick Dale as an influence and mentor. On his off time from playing the clubs on Central Avenue and Santa Barbara (later Martin Luther King) Boulevard during that period, Hendrix often visited Dale at his Del Tone Record Shop in Balboa, where they conversed about Stratocasters, amplifiers, and stage techniques. "Jimi would ask me, 'How do you do this? How do you do that?'" Dale said.

In fact, the famous "never hear surf music again" quip wasn't directed at The Beach Boys. Stories flourished after Dale's rediscovery, when his 'Miserlou' was used in Quentin Tarantino's *Pulp Fiction*, that the remark came about when Hendrix heard that Dale was suffering from cancer and might die. It was said to be Jimi's lighthearted farewell to an old friend.

However, in an earlier, pre-*Pulp Fiction* interview, Dale said it was a humorous farewell to something else. When Hendrix cranked up his amplifier during shows in New York, prior to Chas Chandler's transforming 'Jimmy James' into 'Jimi Hendrix,' some East Coast critics dismissed his high-volume approach as "surf music." Dale said, "It was Jimi saying he'd found his own voice."[18]

Hendrix later dismissed The Beach Boys' 'Heroes And Villains' as "psychedelic barbershop," and admitted, "[I] don't particularly like The Beach Boys."[19] But he did discuss The Beach Boys with Stephen Desper, who engineered at Monterey. "I spoke to Hendrix about how he liked The Beach Boys," Desper said. "He said he wasn't into surf music, but thought Brian was a musical genius."[20]

With the stress over Carl's court case, no new singles to support, and 'Good Vibrations' and *Pet Sounds* fading in their audience's memory, the response to their European tour in May 1967 went from indifferent to uncomfortable. As Carl suspected, the band's inability to reproduce the lush orchestrations of 'God Only Knows' and 'Good Vibrations' onstage left them open to more criticism than they had experienced in the past. To make matters worse, the band toured constantly during this period, only to return home and be ushered into the studio to sing their parts to segments of music rather than songs. They gradually became excluded from Brian's inner circle of influences, and when they voiced their concerns and comments about the music, their comments were viewed as mere naysaying and hectoring to get Brian back on track to 'the formula.'

An appearance at Monterey—for which Brian had been appointed to the board of directors—might have helped. Stephen Desper said a performance by The Beach Boys would probably have knocked out the Monterey crowd. But in San Francisco, as in Europe, the knives were out. From the early gold-rush days, San Francisco had always viewed itself as the cultural capital of California, taking on continental airs while Los Angeles's leading citizens shot each other in the street and smuggled confederate officers southward during the Civil War. After the film industry turned the world's image of California from the foggy elegance of San Francisco to the sunny, palm-lined streets of Hollywood, and Southern California began importing Northern California's water, the two cities would always see the other as rivals. So when Northern California bands and critics saw an opportunity to deliver a critical drubbing to Southern California's biggest musical ambassadors they seized on it with relish. San Francisco now had its own rock'n'roll scene, and most of the world and the record companies would see it first in Monterey.

Over the years, a multitude of other reasons have been advanced for why Brian Wilson pulled out of the Monterey festival. While the promoters originally envisioned Monterey to be a music and art festival, over time they came to view it as an opportunity to elevate pop music to the level of jazz by using the same venue as the Monterey Jazz Festival. "Rock'n'roll wasn't considered an art form as jazz was," said promoter Lou Adler. So the organizers sought somewhere "where we could put rock'n'roll into a venue that is known for jazz, thereby elevating it."[21]

Using the Monterey fairgrounds required the festival to become a charity, with acts performing for nothing. The Beach Boys were unimpressed by the lack of professionalism about the event, at a time when they were already battered, and they stepped aside. Another reason cited is that Mike and Brian shared an interest in health foods and withdrew when festival organizers licensed a major soft drink manufacturer as a vendor; they didn't want to be associated with a product they felt was harmful to people's health. Some also claimed that Brian feared the Northern California hippies would boo the band, as the schedule was top-heavy with the emerging San Francisco bands such as The Electric Flag, Jefferson Airplane, Big Brother & The Holding Company, and Quicksilver Messenger Service.

On Saturday night, filling the slot The Beach Boys were originally scheduled to play, Otis Redding, backed by Booker T & The MGs and The Bar Kays, wowed the audience who had been pummeled into insensibility by an afternoon of San Francisco bands, The Byrds, and Hugh Masekela. On Sunday, audiences got a glimpse of the band that would soon replace The Beach Boys as Los Angeles's musical front-runners when The Byrds'

David Crosby joined his future partner Stephen Stills onstage for a set by Buffalo Springfield.

One further reason why The Beach Boys pulled out of Monterey—and the reason they gave at the time—was Carl's anxieties about his legal battle. On the Tuesday after the festival, he was again in court. He told the court, "I love my country very much but I won't take part in the destruction of people."[22] This time his status as a conscientious objector was accepted, and he was allowed to serve his country in some other capacity. It was left to Carl and his lawyers to sort out with the local draft board what that service should be. This would cause plenty more trouble in the years to come.

Carl's idea was that he should do a concert tour for the troops. He submitted a proposal claiming he had the support of The Beach Boys and that they were willing to perform at "any and all Vietnam installations ... and are willing to render our services without any cost." Offered the opportunity to have the biggest American rock band in the world entertain the troops on USO tours that generally featured fading Las Vegas lounge entertainers, the board instead ordered Carl to begin performing community service at a local veterans' hospital, which meant emptying bedpans, among other things.[23]

When Carl refused to report at the hospital as ordered, he was criminally charged again with breaching the Selective Service Act. He had volunteered to do his duty and serve his country in the best way he could, while still serving his conscience, and The Beach Boys all supported him. So his attorneys challenged the constitutionality of both the war and the Selective Service Act, but the judge rejected these claims.

Eventually, Carl was convicted and sentenced to three years' probation, two of which were to be served as a volunteer in hospitals. There was an appeal, which rejected his lawyers' constitutional arguments but also dismissed Carl's proposal for alternative service as "vague and ill-defined." The case dragged on and on.[24]

What made Carl's case so singular is that, despite contending that the war and the Selective Service System were unconstitutional, he was willing to serve his country and the people who were fighting for it in the best way he knew how without violating his conscience. In the eyes of the law, conscientious objectors who were not part of a major recognized religious movement had little legal standing. But because Carl had the resources and the support of The Beach Boys, independent (non-affiliated) conscientious objectors would at least have some case law to fall back on when pursuing their own cases.

Carl wasn't the only American who had issues with a war that wasn't really a war and a Selective Service System concerned less with protecting America and more with realizing the visions of social engineers. Upon Nixon's election in 1968, the new president said he hoped to defuse the unfairness of the draft by eventually converting to an all-volunteer military. However, with the war in Southeast Asia still raging, that would be impossible to accomplish overnight. So in 1969, Nixon signed into law what many hoped would be a fairer system, a lottery, as had been used in previous wars with success.

Carl's own case would not reach a definitive conclusion until September 16, 1971, when American involvement in Vietnam was much reduced. A United Press International (UPI) story, datelined Los Angeles, reported that Carl would "fulfill his military obligation by touring prisons, hospitals, and orphanages at his own expense." The article goes on to say that US District Court Judge Harry Pregerson had approved the touring plans submitted by Carl and his lawyers to serve his country by improving prisons and lifting morale at hospitals, rather than cleaning bedpans.[25]

According to Stephen Desper, one of the reasons Carl knew this approach would work was that The Beach Boys had experienced the impact their musical performances had in hospitals when the band had, in total secrecy, loaded guitars and bongos into a caravan of cars and quietly and without any publicity performed at local hospitals throughout the country. "That was when I fell in love with The Beach Boys," Desper said.[26]

CHAPTER FOURTEEN

Goin' South

When Brian Wilson finally released *SMiLE* in two formats—the Grammy Award-winning *Brian Wilson Presents SMiLE* (2004) and *The Smile Sessions* (2011)—he said that his biggest impediment to releasing *SMiLE* originally was his realization that he could not have finished it in time. When Grammy-winning engineers and producers Alan Boyd and Mark Linett began reassembling the tapes to create *The SMiLE Sessions*, they found that Brian's epic would have been nearly an hour too long for a single album or nearly a half hour too long for a double album.[1]

When Brian shelved the album in its uncompleted state, "pop music gained one of its most enduring myths, but lost a landmark artwork," wrote Philip Lambert in his 2007 book *Inside The Music Of Brian Wilson*. An old Irish proverb says "God never closes a door without opening a window." When the door slammed on Brian's 'teenage hymn,' a window opened. "The Beach Boys albums of the late 60s displayed a new spirit of collaboration, with artistic control gradually shifting to other group members," wrote Lambert, "especially Carl."[2]

The economics of the music business in the 60s demanded that bands release albums and then tour to support them. Artists like Crosby, Stills, Nash & Young came to their early tours as established stars, but they rarely played the hits they had had in their previous incarnations, and when they did, it was usually in modified form, for instance playing acoustic versions of electric hits like 'For What It's Worth.' In the 60s, record sales drove the industry, tours drove record sales, and bands were expected to create new hits, not dwell on their own history.

With the loss of *SMiLE*, the pressure was on The Beach Boys to deliver a product, and the only real revenues coming in were from the band's tours. So while the picture that emerges from the band's post-*SMiLE* recordings appears to show the demotion of Brian from leader to first among equals, it actually reflects the harsh realities of the 60s music business: whatever The Beach Boys did in the studio, they would have to be able to deliver on stage.

The 16 months between *Pet Sounds* and The Beach Boys' next album would have been longer than the lifespan of most bands. In the period between their greatest success and what history would consider their fall from grace, with the release of *Smiley Smile*, The Beach Boys had experienced marriage, divorce, having children, buying property and—in Carl's case—launching a very expensive legal battle with the United States government. The pressure was on and the stakes were high for the band.

During the build-up to what would have been *SMiLE*, The Beach Boys started their own record company, called Brother Records, a sort of vanity label for band members' various outside musical pursuits, recording other artists such as The Pickle Brothers, and for Brian's more experimental ideas, such as an entire album filled with water sounds. As part of their July 1967 settlement with Capitol Records, Capitol agreed to distribute the Brother products.

Having acquired their own custom-built live sound system, The Beach Boys took another step forward in building their own recording studio in Brian's home—in large part to keep Brian actively involved in the band. The studio, at 10452 Bellagio Road in Bel Air, would come to be known as Brother Studios.

As Stephen Desper set about building the studio in Brian's home, Brian kept tinkering with 'Heroes And Villains.'[3] At one point, the band carried Brian's massive Baldwin organ down to his drained swimming pool, placing a microphone at the deep end to capture its brooding lower tones. However, endless overdubbing and rerecording of the track left its overall sound fuzzy and blurred as opposed to the sparkling crystal-clarity to which Beach Boy fans were accustomed. Released on July 24, 1967, 'Heroes And Villains' stalled at number 12 on the charts.

To add insult to injury, just a week after the release of 'Heroes And Villains,' Capitol put out *Best Of The Beach Boys Vol. 2*. Its 1966 predecessor, *Best Of The Beach Boys*, had been seen by some band members as Capitol's effort to sabotage *Pet Sounds* and get the band back to formula records, or to hedge Capitol's bets in the event the public rejected The Beach Boys new music. The new compilation was not even commercially successful, charting at number 50.

By the summer of 1967, it was clear that The Beach Boys had to get to grips with their recording career again. *SMiLE* was over, but the band adjourned to Brian's house and put together an album using some of the *SMiLE* songs in radically simplified versions, with Carl replacing Brian's lead on 'Wonderful' and chipping in on 'Wind Chimes.' "*Smiley Smile* was a very simple album to make," recalled Carl. "It took a couple of weeks at Brian's house. Tops, two weeks. We had a remote come into Brian's library and we set up a console on his desk with two speakers, ran wires up to the gym, down to the sauna, and out to the pool—anywhere …"[4]

After recording, they went to Wally Heider's studio and edited and mixed the eight-track recordings over one night. The new album, named by Brian, would be called *Smiley Smile*. Before its release, the band made hasty plans for a live album to be recorded in Hawaii, tentatively titled *Lei'd In Hawaii*, to extract some additional mileage out of what was left of their reputation. But the band made a tactical mistake. For the two-night appearance in Honolulu, in August 1967, Brian replaced Bruce Johnston, alternating between bass and his Baldwin organ, which was especially flown out for the tour, leaving Carl to switch between guitar and bass. Still insisting on wearing their early-60s candy-striped shirts and lacking Bruce, they gave a performance so unsatisfactory that they shelved the tapes. While fans were happy to see Brian back in the band, they cringed when he admitted to a reporter that "The Beach Boys are squares" and said that he had "taken some drugs" to fuel his creativity. Trying to position the group as a happy, unselfconscious operation, Brian admitted, "We're not a hip group."[5]

Then *Smiley Smile* was released, on September 18, 1967. The jacket said the record was produced, for the first time, by The Beach Boys. To some it appeared to be the comedy album Brian had long hoped to release on the band's new vanity label. To others, it appeared to be a musical white flag of surrender. To Carl, it was "a bunt instead of a grand slam."

"Describing what *SMiLE* would have been and then comparing it to *Smiley Smile* is unfair," wrote David Leaf. "No record could make up for the disappointment that music fans felt when *Smiley Smile* was released. Expectations had been raised then dashed by the non-appearance of *SMiLE*, and *Smiley Smile*, its titular and musical substitute, was cruelly criticized as *SMiLE*'s unwelcome replacement." By the time the album was released, said Leaf, "The Beach Boys had become cultural dinosaurs … It was into that almost revolutionary vortex of 1967 that *Smiley Smile* was sent forth, an unwanted soldier in the psychedelic rock wars, sentenced to death by critical firing squad."[6]

History has proven kinder to *Smiley Smile* than the cultural tastemakers of 1967, partly because historians have pointed to the fact that The Beach Boys released *Smiley Smile* on their vanity label, Brother Records. If it had not included 'Good Vibrations' and 'Heroes And Villains' (purportedly placed on the album at Capitol's insistence) *Smiley Smile* could be viewed as an album of 'comedy' tracks—in the tradition of 'Cassius Love Versus Sonny Wilson,' 'Our Favorite Recording Sessions,' and 'I'm Bugged At My Old Man'—with a couple of *SMiLE* songs, rather than tracks, thrown in for good measure.

Hipness, like war, means, in the words of Confederate General Nathan Bedford Forrest, "getting there first with the most." For The Beach Boys, in Leaf's words, "*Smiley Smile* was the beginning of their march through the desert. And even though their overseas popularity would not be diminished throughout the remainder of the decade, there was no getting around the fact that at home, The Beach Boys, a decade away from becoming 'America's Band,' were outcasts."[7]

Yet, *Smiley Smile* revealed a glimmer of the future, with Carl singing or sharing lead vocals on half of the album's vocal tracks. It may have been a bunt, but its unintended consequence was to bring 20-year-old Carl Wilson up to bat—and a new era would begin before his 21st birthday. The band was about to answer his question about how a little surf band could perform their newer, more complex music on stage.

* * *

On October 6, 1967, The Beach Boys played a show in Indianapolis that marked the beginning of the end of the 'striped shirts' era. It introduced bassist Ron Brown, whose inclusion in the stage lineup freed Bruce Johnston to play keyboards and enhance the band's ability to do justice to its new material. At the end of the show, they debuted 'Wild Honey,' which would be the title track to their upcoming album.

Six weeks later, in the midst of recording that album, they kicked off their Fifth Annual Thanksgiving Tour in Michigan, supported by Buffalo Springfield, The Strawberry Alarm Clock, The Soul Survivors, and The Pickle Brothers. Replacing the old striped shirts were matching white ice-cream suits. More importantly, The Beach Boys onstage lineup now included Brown on bass and a new keyboard player, Daryl Dragon. He was the son of award-winning composer and conductor Carmen Dragon, and would later be known as the Captain in Captain & Tennille, the successful group he formed with his wife, Toni Tennille.

The tour wound its way toward the East Coast, where Carl—still officially a conscientious objector—and the band performed at the West Point Military Academy and then at a star-studded gala for UNICEF (the United Nations Children's Fund). There they encountered one of the most pivotal figures in The Beach Boys' future. In the front row for The Beach Boys' set, between John Lennon and George Harrison, sat Maharishi Mahesh Yogi, the founder of the school of Transcendental Meditation.

On December 18, three days after the gala, The Beach Boys released their first Capitol album since *Pet Sounds*. On *Wild Honey*, Carl would sing, or share lead vocals, on seven of the album's eleven tracks, emphasising his soulful side. But *Wild Honey* also marked the reality that The Beach Boys now had two almost separate identities: the touring band of musicians and singers, and Brian's choir in the studio.

The Beach Boys were now utilizing the studio at Brian's house. It was built around their live sound equipment, with the addition of a rented multi-track machine. It began as a makeshift affair, but soon they began knocking down walls and building more permanent facilities, at which point it became known as Brother Studios. But the band still ventured out to Brian's favorite recording venues for *Wild Honey*. Working as second engineer to Jimmy Lockert, Bill Halverson recalled The Beach Boys recording at Wally Heider's studio, where "Lockert engineered a lot of the overdubs and mixed a lot of *Wild Honey* and the *SMiLE* sessions. I got to be his second engineer and did some engineering and mixing with them. We also moved some gear to Brian's house and I got to engineer a bit of that, too."[8]

Wild Honey would serve two purposes after the traumas of *SMiLE*. Carl said it was "music for Brian to cool out by," but it also revealed The Beach Boys rediscovering themselves as a band.

"I loved *Wild Honey* because I thought it was getting us back on the track again," said Bruce Johnston. "It was probably the funkiest Beach Boys album, very little production, but a lot of music without any complications. I just remember we wanted to be a band again." *SMiLE*, he added, "had wiped everyone out, and we wanted to play together."[9]

Carl was key to the new sound. "When we did *Wild Honey*, Brian asked me to get more involved in the recording end," he recalled. "He wanted a break. He was tired. He had been doing it all too long."[10]

As with *Smiley Smile*, history has been much kinder to *Wild Honey* than were the critics in 1967. Critics unaware of The Beach Boys' rhythm & blues heritage and influences saw only the obvious 'Four Freshman meet Chuck Berry' approach in their hits, and mocked the band for delving into an idiom that The Beatles and Rolling Stones had 'brought back home' in 1964. This was unfair.

"We all really dug Motown, right?" said Carl. "So Brian reckoned we should get more into a white R&B bag. I also recall around that time the band, and Brian in particular, getting criticized very heavily for sounding like choirboys. I mean, there was one review that said Brian actually sounded like Mickey Mouse. That really tore him up."[11]

Within days of *Wild Honey*'s release, however, Bob Dylan released *John Wesley Harding*. That was followed in rapid succession by The Band's *Music From Big Pink*, The Byrds' *Notorious Byrd Brothers*, and 'Lady Madonna,' The Beatles' homage to Fats Domino. The message in late 1967 and early 1968 was clear: the psychedelic revolution of the year before had run its course. It was time to get back to basics.

Wild Honey rose into the Top 30, and the album yielded a hit single, the Top 20 'Darlin'.' Soulfully sung by Carl, it became the band's concert opener for decades. The song was rewritten from an earlier single called 'Thinkin' 'Bout You Baby,' which Brian and Mike had written for a singer named Sharon Marie. As 'Darlin',' it was intended by Brian for a band called Redwood, formed by his friend Danny Hutton (who later changed their name to Three Dog Night). Brian had always taken on outside production projects, often with very little success. For Redwood, Brian had produced 'Darlin'' and 'Time To Get Alone,' which would end up on The Beach Boys' last Capitol album, *20/20*. The bills were piling up, however, and Mike insisted Brian finish the song as a Beach Boys track.

The critical response to *Wild Honey* was lackluster at best, although *Crawdaddy*'s Paul Williams would later lavish praise on it, while also citing The Doors' Jim Morrison as a fan.[12] Carl lamented the album's lukewarm reception. "It didn't have all of the polish and pizazz, but it brought out our rhythm & blues influences that had always been there, but people had overlooked."[13]

Even though *Wild Honey* was the first real Beach Boys album since *The Beach Boys Today!*, and despite the back-to-back debacles of *SMiLE* and *Smiley Smile*, one thing hadn't changed. "Brian was the driving force the best that I could tell," Bill Halverson said.[14]

As 1968 dawned, The Beach Boys were a band again onstage and in the studio. They had a hit single and a Top 30 album on the charts. As a performing unit, The Beach Boys broke new ground by adding additional musicians so they would now be able to perform their more complex songs onstage.

On December 21, 1967, Carl Wilson turned 21 years old. He had spent most of his youth being one of the biggest rock stars on the planet. He was married, owned a home, and faced time in federal prison. The world of music had changed and the unobtrusive lead guitarist, who dutifully filled out the harmonies his older brother made him sing, was now the lead vocalist on three of The Beach Boys' recent hit records: 'God Only Knows,' 'Good Vibrations,' and 'Darlin'.'

Now, two new characters would enter The Beach Boys' orbit in 1968. One brought a message of inner peace. The other was a murderer.

CHAPTER FIFTEEN

Passing By

Alcoholic drinks and lighter drugs such as marijuana have long been favored social lubricants for musicians, and music is the most social of all of the arts: musicians have to play together to create music and, for the audience, most public performances involve either gathering to listen or taking part in the mating ritual of dancing.

Using drugs to enhance creativity extends far back beyond the 60s, but a new wave began in 1964 when Bob Dylan assumed The Beatles used drugs after mishearing the words of 'I Want To Hold Your Hand': he heard "I can't hide" as "I get high." The Beatles pointed out his error but owned up to a history of drug use dating back to 1961. It was then that singer Tony Sheridan had offered the band diet pills called prellies: they were phenmetrazine, an appetite suppressant sold under the name Preludin. He said the pills would keep them awake during their grueling eight-hour sets in Hamburg's red light district. However, it was Dylan who introduced them to marijuana.

Brian may have been the first Beach Boy exposed to marijuana, during the early surfin' period. Given Southern California's proximity to Mexico (a chief growing area) and marijuana's reputed relaxing and mind-expanding properties, it soon became the illicit substance of choice among Southern California's musical community. Also important were the so-called 'natural' psychedelics, such as mescaline, peyote, or 'magic' (psilocybe) mushrooms, which grew wild in the great Southwestern deserts and which were used in Native American religious ceremonies.

In the 60s, popular songs addressed the drug experience in three ways: directly, as in Dylan's 'Mr Tambourine Man' and 'Rainy Day Women #12 &

35'; indirectly, as in The Byrds' 'Eight Miles High' (a song about a dismal visit to London, but using the word 'high' to generate controversy); or foolishly, as in Donovan's 'Mellow Yellow,' about the rumored psychedelic effects of smoking banana peels or saffron. However, the biggest impact came not from the drug experiences themselves, but from what guitarist Stephen Stills called the "marijuana mentality," where musicians improvised over simple key changes for longer—and sometimes interminable—periods of time.[1]

This became the period where songs began featuring extended solos or became available in 'long versions.' *Wild Honey*, in contrast, may have been a harbinger of the back-to-basics movement that sought musical retrenchment after the excesses of the psychedelic era. It may have set the stage for the later successes of The Band, The Flying Burrito Brothers, and even for The Beatles' *Let It Be* album. But its shorter, more focused songs and keyboard-centric arrangements didn't fit a musical landscape in which bands like Quicksilver Messenger Service or The Paul Butterfield Blues Band regularly transformed old blues tunes into epics of guitar improvisation onstage and in the studio.

The psychedelic era introduced the idea that weird, surreal, or seemingly disconnected stream-of-conscious lyrics could have meaning. The Strawberry Alarm Clock exploited this to great success when their managers took the chord changes from one of their early surf band instrumentals and stitched together 'lyrics' from a rhyming dictionary to produce the psychedelic classic 'Incense And Peppermints.'

Aside from their immediate or cumulative physical impact, drugs have ill effects because they are generally illegal. Not only do they make users into criminals, they provide an entrée for much more experienced, and potentially dangerous, criminals into their social and professional circles. For musicians who publicly or privately decried drug use, such as Dick Dale or Frank Zappa, dealing with musicians or audiences who did take drugs often introduced them to a slew of issues. And by 1968, most musicians or audience members had at least experimented with drugs to some degree.

Many users who experimented had, in Brian's phrase, "experimented themselves right out of action."[2] Bad trips were a common occurrence among LSD users, and dope smokers frequently found themselves sickened or scammed with bags of oregano or lawn trimming passing as marijuana. Worse yet, some musicians never returned from their trips, joining the list of famous 60s 'acid casualties,' including Moby Grape's Skip Spence, Fleetwood Mac's Peter Green, and Pink Floyd's Roger 'Syd' Barrett. Other drug users faced prison time, including, in 1967, The Rolling Stones' Mick Jagger, Keith Richards, and Brian Jones.

By the end of the Summer of Love, many musical creators were looking for a legal alternative to drugs—and some of The Beach Boys found it.

While Carl was known to be the band's most spiritual member—the recording of *Pet Sounds* often saw Carl and Brian praying together—it would be Dennis who first alerted The Beach Boys to the Maharishi Mahesh Yogi and Mike who became his most devout disciple. Born Mahesh Prasad Varma ('Maharishi' is an honorific title, meaning 'great seer'), the Maharishi, born 1918, was an Indian mystic who developed his own religious or quasi-religious movement based on a technique known as Transcendental Meditation (TM). An inveterate collector of celebrities, he claimed to have introduced more than five million people to his technique, and promised it would bring about world peace.

The Beach Boys met the Maharishi at the UNICEF gala in Paris in December 1967. Mike flew off to London after the gig, but the others stayed on. He was surprised to receive a call from Dennis, informing him that the Maharishi had agreed to teach them the technique and urging him to come back. Mike would become TM's greatest advocate within the group and perhaps in the wider world.

Yet while the Maharishi's practice of Transcendental Medication spared some of The Beach Boys the ravages of drugs, it created a schism within the band so severe that they eventually traveled on two airplanes—one for substance abusers and the other for TM devotees.

"I learned TM in December 1967," Mike Love said, "and that was it with marijuana for me. Alcohol and marijuana and other drugs may be relaxing or invigorating or whatever, but you can get plenty relaxed through meditation without the negative side-effects."

Love went on to say that TM in the band "created a 'them and us' situation. Bruce and Alan and myself didn't [take drugs] and the Wilson brothers did. Tragically, with Dennis, it led to his early demise. With Carl, he'd been smoking since he was 13 or 14 and contracted lung cancer. That was a bummer. The tragedies have affected us emotionally, and like anybody's family you're going to have loss."[3]

Carl practiced TM, yet ended up in what Mike termed the 'them' faction of The Beach Boys. This was most likely because, under threat, he would close ranks with Murry's other sons to protect them. In fact all of the members practiced TM to some degree. Spirituality, rather than organized religion, became a serious matter for a band who made music because, in Brian's words, "music is God's voice."

Carl's attitude to TM was revealed later in the year, in a long interview conducted by *Back To Godhead*, the organ of the Krishna Consciousness Movement, better known as Hare Krishna. Interviewed before a concert in New York in October, along with Dennis and Mike, Carl spoke eloquently of meditation and faith in general.

"I was introduced to transcendental meditation, and I found it to be a great thing for me," Carl said. "You know, nowadays we don't really have a feeling of wellbeing as much as they did at other times. Of course, it isn't something that we really know about, you know. You just meditate, and through a long period of time you develop something, a state of awareness that is really good. It's really just natural. But I definitely feel the influence and the help of it when I do meditate. And when I don't, I miss it. I stopped meditating for about a month, a month and a half, and then I really noticed it."

The goal of his meditating, Carl added, was "bliss consciousness. I'm sure that all forms of meditation are really designed to do the same thing. To bring you to a higher state of awareness something above the everyday life. To bring you closer to God … I've always felt the divine power running through me. And I felt the love a lot … And when I found meditation I felt it more, and I felt it all the time. It wasn't just a once-in-awhile thing. That's an important thing that you can feel it whenever you want."

Concern for the environment drove much of Carl's spiritual journey in those days before 'ecology' became a fashion statement. Noting that the band had earlier been singing the old spiritual hymn 'Didn't It Rain?' about the Biblical story of Noah's Ark, Carl said, "We could experience the same thing … people were treating the earth bad, and they were abusing it and putting a lot of pressure on the earth in different places like in Manhattan, and like in Los Angeles for example. It's just a bad thing to do to nature. It's sinful, really."

Yet to Carl, TM was about more than just being relaxed and self-aware. "I always knew that there was a Supreme Being, and I always had a lot of peace of mind about that. And I've always thought of God as the protector … I've always known that inside. I know that meditation can probably make someone feel it more."[4]

After an afternoon concert sharing the stage with Buffalo Springfield in Portland, Oregon, on February 4, 1968, The Beach Boys touring band took a two-month hiatus. Mike took the opportunity to fly to the Maharishi's retreat in Rishikesh, India, to take meditation courses. There he joined The Beatles and their significant others, Donovan, and the Farrow sisters, Mia and Prudence. (John Lennon wrote 'Dear Prudence' there, employing the fingerpicking technique taught him in India by Donovan.)

TM became a major theme in the lives of The Beach Boys. They would celebrate it with not one but three songs, 'Transcendental Meditation,' on *Friends* (1968), 'All This Is That' on *Carl And The Passions "So Tough"* (1972), and 'The TM Song' on *15 Big Ones* (1976). During downtime from their meditating, Mike struck up a conversation with The Beatles and suggested they write a song about English girls, mirroring what The Beach Boys had done with 'California Girls' or 'The Girls On The Beach.'

The comment inspired McCartney to write an affectionate satire on The Beach Boys' obsession with girls, with a wicked twist. Whereas The Beach Boys clearly celebrated American girls as the most beautiful in the world,

McCartney celebrated their opposite: Soviet-era Russian women who were strangers to makeup and fashion. He even took a jab at The Beach Boys' record of borrowing from their hero Chuck Berry, by titling the song 'Back In The USSR' after Berry's 'Back In The USA.'

While Mike hobnobbed with The Beatles, the remaining Beach Boys commenced work on what would be their first stereo release: *Friends*. Gone was the creative whirlwind of the early cra. Now four of The Beach Boys were fathers, the songs were more reflective of their domestic lives and concerns.

"I have heard some songs about parents and babies before and I was challenged to write a song that describes the feeling of love for my daughters," wrote Brian in his liner notes for the 90s CD reissue of *Friends*. "'When A Man Needs A Woman' is a good example of that.

"This album was our best production to date. It had perfect instrumental tracking with no mistakes," he concluded.[5] *Friends* featured 'Busy Doin' Nothin',' a slice of Brian's life set to a gentle Latin jazz backing, the gorgeous waltz-time 'Friends,' the wordless 'Passing By,' and Dennis's first songwriting efforts, 'Little Bird' and 'Be Still.' Brian declared that *Friends* was his favorite album, due to its warmth and relative simplicity.[6]

Friends also revealed another step in Carl's journey from lead guitar to lead singer. Vocally, *Friends* showed a new musical democracy with the band members sharing lead vocals on individual songs; they even imported Murry to sing the bass notes in 'Be Here In The Mornin'.' As with *Wild Honey*, the songs clearly had keyboard origins; the one instrumental, 'Diamond Head,' features Hawaiian steel guitar and ukulele, and no electric guitar solo.

* * *

In February 1968, while Brian started work on the *Friends* album, The Beach Boys hit the road again with Buffalo Springfield (then featuring Stephen Stills, Neil Young, Richie Furay, Dewey Martin, and Jim Messina) for a series of concerts beginning in Washington State. After a break in March, The Strawberry Alarm Clock (then featuring future Lynyrd Skynyrd guitarist Ed King) were added to the bill. The tour ended in Memphis, Tennessee, at the end of April. Mike and Carl both became fans of Buffalo Springfield, watching their sets from behind the stage and adding Springfield's 1967 'Rock & Roll Woman' single as a cover tune into the set. Few bands played their rivals' material in concert in those days, and with the exception of 'For What It's Worth,' Springfield's singles didn't get a lot of play outside of Los Angeles. As they would with an unknown singer Elton John in 1970, The Beach Boys used their shows to support other artists. In their downtime, Mike Love and Neil Young "became inseparable on that tour," Stills later recalled. "That's the tour where Mike Love was talking Neil into quitting the band, just because he thought it was cool to be able to talk anybody into anything. But that was an interesting tour."[7]

On the first dates of the tour, Carl noticed a difference in the audience's response to the band. "There are no riots out there like there used to be," Carl said to an interviewer. "I think the kids are growing up."[8] Carl's words would come back to haunt him the next day, April 4, as the band landed in Nashville. In preparation for a planned march to Washington, Dr Martin Luther King Jr and his entourage had stopped in Memphis to support a sanitation workers' strike. The civil rights leader had given a prophetic speech the night before at the Mason Temple Church, saying, "I've seen the promised land. I may not get there with you. But I want you to know tonight, that we, as a people, will get to the Promised Land." The next night, Sunday April 4, on the balcony of the Lorraine Motel, a sniper's bullet ripped through his neck and killed him. Over the course of the next few days, rioting consumed more than 100 American cities.

"We were sitting in Nashville and Dr Martin Luther King, Jr. was assassinated in Memphis," Mike recalled. "Almost immediately more than half the shows were canceled, because a lot of those cities were burning and the National Guard came out. We lost a lot of money. I was thinking to myself, 'Had I stayed in India we would have rearranged the tour and not been right in the middle of that thing.'"[9]

As the riot-torn cities set about cleaning up the mess, the tour resumed three days later, unmarred by incident except for one occasion when members of the three bands formed an informal posse and pounced on a guitar thief who had attempted to steal Stephen Stills's Les Paul guitar.

"After one show some guys on the road crew were putting some guitars in the luggage bay below the band bus," wrote Ed King. "A few of us from the three bands (I think I can recall Neil Young & Alan Jardine) were standing out in back of the coliseum when this older station wagon pulled into the parking lot. One of the guys in the car jumped out, ran over to the bus and grabbed Stills's Les Paul from the luggage bay, ran back to the car, threw the guitar in and they started to drive off. Good thing it was still in the parking lot ... they couldn't go that fast.

"We saw this and started running toward the station wagon. Like I said, I can't recall who did what but someone broke the back window out, someone else jumped in and stopped the driver and Young was able to retrieve the vintage guitar. The rest of us pulled the occupants out and stomped on them for a while. But the important thing was that we were able to get Stills's guitar back!"[10]

Picking up the pieces of an interrupted tour wouldn't be the last hurdle The Beach Boys faced that spring. A second occurred when they had to cancel an ill-conceived tour with the Maharishi after five dates, because the Maharishi had to pull out to focus on a film project. (Audiences, already small, would walk out of auditoriums after The Beach Boys and before the Maharishi: Mike said later that perhaps a lot of them weren't ready for meditation.) The cost of the debacle to The Beach Boys was estimated to be between a quarter- and a half-million dollars, the equivalent to something like $4 million today.[11] They canceled the tour at a time when their contract with Capitol Records was coming to an end, without any other offers pending.

The cancellation, in conjunction with the missed Buffalo Springfield/Strawberry Alarm Clock dates, added to the financial woes they'd experienced with their albums and singles failing to perform. In fact, their most recent single, 'Friends,' released on April 8, charted no higher than number 47 on the pop charts. The album, released in June, would be their worst chart showing to date, failing even to enter *Billboard*'s Hot 100.

Losing money was not the worst thing that happened to The Beach Boys in 1968, however. One day in April, as Dennis cruised down the Pacific Coast Highway in his Ferrari, he stopped and picked up two young girls, hitchhiking. A couple of days later he met them again and brought them back to his house on Sunset Boulevard for an afternoon of casual sex. They called themselves 'Yeller Stone' and 'Marnie Reeves.' Throughout their visit, they kept telling Dennis about a 'prophet' they referred to as 'the soul.' Dennis left them to go to a recording session for *Friends*. When he returned, in the early hours of the morning, the soul was waiting for him. He introduced himself as Charles Manson. He had filled Dennis's house with his followers, many of them young and female and known as the Family. They would stay five months.

* * *

When Charles Manson insinuated himself into the world of The Beach Boys, he fancied himself as a musician and songwriter. Neil Young, who met him through Dennis, said he was more like "a song spewer." Like many within The Beach Boys' circle, Young heard Charlie's songs and once cautioned Reprise Records' head Mo Ostin: "This guy, he's good. He's just a little out of control."[12]

For decades, people have viewed the Dennis/Manson relationship through the lens of Dennis's wild-child personality. Today, he would be forgiven his sins as a sex addict and the offspring of a highly dysfunctional family. But in the world of rock'n'roll, he was just 'crazy Dennis.'

While the Wilson household in which the brothers were raised was clearly a musical household, it was not a literary household. While Brian was known to consume books, they were usually trendy spiritual awareness books written by what *Pet Sounds* lyricist Tony Asher termed "marshmallow mystics."[13] Unlike those of his contemporaries, Brian's writing partners seldom shared the musical burden and served primarily as wordsmiths.

Dennis often said that "Charlie doesn't have a musical bone in his body," but Manson did exhibit a talent that Dennis didn't possess: writing lyrics.[14] With Brian's songwriting contributions coming in shorter bursts, the other members of the band found themselves in the position of either contributing songs themselves or trying to work with Brian to generate more songs. The problem with being a songwriter in The Beach Boys was that one's songs would always be held against the standard of a genius. Yet something had to be done.

Worse still, at some point in the summer of 1968, Brian was either committed to a psychiatric hospital or checked himself in for treatment. The Beach Boys had only one album left to run on their Capitol contract before they would find themselves without a label. To bridge the songwriting gap, Dennis had come up with two songs for the *Friends* album and now, for the final Capitol Beach Boys, brought to the table a Charles Manson song originally titled 'Cease To Exist,' later amended by Dennis to 'Never Learn Not To Love.'

Manson and his Family managed to penetrate The Beach Boys' inner and outer circles. One night, the straight-arrows, Bruce and Mike, found themselves at a dinner party with the Family in which they were the only ones wearing clothes. Newly married, and still at odds with the Selective Service, Carl is said to have limited his involvement to recording some Manson demos at Brian's house, to which Brian himself allegedly contributed on at least one occasion. Dennis introduced Charlie to a number of people who could help gain what Manson wanted most: a recording contract. One day he took Charlie up to 10050 Cielo Drive in the Hollywood Hills, home of his friend, the record producer Terry Melcher. Melcher agreed to give Manson's music some consideration. A year later, Charlie sent his gang to the house to slaughter the house's new tenant, the actress Sharon Tate, her unborn baby, and four friends. Among the murderers was Marnie Reeves, whose real name was Patricia Krenwinkel.

And yet, Carl would much later look back on this period in The Beach Boys' story with little fear or rancor. The period after *SMiLE*, in Carl's recollection, was a time when The Beach Boys were all starting families. He always loved children, and soon his reputation in the family was to be Papa

Bear, looking out for all of his nieces and nephews.[15] When it emerged that Manson had ordered the killings, and that Dennis might face repercussions from members of his death cult, Carl and Annie hid him in their home in Coldwater Canyon.[16]

Supplemented with additional stage musicians and an occasional five-piece horn section, The Beach Boys returned to touring after the debacle of the Maharishi tour. Released in July, *Friends* peaked at number 126. Capitol would follow that failure by releasing two more Beach Boys albums that summer: *Best of The Beach Boys Vol. 3*, which only charted at number 153, and *Stack-O-Tracks*, a weird collection of 15 Beach Boys instrumental tracks without vocals, with a booklet of lyrics, lead lines, basslines, and guitar chords. Designed to allow guitarists to learn to play along with The Beach Boys, the experiment failed miserably and it became the first album bearing The Beach Boys' name to fail to chart. On the other hand, their most recent single, released in July, did quite well. A nostalgic Brian and Mike collaboration called 'Do It Again,' it charted at number 20 as well as being a British number one.

Playing to smaller venues, in areas most likely to attract a friendly crowd, The Beach Boys found themselves confronted with a problem that would dog the rest of their careers: the oldies—the early surfin' and hot-rod singles—generated the best responses from the audiences, while simultaneously generating the critics' nastiest vitriol. Even though the average age of The Beach Boys was more than a year younger than The Beatles, one critic savaged the band as a bunch of "aging millionaires."

Dennis moved out of his house on the Sunset Strip in August and left it to the Manson Family. After a menacing encounter with Charlie, he let the lease lapse, avoiding a confrontation, and the Family were evicted. For Carl, however, the toughest year The Beach Boys had experienced would give way to a year in which he would finally come into his own, creating a hit record with a credit that read 'Produced by Carl Wilson.' It was a record he made to help his older brother heal.

CHAPTER SIXTEEN

I Can Hear Music

Whether the pleasures of the flesh, genuine artistic interest, or both fueled Dennis Wilson's friendship with Charles Manson, the relationship ended for good in December of 1968, when Dennis finally committed one of Manson's songs to vinyl as the flip side to their single 'Bluebirds Over The Mountain.' While on tour, Dennis had told *Rave* magazine that Manson, whom he referred to as The Wizard, "may be an artist for Brother Records."[1]

However, capturing Manson on magnetic tape proved to be a difficult experience for Dennis. "Charlie would not be produced," said Stephen Desper, noting that Manson ignored Dennis's direction. Manson "was not a professional artist."[2]

'Bluebirds Over The Mountain' was a cover of a 1958 Ersel Hickey rockabilly classic (although their arrangement drew from Ritchie Valens's later version). It featured what may be the first distorted lead guitar on a Beach Boys record, played by touring band bassist Ed Carter, one of Bruce Johnston's former bandmates before he joined The Beach Boys. Produced by Bruce, the upbeat single featured a distinct rhythm & blues horn section and fuller vocals, more akin to The Association than The Beach Boys. It was quite representative of the band's stage act at the time. It was also a resounding flop, reaching only number 61 on the *Billboard* chart and number 33 in the UK.

On the flip side was 'Never Learn Not To Love,' a song credited to Dennis Wilson with no mention of Manson (an oft-repeated rumor is that Manson gave Dennis the song in exchange for taking the entire Manson Family to a Beverly Hills doctor to be treated to what Dennis called "the largest gonorrhea bill in history"[3]). It had originally had been written by

Manson as 'Cease To Exist.' To transform Manson's turgid tune into a Beach Boys record, changes had to be made, which didn't please Manson. In his original, the song features an introduction that makes it clear it is addressed to a "pretty girl," but Dennis discarded that. The lyric "Submission is a gift / Give it to your brother" was changed to "Give it to your lover" for clarity.

The changes enraged Manson, and he resorted to threats, such as leaving a bullet at Dennis's home with a message that it had either his or his stepson Scotty's name on it. Dennis's involvement with the Family "really scared me," said Bruce Johnston. "I thought, 'Oh my God, someday something's really going to happen to Dennis and he won't be here.'"[4]

The album on which the song would later appear, *20/20*, released in February of 1969, offers a somewhat macabre historical footnote, as probably the first pop album in history to feature songs written or co-written by three convicted murderers: Charles Manson, Phil Spector, and Huddie 'Leadbelly' Ledbetter. Yet despite its overall weakness, it is treasured among Beach Boys devotees as the first album to feature tracks such as 'Our Prayer' and 'Cabinessence,' intended for the *SMiLE* album. As The Beach Boys would find themselves doing over the next decade, the band—usually Carl along with Stephen Desper—ransacked the band's archives looking for tracks that when reworked would give Brian Wilson songwriting credits on the albums. For 'Cabinessence,' Carl transferred the tapes to more modern recording equipment, and he and Desper carefully overdubbed new vocals over the unfinished tracks.

In the fall of 1968, The Beach Boys wrapped up their tour of the American south and performed a number of charity concerts, hoping to convince the authorities that Carl served his country better as a musician than by changing bedpans, as ordered by the courts. Even in a year in which they had charted four hit singles—two of them Top 20—critics complained about the abundance of oldies in the set, but those oldies still generated the biggest applause.

While Brian had freely admitted that The Beach Boys were "squares" during their ill-fated trip to Hawaii, Carl later took a more philosophical view of the band's reversal of fortune in the late 60s. "We were used as a reference point as to what was 'lame' about the time. It was nonsense, but people still associated us with cars and surfboards. When the hits stopped coming, we all felt a lot of pressure. It was back to the real world after the fairy tale."[5]

Things would change in December when they flew to Europe, with Desper manning the console and three backing musicians: Ed Carter on bass, Mike Kowalski on percussion, and Daryl Dragon on keyboards. When they arrived in Europe, they hired a five-piece horn section. Carl's little surf band had now grown to 13 onstage musicians.

Making a whirlwind round of concerts and television appearances, The Beach Boys performed in the United Kingdom, West Germany, Belgium, and the Netherlands. A performance at the Finsbury Park Astoria in London in December 1968 would be issued in the UK in 1970 as *Live In London*. In 1975, Capitol repackaged the album, ignoring the date of the concert and releasing it in the USA as *Beach Boys '69*.

After a December 18 recording session for the BBC's *Top Of The Pops* television program, Al invited Carl to come see an exciting new band from South Africa performing at a London nightspot called Blaises. They called themselves The Flames. Soon, two of them would be called Beach Boys.

* * *

The year 1968 had gone badly for The Beach Boys. Bills piled up from the canceled concert dates and they had to absorb the added costs of expanding the touring group just to be able to perform the new music. According to writer Brian Chidester, "The Beach Boys situation, sans [Brian], became desperate. A forged signature apparently put Wilson's mansion up for collateral in order for the band to acquire additional recording funds needed to complete their last Capitol Records album."[6]

After *Friends*, Brian had nearly abdicated his role as The Beach Boys' leader and sought out other musical projects—many of which would end up on subsequent Beach Boys albums—such as early versions of 'Sail On

Sailor' and 'All I Wanna Do.' Yet it would be Carl who, in March 1969, would deliver the last successful Beach Boys single of the 60s when he resurrected an old Ronettes tune.

Co-written by Jeff Barry, Ellie Greenwich, and Phil Spector, 'I Can Hear Music' was an obscure single that Spector had passed off to his co-writer Jeff Barry to produce. The original version was released in 1966, at a time when Spector, hoping to find a rock group to compete with The Beach Boys and the folk rock bands of the mid-60s, had largely abandoned his girl groups in favor of artists like the Modern Folk Quartet or The Bobby Fuller Four.

Without Spector's involvement, the original reached few listeners. For The Beach Boys' version, Carl discarded the flatulent horn introduction and replaced the listless beat with a smoother, more linear tempo. The a capella section bursts from the song like joy that can no longer be suppressed and the song resumes its journey to the final fade-out with Carl's inimitable vocal soaring over the top of it. The production credit read 'Produced by Carl Wilson.' Brian's only involvement in the song was to be astonished when he first heard it.

Just as John Lennon wrote The Beatles 'Dear Prudence' to get Prudence Farrow to leave her meditation tent and "come out to play," Carl hoped to trigger Brian's creative urge again with 'I Can Hear Music.' It didn't hurt The Beach Boys' fortunes when it charted at number 24, following the dismal showing of 'Bluebirds Over The Mountain.' It peaked just in time for Carl and Annie to welcome their first-born son Jonah into the world on March 22. Brian would make one more stab at a single before 1969 was over, but Carl's first production credit granted him new leverage within the band as The Beach Boys entered a new world of 16- and 24-track recording, synthesizers, and quadraphonic sound.

Meanwhile, in the opening days of 1969, The Beach Boys readied for another touring season—and this time they would make history as well as music. After a seven-week tour that began in the Pacific Northwest and ended in Texas, Carl flew home to be with Annie as she prepared to give birth to Jonah. With mother and baby resting comfortably after a few weeks, Carl and the band hit the road again, where they performed more charitable concerts mixed in with their regular schedule. Whereas before The Beach Boys had performed these concerts with no attendant publicity, the events now had to be publicized as, in Brian's words, "an unofficial way for the group to pay off our debt to the American government for allowing Carl to become a conscientious objector."[7]

On April 13, The Beach Boys pulled off one of the wickedest inside jokes in rock'n'roll history when they headlined a 'Decency Rally' in Oklahoma sponsored by local high schools. It was intended, according to its conservative organizers, "to show that not all teenagers support the protest movement popular with some youths today." They took the show seriously, and probably averted a riot when they sang their a capella version of Bobby Troup's 'Their Hearts Were Full Of Spring' to calm the restive crowd.

The decency enthusiasts would not have been impressed if they'd listened closely to the band's most recent album, *20/20*, which was still on the charts at the time of the concert. It featured a snippet of what may have been the first live sex ever pressed into the vinyl of a major band's album. During the recording of Dennis's raucous 'All I Want To Do' (not to be confused with Brian's and Mike's 'All I Wanna Do,' which would appear on the *Sunflower* album) at Capitol Studios, Dennis had run down to Hollywood Boulevard and procured a prostitute, brought her back to the studio, and supplied her with headphones so they could have sex in time to the music. The resultant sound effects ended up on the fadeout of the track.

On April 18, The Beach Boys accepted an invitation to perform at the Hawthorne High School Prom, held in the Beverly Hilton Hotel in Beverly Hills. It was almost a charity gig as they only received $900 for the show. They arrived in tuxedos and performed to a stunned crowd of fellow Cougars.

Before heading out to Europe for another tour, during which they would play four shows in Czechoslovakia (becoming the first American rock'n'roll band to appear behind the Iron Curtain), The Beach Boys took a last shot at a hit single on their old label. 'Break Away' was, uniquely, co-written by Brian and Murry, credited here as 'Reggie Dunbar.' Released by Capitol in June, it became their lowest-charting single in the USA since 1962's 'Ten Little Indians' (it was, however, a substantial hit in the UK, reaching number six).

'Break Away' provided a bitter conclusion to The Beach Boys' Capitol years. Two months earlier, the band had sued Capitol for $2 million, claiming underpayment of royalties and production fees for Brian. In the resulting settlement, The Beach Boys would only retain ownership of albums released since *Beach Boys' Party!* In the record industry, The Beach Boys were now considered the musical equivalent of box-office poison. Brian's unreliability and Dennis's rock star antics provided loads of great cocktail chatter, but for most in the industry, it was over for The Beach Boys.

The doyen of Beach Boys historians, David Leaf, later wrote that 'Break Away' was "easily the greatest Beach Boys 45 that wasn't a hit … a dazzling record, full of sensational vocals, great hooks and meaningful lyrics." It also featured a wonderful Carl vocal on the verses, with Al taking the chorus. (An early version had Brian on the first verse, but he withdrew in favor of Carl.) Radio stations, though, balked at playing the record, and some complained that the record sounded less like The Beach Boys than like 'The Beach Men.'

"I was really disappointed and frustrated by how this one ended up," Al Jardine said later. "We knew we had 90 percent of a good record, but typical of his late-60s mentality, Brian under-produced and undersold the ending of the record."[8]

The creation of 'Break Away' was not helped by the fact that, during the sessions at the house, Murry showed up to hear the song he'd written with Brian—helping shape some of the most poignant lyrics of Brian's career, with their references to "voices in my head"—and check on its progress.

In Desper's account, Murry's endless hectoring and constant micromanaging of the recording increased the stress level to the point that the results of the entire session had to be erased and new work begun afterward. (One of Murry's suggestions, raising the level of the vocals at around 1:30 and adding reverb, made it to the final mix.) In the end, it was Carl who stepped in to salvage the record. He suggested that the song be speeded up slightly, a move that Desper recalled as improving the rhythmic pulse of the song.[9]

Recording 'Break Away' may have just worn Brian out. The song would not appear on an album for six more years, and even then it was for a Capitol compilation, not an official Beach Boys release.

As The Beach Boys set out in search of a new record company, Carl was having the greatest success at replacing Brian in the studio, at least temporarily. 'I Can Hear Music' had shown that, at 22 years old, he could deliver records for the modern stereo world and translate them for live performance.

The sorcerer's apprentice had proved himself worthy of the sorcerer's cap. For the band's first decade, Brian had ruled, but as he once again receded into the background, Carl emerged as the leader in the studio as well as onstage. The problem was that the band's next record company would not care for the new order.

CHAPTER SEVENTEEN

It's About Time

In 1969, The Beach Boys were still accused of being 'lame' and unhip. This at a time when their lead guitarist and onstage leader was—alone major rock stars—fighting against the draft because it conflicted with his pacifist beliefs. But the tide was turning again.

A high point was the two shows they played for thousands of fans at the Lucerna Music Hall in Prague, Czechoslovakia, in June of 1969, just as their contract with Capitol had finally come to an end. In the Soviet states, behind the so-called Iron Curtain, rock music was strongly discouraged lest it turn listeners into rebels or 'beatles,' which is what the Russians called hippies. The Beach Boys represented the first contact Eastern European teenagers had had with live western pop. Some of them had heard the hits, crackling over their radios; now they saw and heard them played live. In Prague, after tickets sold out, 6,000 fans gathered outside to hear wisps of music seeping through the doors.

Yet they returned home with no record label, and their latest single, 'Break Away,' had barely registering in the pop charts. The Beach Boys soon got a sense of how far they'd fallen in their own country. During a July 20 show in Troy, New York, on the day of the moon landing, they had to interrupt their set while a local disc jockey brought on a tiny black-and-white television broadcasting Neil Armstrong's giant leap for mankind. The band then set out on a smaller-scale tour of colleges and venues that didn't often present star-level talent.

During the summer of Woodstock, The Beach Boys were considered an oldies band by most, and the effects of being banished to the hinterlands of pop influence became clear in July when promoter Fred Vail signed contracts for the band to play the Steel Pier in Atlantic City, New Jersey. From the earliest days, formal Beach Boys contracts had always promised to present "Carl Wilson and four musicians known as The Beach Boys"—Carl being recognized as leader of the touring band. Here the band arrived to find the posters promoting the event as "Carl Wilson" in large print with "and The Beach Boys" in much smaller type. "[Mike] Love must have been having a hemorrhage when he saw that!" laughed Vail.[1]

The band had begun recording material for a new album in July at Brian's house. They had not yet secured an offer from a new record company. In November, they signed with the Reprise division of Warner Bros Records, which agreed to co-branding with the band's own Brother Records. Warners insisted on the involvement of Brian in all future Beach Boys recordings, to which the group concurred. According to Brian Chidester, "Mo Ostin, head of Warner Bros at the time, said of the chance to sign The Beach Boys away from Capitol, 'The only signature I care about getting on that contract is Brian Wilson's.'" The eldest Wilson brother, "as the goose that laid the golden egg, was marched into a conference room in white undershirt and tousled hair, where photographs show him scribbling his John Hancock with pronounced disdain."[2]

The same month, Murry sold Brian's Sea Of Tunes publishing company to Irving-Almo Music, the publishing division of A&M Records, for $700,000 in cash. Convinced that Brian's songs had little value for future artists, or perhaps seeking retaliation for past indignities, he left Brian with only a handful of songs from the collection, while Almo executives tried to turn the old surf tunes into commercials.[3]

By some accounts, Brian resisted being locked into a contract with a major record label. Unlike The Beach Boys' early relationship with Capitol, the Brother/Reprise years didn't begin with a string of hit singles moving effortlessly up the charts. Through the late fall and winter, the band toured small venues to little enthusiasm, but started 1970 with a great deal of recording. 'Add Some Music To Your Day,' the first single from what would eventually be *Sunflower*—the first song lineup of the album was rejected by

Warners—was released in February. Despite its gorgeous vocal arrangement, featuring the whole band except Dennis, and with Carl providing the heartfelt middle-eight ("Music / When you're alone / Is like a companion / For your lonely soul"), it reached only number 64 in the US and failed to chart in the UK, always The Beach Boys' most reliable market. Two further singles from the album, 'Slip On Through' and 'Tears In The Morning,' would fail to chart at all.

Meanwhile, the band was touring again, including to New Zealand and Australia. Carl was continually asked about the absent Brian but preferred to turn the conversation to music. "The music we do now is just for fun," he told an Australian reporter. "In a way we had to catch up with Brian. We've been developing rapidly as a group and as individuals in the last year. I guess we've gone into another whole cycle. We're much stronger, independently stronger. I'm a much better singer now than I used to be."[4]

Sunflower, having finally been approved by Warners, appeared in August of 1970. For the devout, *Sunflower* is to The Beach Boys as *Pet Sounds* was to Brian Wilson. While *Pet Sounds* served as Brian Wilson's tour de force, *Sunflower* introduced The Beach Boys as a solid unit of creative songwriters and musicians. For the decade previous, most people compared The Beach Boys to The Beatles, when a more apt comparison would have been between Brian Wilson and his contemporary Frank Zappa. Both sought respect as composers rather than mere songwriters; both had their own orchestra (Brian had The Beach Boys, Zappa had the Mothers and his later Zappa bands); and both had their instrument: the recording studio.

The big difference in 70s recording was stereo. Monaural or mono recording was now a relic. Where engineers and producers once recorded with a mono mix as the end goal, now engineers sought stereo mixes and only spent time on mono mixing for singles. Stereo had become essential, yet the greatest record producer in Hollywood couldn't hear it. According to The Beach Boys' new engineer, Stephen Desper, it would be Carl's first duty to help Brian navigate this new approach to sound.

From the time he left the United States Army Signal Corps in 1964,

Desper had experienced a huge range of engineering tasks, from John F. Kennedy's speech in Berlin, through Jimi Hendrix's Monterey Pop debut, through two years of Frank Zappa's studio recording and tours. Over that time, he had recorded virtually every instrument from alphorn to zither. "He was a genius engineer," Brian told Alan Boyd. "Oh my God, he was."

Desper hailed from a rare line of engineers like Dave Gold or Zappa's mentor Paul Buff. They were more than engineers: they were sonic futurists, inventors and innovators as well. In Desper, said Boyd, The Beach Boys found a chief engineer and mixer whose own imagination and sense of adventure were equal to their own. "They inspired each other."[5]

Sunflower stands as the only Beach Boys album that can legitimately be compared to the work of The Beatles—a compendium of songs and performances by a group of gifted songwriters and musicians. The comparison was not lost on reviewers of the time, particularly in *Rolling Stone*, where the reviewer singled out the recording techniques on *Sunflower* as superior to the production job done on *Abbey Road*. And this at a time when calling anything better than The Beatles amounted to cultural blasphemy.

Carl's fingerprints were all over the album, although he had only one writing credit. *Sunflower*, wrote Brian Chidester, was "in fact, largely produced by the youngest Wilson brother, Carl."[6] When *Endless Summer Quarterly* devoted an entire issue to the making of *Sunflower*, Al Jardine said of the album, "Carl and Dennis had quite a lot of material on it. It was kind of a Wilson Brothers album when you think about it. I really wish the two of them had collaborated and put out an album like that together."

Carl was characteristically modest. "*Sunflower*, I'd say, is the truest group effort we've ever had. Each of us was deeply involved in the creation of almost all the cuts."[7]

Jardine noted that, while Carl was part of the songwriting team that delivered Dennis's classic rocker 'It's About Time,' "Carl's name isn't on the song credit—which is really weird. I distinctly remember sitting with Dennis and Carl writing that song."[8]

Always humble, quiet, and gentle, Carl Wilson carved his leadership path by creating partnerships throughout The Beach Boys' career. Working with Mike, Carl made the live shows work under the most arduous of circumstances. In the studios with Brian, Carl served as his creative second-in-command. Now, with Desper, Carl had forged a creative partnership that would reconcile the complex chorale of 'Cool, Cool Water' with the raucous simplicity of '409,' finding a new audience while retaining the old crowd who couldn't get enough of their uplifting melodies and harmonies.

Carl's vocals on *Sunflower* are among his best. On Brian's 'This Whole World,' reaching effortlessly into falsetto, he creates one of the record's high points. Elsewhere, he sang lead on the raucous 'It's About Time,' and 'Our Sweet Love,' a tender ballad co-written with Brian and Al. In his production capacity, he created with Desper what *Rolling Stone* called the "mind-wrenching" echo that adorns 'All I Wanna Do.'

Carefully assembled from elements of Brian's 'I Love To Say Da Da,' part of *SMiLE's* 'Elements Suite,' 'Cool, Cool Water' stood apart from the rest of the album as more of a tone poem than a song, and critics and fans seized on it as a vestige of *SMiLE*. Because it was the first Beach Boys track to utilize a synthesizer (a modular Moog system), Desper promptly joined the Musicians' Union as a synthesizer player and programmer.

With a new record company, the pressure was on to deliver Brian Wilson material. The terms of their new contract indicated that, at some point, the band would deliver *SMiLE*. However, at this time, said Desper, "Brian was ill and depressed, so Carl brought down all of the existing tapes to see what could be salvaged."

Now the entire band joined in to turn 'Cool, Cool Water' from a fragment to a masterpiece. They created a 'great wave' sound to bridge the sections, by patching together white, pink, and brown noise generators. Then, Desper recalled, they "further processed the resulting sounds to control the side-to-side and back-to-front movements. … The keyboard was used to further shape the sound and allow it to be played like an instrument."

Mike, of course, had to inject his dry sense of humor into the song when he sang "cool water is such a gas," as the band tried to recreate "the sonic equivalent of water evaporating into air—into a gas." The end result, Desper said, would "tie the two segments together, enveloping the listener with a climax timed to dissolve into the start of the final section's bass notes." The Beach Boys were involved in the final mix as well, with various members assigned to specific tasks such as flipping switches or assigning levels or echo sends. The final mix allows the listener to "zone in on specific parts or just be awash in the beauty of a relentlessly transforming structure."[9]

Over the decades, *Sunflower* has achieved its own kind of mythology. While several proposed track lineups were rejected, Carl's concept for the cover came about early on. The album was never intended to be anything but *Sunflower*, said Desper. One evening, while leafing through a stack of citrus crate art, Carl found the sunflower image from a nearby Redlands, California, packing house. His future brother-in-law Ricci Martin (for whom Carl and Billy Hinsche later produced an album) was then enlisted to snap the cover photo of The Beach Boys with their children posed on a lawn, with Carl's son Jonah hoisted up on his father's shoulders while Brian fiddles with his daughter Carnie's pink bonnet. Matthew Jardine, still a long time from replacing Brian on the road, stands next to his father Al, and Mike kneels next to daughter Hayleigh and future Beach Boy Christian.

The album was released in August 1970, in a special gatefold cover showing the individual Beach Boys posed in costume. While Carl only appears in a portrait, unused photos of the session reveal him to be standing next to a horse and a guitar, dressed like a 1930s singing cowboy. Mo Ostin provided a brief introduction, celebrating the importance of The Beach Boys and the pride with which the Warner/Reprise family of labels welcomed the band to their new label.

More importantly, the liner notes offered extensive detail about the "true stereophonic" technology used to record the album, a highly unusual disclosure at the time, designed to appeal to the growing hi-fi market. Its importance would become apparent when Brother/Reprise released the Carl Wilson-produced *The Flame* album in March and then The Beach Boys' *Surf's Up* in August 1971.

Sunflower reached only number 151 in the US and 29 in the UK. It did, however, achieve a degree of critical acclaim. *Rolling Stone*, which had been both hero and villain in the Beach Boys story, gave the record a stellar review and said the band had "finally produced an album that can stand with *Pet Sounds.*"

* * *

In October, equipped with a new manager in the shape of Jack Rieley, a former disc jockey, the band played the Big Sur Festival in Monterey, California, on the same bill as Merry Clayton, Joan Baez, and Linda Ronstadt. It was the start of Rieley's strategy to make the band "hip." They played songs old and new and were very well received. (Dennis was missing, filming his only movie role, *Two Lane Blacktop*, with James Taylor and Warren Oates.) It was in keeping with the band's new image, that Carl grew the full beard he would favour for the rest of his life.

On November 4, 1970, lines snaked out the door of the Whisky A Go Go on Hollywood's Sunset Strip, around the club, and up North Clark Street into the residential neighborhoods. Some Hollywood watchers estimated them as the longest lines reported to date. Along the Clark side of the building, the Whisky posted photos of the individual Beach Boys performing that night. One of the photos showed Brian Wilson.

The crowd was slightly older than the usual crowd at the popular Los Angeles clubs. The Whisky generally featured a mix of new bands and older 'boutique' bands whose album sales never quite launched them into the civic halls and arenas. Buffalo Springfield, The Doors, Led Zeppelin, Cream, and many more bands that have long since achieved legend status played here at some point in their careers.

This night was different, however, as the Whisky was playing host to a four-night engagement by the band that was once the biggest rock'n'roll act in America. Much of the curiosity driving the long lines was whether or not the audience was going to witness a phoenix-like rebirth or the final death throes of The Beach Boys.

The first time The Beach Boys played along the Sunset Strip, eight years previously, they were a struggling surf band. That night Brian spilled hot chocolate on a girl called Marilyn Rovell, later to become Mrs Brian Wilson. The last time The Beach Boys played in Los Angeles, on June 25, 1966, at the Hollywood Bowl, they were riding the crest of unimaginable success and on their way to more. Now, the marquee out front simply read 'The Beach Boys—The Flame.'

The line began moving into the club, renowned for its rowdy crowds, unwilling to listen at anything less than ear-splitting volume. Some in the audience were drawn by morbid curiosity. In June, Charles Manson and members of his Family had begun their trial for the murders that had held Los Angeles in a vise grip of fear for nearly a year. The media pointed to Dennis as the Family's entrée into the entertainment world, despite the fact that Family member and aspiring actor Bobby Beausoleil, and some of the Manson girls, had made inroads into the movie community far earlier.

The opening act was The Flame, whom Carl had met in London in 1968. He had subsequently signed them to the Brother/Reprise label. Originally The Flames, they comprised four South African musicians: three brothers, Edries, Ricky, and Steve Fataar, and guitarist/singer Blondie Chaplin. They offered a strong performance of guitar-based rock'n'roll, revealing English influences such as The Beatles and Traffic.

As The Flame left the stage, conversation resumed until three middle-aged men clad in tuxedos rose from the crowd. Two raised violins to their chins and the third began playing his accordion. They strolled, smiling, among the tables of the astounded audience. As they finished, Jack Rieley walked on to the stage and announced in the measured, stentorian tones of a late-night FM disc jockey that a big event was about to occur. He mentioned the band members individually, beginning with Brian. So it was true: he would be there.

As Rieley left the stage, The Beach Boys appeared, out of their customary and sadly dated uniforms and simply dressed in street clothes. They took their places on a stage crammed with three keyboards, a massive synthesizer, multiple microphones, and eight musicians. They were joined by a brace of horn and percussion players on a temporary riser on the side of the stage. Carl appeared, sporting a full beard, and counted off the band. With the exceptions of 'Help Me, Rhonda' and 'Surfer Girl' (on which Brian sang lead on the first night to a delirious reception), the set list consisted almost entirely of material from their post-1966 years. That included a healthy smattering of songs from *Sunflower*, including 'Forever' and 'Cool, Cool Water,' which was performed on conventional instruments when the synthesizer wouldn't cooperate. Mike offered a pointed remark about not being able to find a copy of *Sunflower* at the little hippie record store across the street. Bruce Johnston took his solo spot by performing 'Your Song' by a new singer-songwriter, Elton John, who was just beginning to gain traction on the national charts after his successful debut in Los Angeles a few months before. For 'Vegetables,' the band picked up a basket filled with produce and tossed carrots into the crowd.

On the second night, though, Brian neither sang nor spoke. Instead he sat silently at a Wurlitzer electric piano and pounded out chords throughout the evening. Al accommodated him by taking the solo vocal on 'Surfer Girl.' Brian merely sat and played piano, forcing keyboardist Daryl Dragon off to the side of the stage on an old upright.

The big surprise of the first show was an old Coasters favorite from the band's Pendletones days, 'Riot In Cell Block Nine,' complete with screaming siren sounds and a searing guitar solo by Carl. They closed with one of the rockers from *Sunflower*: 'It's About Time,' written by Dennis with help from Carl, who also sang it. They exited the stage to wild applause, although an unanswered question—"I don't know, did *you* like it?"—seemed to hang in the air. Before the applause subsided, The Beach Boys resumed their places onstage and ripped through an encore of Beach Boys oldies, ending with a rapid-fire rendition of 'Johnny B. Goode.' It was so fast that one reviewer noted that the horn players were staring in disbelief. The Beach Boys, it appeared, were back.[10] Yet the show also revealed what industry insiders suspected. Brian was now a 'beloved entertainer,' making cameo appearances onstage and in the studio. He had carved his niche in The Beach Boys' previous incarnation. No longer an actor in the play, he had become the man who appeared when the audience shouted "author, author."

The Beach Boys had become seasoned and tough under the most difficult of circumstances, delivering performances of such complexity and sophistication that many musicians avoided playing their songs. The band raised the bar with every performance. But after the Whisky show, Brian began to fade into the background again. For the next Los Angeles area concert, the Santa Monica Civic Auditorium in February 1971, the band vamped on 'Surfer Girl' while they tried unsuccessfully to inveigle Brian out onstage for a vocal. When Brian demurred, Al—as always—filled in admirably. In December, at a show in Long Beach billed as their tenth-anniversary celebration, Brian rose out of the audience and clambered onstage for an impromptu (and truncated) version of 'A Day In The Life Of A Tree' with Jack Rieley, then returned to his seat.

History is replete with tales of artists who find themselves victims of a massive early success they cannot replicate later in their career. Library shelves groan beneath the weight of biographies of writers like Raymond Chandler, F. Scott Fitzgerald, and James M. Cain, who continued writing long after being regarded as artistically spent. Everything The Beach Boys did after 'Good Vibrations' would be compared to everything that came before. To crowds who cherished their glory years, the *Wild Honey* and *Friends* material in which they were trafficking would always come up short.

Yet The Beach Boys weren't ready to be consigned to the dustbin of history in 1970, and probably the greatest of their fortunes, after having a genius songwriter and producer for their leader, is that their onstage musical director began as a mere teenager and entered a new world of recording at exactly the right time for someone of his gifts.

Carl was probably the most technologically proficient of the band, and by the 70s, he was developing the keyboard skills required by a new generation of listeners accustomed to the gentle tunefulness of singer-songwriters like Joni Mitchell and Jackson Browne.

Unlike his brothers, Carl had strayed from his early piano lessons once he discovered the guitar. Yet as The Beach Boys progressed, the demands on Carl's guitar playing derailed any plans he might have had to follow the surf guitar veterans who had graduated to rock'n'roll guitar god status, including Stephen Stills, Neil Young, and Ed King. Like Guitar George in Dire Straits' 1977 'Sultans Of Swing,' Carl knew "all the chords" and didn't want to "make it cry or sing."

As a keyboard player, Carl "had a great knowledge of very crude chords that he learned from his brother Brian," according to the classically trained keyboard player Gary Griffith, who began touring with The Beach Boys in 1977. "He wasn't a fabulously skilled player, but he knew voicings that worked very well."[11]

One of the keys to Brian's playing, as Billy Hinsche has pointed out, was that Brian frequently moved the bass notes in a chord around to enhance chords or create a series of complex chords from simpler ones. In the 60s, Carl learned this technique well and learned to apply it to guitars. He often called his keyboard technique a simple matter of placing his hands where they felt good and where he liked the resulting sound. But now, becoming a multi-instrumentalist at a time when multi-track recording technology was moving from 8 tracks through 16 to 24, Carl was ready to move into Brian's territory as a producer and songwriter as well as leader.

Being the youngest and most artistically aware member of The Beach Boys, Carl sensed what a great many musicians sensed in the 70s: as the guitar grew into more and more of a solo instrument, keyboard-based songs were capturing the public's attention. Major groups of the early 70s, such as The Beatles, found that their keyboard-based songs such as 'Let It Be' now rivaled the success of their guitar-based songs. The growing Laurel Canyon crowd, headed by Joni Mitchell, always featured piano songs in their sets. Carole King used her piano to help make James Taylor a star, before releasing her own album, one of the most successful of the early 70s.

In 1970, the world was no longer divided neatly into songwriters and performers. Today, the performers wrote the songs and in Los Angeles, where lead guitarists once ruled, a new type of musician emerged: the multi-instrumentalist who composed on a variety of instruments. Hit albums by Los Angeles rock acts like Crosby, Stills & Nash also created a new template for bands who could mix acoustic and electric music. While The Beach Boys had technically only delved into acoustic music with *Beach Boys Party!*, at Beach Boys shows in the 70s, Carl would stand alone onstage with nothing but his Gibson Dove acoustic guitar and perform 'Caroline, No,' after introducing it as "one of the most beautiful songs Brian has ever written."[12]

In the early days of rock'n'roll, keyboard-based bands were few and far between. Most piano players had to put up with whatever piano the venue had on hand, and organ players had one of two choices: either lug a heavy Hammond or Lowrey organ onstage and feed it into a Leslie speaker, or choose a lighter, more portable model, like a Farfisa or Vox Continental, and sound like every other band who played a similar instrument.

But a new wind was blowing in the music world. Where Brian once carefully married two or more instruments to create a sound that was an amalgam of the two, now a new generation of electric keyboards was able to create those sounds with technology, just as guitarists had earlier in the 60s.

Among the first of the multi-keyboard bands to emerge in the 60s were The Seeds, who like their friends The Doors used a Fender Rhodes piano bass in place of a bass player onstage. The Seeds' keyboardist Daryl Hooper became one of the earliest proponents of multiple keyboards on the LA scene when The Beach Boys were still a guitar band. Once guitars moved from a period of innovation to a period of refinement, electronic keyboards became the new voice of rock'n'roll, and Carl was ready.

According to Hooper, old technology like the Fender Rhodes and Wurlitzer pianos, designed in the 40s and 50s, produced sounds that were "simple and sufficient to fill in a rhythm track, but there wasn't a pronounced 'sound' back in the 60s. The sound of the 60s was really the guitars." Now new instruments were arriving: namely Mellotrons and synthesizers. The first Moog instrument was demonstrated at the Monterey Pop Festival in 1967. These filled the gap to the point where "keyboards started being influential to the music." In the studio, greater track numbers meant that keyboard players could "stack" the new sounds to create textures never heard before. The world of music was changing and The Beach Boys were ready for it.[13]

By the end of 1970, The Beatles had delivered their final album and announced to a stunned world that they had broken up. The baby boom generation now faced a musical world without them. Sensitive singer-songwriters were the musical genre of the moment in Los Angeles, and the wholesale musical reconstruction that began with *Wild Honey* now opened up to a wave of country-rock bands, blues bands, and artists fusing jazz and rock, such as Miles Davis, Larry Coryell, John McLaughlin, and others.

AM radio stations tightened up their formats, and singles were selected for their ability to 'hook' listeners, leaving singles by artists like James Taylor and The Rolling Stones to do battle with one-hit wonders like The Tea Set, Shocking Blue, and The Five Man Electrical Band. Singles were now viewed as supplemental publicity efforts to promote an album rather than stand-alone artistic statements. FM stations, less constrained in their formats, helped to exacerbate the growing divide between casual listeners and more serious devotees. The album became the statement of choice for 'serious' artists, and the first year of the 70s saw the release of a plethora of now-classic albums by The Beatles, Van Morrison, Led Zeppelin, Crosby, Stills, Nash & Young, Black Sabbath, Carole King, Derek & The Dominoes, and The Doors, among others.

While the world waited for Brian to get out of bed and finish *SMiLE*, or start another masterpiece, The Beach Boys were on the road, honing their skills and experiencing firsthand the impact their music had on listeners. They not only listened to the competition, they performed songs by The Beatles, Elton John, and Buffalo Springfield in concert. Their set lists included some of the most complex pop songs ever written, and they delivered live performances better than many other bands' recordings. As songwriters, they had not merely learned from the master; they now wrote songs hoping to inspire him to get back into the studio.

CHAPTER EIGHTEEN

Feel Flows

Like most kids growing up on the East Coast in the 60s, Chip Rachlin didn't really relate to songs about surfing and cars. "Everybody was a fan of The Beach Boys," he said, "but it didn't resonate with me." He only became a fan when "The Beach Boys got into greater harmony and layers."

Like so many others, he had been profoundly affected when he saw The Beatles on *The Ed Sullivan Show*. "I put down the clarinet," he said. Some years later, he went to see The Beach Boys at the Steel Pier, Atlantic City. While waiting for the show to begin, "I looked over and saw the original five Beach Boys in their striped shirts readying to go onstage." Seeing The Beach Boys in person was a life-changing moment. "It was like nothing I'd ever imagined," he said.

With rock'n'roll consuming his soul, Rachlin carved out a niche in the entertainment business promoting dances and writing newspaper columns about music. By his senior year in high school, he found himself co-promoting the world's largest county fair in La Port Indiana. Finding he had a gift for promoting rock'n'roll shows, he found work promoting shows at the Fillmore Auditorium until one day he looked up to see a huge figure in the doorway. "He literally filled the doorway—he had this big 'Jewfro'—and he comes over to my desk, whips out a six inch knife and says, 'Hi, I'm Michael.'"

The knife-wielding hulk turned out to be Rachlin's future partner, Michael Klenfner. Together, Rachlin and Klenfner set out to introduce the world to an exciting new band promoting an exciting new album. They were called The Beach Boys.

In 1971 in New York, "the attitude was that The Beach Boys are 'unhip,'"

Rachlin said. "And Klenfner and I were out to disprove it." The venue they chose to reintroduce The Beach Boys to the world was audacious: Carnegie Hall. At rehearsal, Rachlin walked through the doors to see The Beach Boys "noodling around onstage; there were the five Beach Boys and seven or eight musicians. I was introduced to Carl. I was probably kind of dumbstruck. It was absolutely extraordinary."

That night, February 24, 1971, The Beach Boys gave a New York debut to their new-look band, featuring support musicians Ed Carter, Daryl Dragon, and Dennis Dragon, and a five-piece horn section. The show began with legendary New York Disc Jockey Pete Fornatale, a friend of Klenfner's, walking out onstage carrying a surfboard. "He gave one of the most eloquent introductions in history," said Rachlin. "He said, 'Growing up wouldn't have been much fun without The Beach Boys.' It was an evening that changed my life."

The concert reviews ranged from positive (in *Billboard*) to delirious (*Rock* magazine). As with their Santa Monica Civic Auditorium concert four nights earlier, the set list leaned heavily toward the new music, with a smattering of oldies scattered throughout the set. Gone were the striped shirts, ice-cream suits, and banks of Dual Showman amps. The new Beach Boys were a rock'n'roll orchestra, delivering a decade's worth of hits, along with exciting new music from *Sunflower*.

As The Beach Boys moved on for a concert in Ohio, Rachlin called his boss Herb Spar and said, "I think we should represent them." Spar agreed. When Rachlin asked how he should go about signing the band, Spar replied, "Fly to Boston and hang out with them until they say yes or tell you to go fuck yourself." So Rachlin did what he was told. "They let me hang out and they allowed me to come on their tour bus. I started to figure out the dynamic of the band."

Rachlin found Carl to be "very gracious, but distant. He listened." Dennis met Rachlin in his hotel room and said, "You gotta know who I am." He let Rachlin know The Beach Boys were "more than just Carl, Mike, or Brian." Rachlin's gambit worked better than he had anticipated. The Millard

Agency was given a 90-day period to represent The Beach Boys—and the relationship lasted for 17 years.

The band's new manager, Jack Rieley, laid out the concept for the new-look Beach Boys. The concept, said Rachlin, "was art, art, art, and golden oldies. I think Jack traded on the myth of *SMiLE*—as he should have—and the legend of 'Surf's Up.'" Among The Beach Boys, Rachlin immediately gravitated toward Carl. "He was a nice guy about my age … and Dennis *was* a little crazy."[1]

While sales for *Sunflower* and the singles extracted from it were still in the doldrums, The Beach Boys' concerts from the early 70s injected them back into the cultural bloodstream. Audiences were shocked to find the band they'd grown up with on the radio were a bunch of young guys, about the same age as the other major acts at the time, but with a decade's worth of performing experience beneath their belts.

The Fillmore connection through Rachlin and Klenfner, and through their new record label, helped The Beach Boys deliver their next great concert of 1971. At a Grateful Dead show at the Fillmore East on April 27, Jerry Garcia announced, "We've got another famous California group here: this is The Beach Boys." After a few minutes' tuning, The Beach Boys joined the Dead (a band who could be described the anti-Beach Boys) for an extended jam on a couple of favorite oldies, The Coasters' 'Searchin'' and 'Riot In Cell Block Nine,' complete with siren sounds, courtesy of Mike and his custom-made ribbon-controlled Moog synthesizer.

Then The Beach Boys played their numbers, beginning with a powerful 'Good Vibrations,' led by Carl. "We're very grateful that there's something called the Grateful Dead," Bruce said, before launching into 'I Get Around,' a lightning-paced performance that gobsmacked an audience accustomed to the meandering, stoned performances of the Dead. Then the two bands pooled resources again for 'Help Me, Rhonda,' featuring Carl on lead vocal and played as a mellow, country-flavored shuffle. They closed with rousing renditions of Merle Haggard's 'Okie From Muskogee' and 'Johnny B. Goode.'[2]

"I was amazed at my good fortune to be around these guys," Rachlin said, "not in a showbiz way, but as a 'kid on the boardwalk' way."

Rachlin's bond with Carl grew during that time. He was one of the few industry insiders who witnessed the Hollywood scene they were part of while penetrating Carl's jealously guarded privacy. "We talked about everything," Rachlin said. "I wound up going on the road for a time. Where I got to know him was on my first trip to Los Angeles in April 1973, where they played the Palladium." On a trip to the famous Martoni's Restaurant, Rachlin found himself sitting with The Beach Boys when "out of the corner of my eye I see Phil Spector. It was like seeing Chaplin."

Spector merely grimaced back at Rachlin, so Bruce offered to intercede. Returning to the table, Bruce explained that Spector "thought you were John Sebastian [of The Lovin' Spoonful] and was pissed at you for not coming over and saying hello." The next morning, Rachlin awoke, "still on New York time." Carl had invited him to visit the Coldwater Canyon home he shared with Annie and Jonah. He arrived at 8:30am to find the Wilsons still asleep. Once they were awake they welcomed Rachlin, and everybody hung out by the pool, playing with Carl's "big fluffy white dogs. That's how I got to know him."

For Carl, said Rachlin, "The Beatles were always part of the conversation. Carl liked the whole rockabilly side of things, that 50s style. He loved [jazz flautist] Charles Lloyd. When Elton John first came out, Carl was the first to turn me on to Elton. I don't know that your usual cast of guitar heroes mattered to him."

Carl had two concerns about The Beach Boys, however, as Rachlin discovered. The first was that "Brian had already started to crumble and Carl started to morph into the role of co-producer. Carl became the *de facto* Brian." The second was "the formula versus doing something new."[3]

* * *

As the dust settled from the triumphs of 1970, The Beach Boys were a new band, and after Bob Dylan lauded their set with the Grateful Dead earlier in the year, their hip credentials were secure. It was now acceptable to like The Beach Boys. While the media shrugged off Carl's battle with the Selective Service System, performing for causes such as prison reform did much to endear the band to audiences of the early 70s. Their record sales failed to reflect this new attitude, however, and while concert grosses grew, the singles from *Sunflower* sputtered. Like *Pet Sounds*, *Sunflower* met Mark Twain's definition of a classic: something everyone knows about but nobody listens to.

Yet for Carl Wilson, the period between *Sunflower* and the release of *Holland* little more than two years later provides a glimpse of the artist that could have been. While he would spend the next quarter century delivering fine music with The Beach Boys and other artists, only on 1971's *Surf's Up* would the world see what Beach Boys insiders already knew. For once, Carl would step out of his role of brother, cousin, bandleader, co-producer, and co-writer and into the spotlight as a songwriter and solo performer.

Of all of the people who entered The Beach Boys' orbit in the 70s, few would have the impact of Jack Rieley. For all his faults, Rieley's period with The Beach Boys turned the band around in the early 70s. More importantly, while Carl had written with all of The Beach Boys, with Rieley, his songs would be Carl Wilson songs, rather than Beach Boys songs.

"'Long Promised Road' was the first Beach Boys lyric I wrote," Rieley told author Ken Sharp. "Carl asked me to have a hand in writing lyrics. I felt very strongly that I was on to something lyrically. Van Dyke was writing ethereal lyrics … I was writing personal lyrics; not love songs in a traditional sense but love songs nonetheless, but with a sense of poetry. For the lyric, I was trying to tell the tale of life and love that we all go through at different times in our life, and I hope that I succeeded.

"I wanted so much to see Carl really stretching out and making something really extraordinary. His vocal is so precious. There's that screaming deep guitar in the song, which in my opinion is the anchor that holds the song together and gives it relevancy beyond the first minute and thirty seconds. This was a period where Carl was also dabbling and experimenting with chemicals and I did as well. It enhanced that song."[4]

Whether the chemicals helped or not is open to debate. Many criticized Rieley's lyrics as little more than drug-soaked meanderings or characterized Jack as sort of a poor man's Van Dyke Parks. Yet while his lyrics for 'Long Promised Road' may not have been of *SMiLE* standard, the fact is that for the first time they allowed Carl to be singled out as a composer and a producer.

'Long Promised Road' is an encapsulation of Carl's musical strengths. His serene 'God Only Knows' voice begins the song with a lament about answering "future's riddle" then steps up gradually until the rocking chorus "hits hard at the battle that's confronting me." The keyboard-based track reveals a new Carl, no longer just the lead guitarist but pulling together his gifts as a multi-instrumentalist and producer. The acoustic piano grows into an electronic symphony with breathless flanged synthesizer lines rising and falling while a heavily distorted lead guitar challenges a synthesizer line for the listener's attention.

In any discussion of The Beach Boys, Rieley's influence on the band provokes controversy. To some, he served an important part in bringing the band's various anti-war, health, and pro-environment passions to the forefront to help them connect with 'aware' audiences who shared the same sentiments. To others, there was a sense that the band protests too much.

Backed by 'Deirdre,' a Bruce and Brian song from *Sunflower*, 'Long Promised Road' was issued in May 1971. Like all of their recent singles, it sank before it could hit the charts.

Over the decades, the *Surf's Up* album would gain a reputation as a flawed masterpiece. It set the template for The Beach Boys' future album releases, showing the members becoming more confident in their own songwriting while Brian receded further into the background. The relative failure of *Sunflower* had eroded the unity that they had once known. With only two exceptions, most of The Beach Boys' albums would be cobbled together from individual band members' projects or discarded tracks from the vaults repurposed for later use.

And yet The Beach Boys had now become, in record company terms, a prestige act—critical darlings rather than mere popular hit-makers. Their concerts became cultural events, even as their record sales stiffed. Worse yet, by 1971, Capitol had deleted almost the entire Beach Boys catalogue in the United States, with the exception of *Friends* and occasional greatest hits packages. For Beach Boys fans, their concerts became the only game in town.

As the band set out to put together the album to follow 'Long Promised Road,' the pressure from Warner Bros didn't relent. Rieley's insistence on mythologizing 'Surf's Up' backfired when pressure from Warners forced its inclusion on the upcoming album. With no record sales to fall back on, and now operating a full-time recording studio with a staff engineer, The Beach Boys were feeling the financial pinch—even Brian.

"If they call that album *Surf's Up* we can pre-sell 150,000 copies," said Van Dyke Parks, the song's lyricist, in an interview. "And Brian can keep his house on Bellagio."

'Long Promised Road' may have been Carl's maiden voyage as a songwriter, and 'Surf's Up' may have been the centerpiece of the album, but 'Feel Flows' stands as the track that finally fulfilled the promise of the electronic revolution that defined Southern California music in the late 50s and early 60s.

"I played piano first and then I played organ," Carl told Tom Nolan. "I played piano twice, overdubbed it, and used a variable speed oscillator to make the track different speeds so that the piano would be a little bit out of tune, sort of a spread sound … say at 60 cycles and then 59. So that makes the piano sound like the effect of a 12-string guitar, you know? When the two strings are at the same octave but just a tiny bit out of tune? You know that real ringing sound?

"And then I put the organ on and put it through the Moog at the same time, so that one side of the stereo had the direct organ sound and the other side had the return through the Moog synthesizer. It's sort of like a vibrato, but the frequency changes, there's a tone change, like a graphic tone … you can amplify any particular part of a sound spectrum, like from 50 cycles to 10,000 cycles. The Moog did that automatically; there's a component called a sequencer and you can time it to react and go through a series of circuits

220 • KENT CROWLEY

all connected to a different frequency, and it does that back and forth. And therefore it sounded sort of like a vibrato or a wah-wah, sort of both at the same time.

"Then I put on the bass, played the bass guitar. Then I put on the Moog for that part where the piano comes in by itself after the instrumental part, you know? Then we put on the bells, and a guy named Woody Thews played percussion on it, and I sang it. I put the guitar on about the same time.

"Then I think it was the next day Charles Lloyd came by and we did the flute and saxophone. And I might add, he heard it one time and then started playing; he started recording right away. It was really a thrill for me to have him play on it 'cos he's a gifted musician. It was really great. And then the next session we did the vocals, the background part, and that was it."[5]

At a time when jazz musicians were turning to rock for inspiration, Carl scored a musical coup by having Charles Lloyd sit in on 'Feel Flows.' Born in Memphis of African, Cherokee, Mongolian, and Irish descendants, Lloyd took up the saxophone and later flute as a boy and served his jazz apprenticeship with some of the most respected and formidable jazz artists of the 20th century. After leaving Cannonball Adderley's quintet, he formed one of the legendary ensembles of the 60s with a young pianist named Keith Jarrett, drummer Jack DeJohnette, and bassist Cecil McBee. Together, they produced the critically acclaimed *Dream Weaver* (1965) and the first million-selling jazz album, *Forest Flower—Charles Lloyd At Monterey* (1967). *Downbeat* magazine named Lloyd 'Jazz Artist of The Year' and he became one of the first jazz artists to share the bill with rock bands at the Fillmore West. Lloyd shared a love for TM with The Beach Boys and various configurations of the band would play on two of his later albums in the 70s.

Yet the centerpiece for *Surf's Up* would be the legendary *SMiLE* track that had attained mythic status after being played on the Leonard Bernstein television special in 1967. Once again, economic realities trumped artistic pursuits. Over Brian's objection or indifference (accounts vary), Carl once again ransacked the vaults to bring an unfinished *SMiLE* track to fruition, as he had done with 'Cool, Cool Water' and 'Cabinessence.'

The first difficulty Carl and Stephen Desper encountered was in the format. Brian had begun recording *SMiLE* as four tracks were giving way to eight tracks. Now, 16-track machines, utilizing two-inch tape, were the industry standard. Once usable copies of 'Surf's Up' were located, "listening under the microscope of a studio monitor found the tracks to be inconsistent in level and full of dropouts," wrote Desper. "Some parts of the tape had folds or creases along the vertical, causing tracking problems. Further, excessive compression of the dynamics for use in broadcasting caused the room background noise to modulate."

According to Desper, "Carl could not talk Brian into just re-singing his part, so had to go with what he had on hand." In sections where the tape could not be salvaged, Carl himself sang Brian's parts. "Maybe 30 percent of that is Carl—that part you think is Brian."[6]

Released on August 30, 1971, *Surf's Up* contained the legendary title track along with two further Brian classics, 'A Day In The Life Of A Tree' and the sombre elegy 'Till I Die.' Probably the most controversial track on the album was 'Student Demonstration Time,' Mike's contemporary reworking of 'Riot In Cell Block Nine,' which featured one of Carl's most blistering guitar solos.

Rereleased in October, backed this time with 'Till I Die,' 'Long Promised Road' finally broke the band's nineteen-month absence from the singles charts, peaking at number 89, just in time for Carl and Annie to announce the birth of their second son Justyn.

* * *

The year 1972 should have been Carl Wilson's moment. He had established himself as a producer, composer, multi-instrumentalist, and performer. Thanks in large part to Carl, The Beach Boys finally had an album and a single on the charts. They headlined a television special, *Live In Central Park*, on ABC TV and celebrated their tenth anniversary in Long Beach, California, the site of one of their first shows.

Yet problems were beginning to emerge as 1971 wound to a close. The

222 • KENT CROWLEY

Beach Boys of 1972 would be a far different band, making far different music, to the band who delivered *Sunflower* or *Surf's Up*; and their biggest disappointment to date would put Carl's name front and center.

After the establishment of the new, hipper look for The Beach Boys, a new lineup appeared: two Wilsons, two South Africans, named Ricky Fataar and Blondie Chaplin, and stalwarts Mike Love and Al Jardine. The depth to which Brian had receded into the background was made clear when photographers had to montage an older photo of Brian over the new band to make it appear that he was still involved.

Carl And The Passions "So Tough" was The Beach Boys' third Warner Bros album and their second, after *Surf's Up*, recorded in what Desper called "people's quadraphonic," a system enabling listeners to enjoy a surround-sound effect using only two extra speakers and some speaker cord. It was also their second since 1966, along with *Friends*, that included neither resurrected *SMiLE* songs nor rehabilitated recordings from those sessions. Instead, as musician and writer Andrew Hickey pointed out, with two rockers by Brian, two Love/Jardine songs about meditation, two Flame tracks, and two Dennis Wilson ballads, it "could be the work of four different bands. Carl Wilson is, largely, the common denominator, working with everyone to get their tracks into shape."[7]

The Flame had broken up after recording, but not releasing, their second album, which Carl produced. Carl asked drummer Ricky Fataar to step in for Dennis on the drums as the middle Wilson brother had suffered a severe hand injury a few months before. Meanwhile, tensions mounted between Bruce Johnston and Rieley, who had been Brother's head of public relations since August 1970 and was now about to replace Nick Grillo as the band's personal manager, and Bruce departed after seven years as a Beach Boy. To replace Bruce, Rieley asked Chaplin to play bass and guitar, and on March 16, 1972, Fataar and Chaplin became official Beach Boys.

The two former Flame members brought new vocals and new instruments to the band. Where Carl and Al focused on supporting the songs, essentially as rhythm guitarists, Blondie brought a new lead guitar sensibility to the band. Where The Beach Boys of 1971 could have been considered an 'art rock' band, now they were back to being solidly rock'n'roll.

Dennis's hand injury not only sidelined him as a drummer, but as a songwriter, which didn't go unnoticed by critics of *Surf's Up*. Yet by the spring of 1972 he had recovered enough to play keyboards and had been working with Daryl Dragon on solo projects, two of which would be shanghaied by the band to fill out the album.

Carl And The Passions "So Tough", released on May 15, was named to honor Carl's involvement in pulling the album together, reviving a temporary band name used to get Carl to play guitar for one of Brian's school assemblies. Yet it quickly fell into the 'love it or hate it' category of Beach Boy albums. While there are no bad tracks on the album, the tracks that constitute 'good' are often a matter of taste. After the blissful sonic experiments of *Surf's Up*, *Carl And The Passions "So Tough"* sounded more like The Band or The Flame. Carl produced the only real singles-worthy track on the album with 'Marcella.' Yet 'Marcella,' like so many Beach Boys songs before and after, was an updating of an earlier Brian Wilson song, this time one called 'Beatrice From Baltimore.' While critics singled it out as the standout track on the album, when it was released as a single in June, it continued what was becoming a long tradition of misses.

The album had its admirers, however. Elton John wrote later that *Carl And The Passions "So Tough"* "is perhaps the 'loosest' of all The Beach Boys albums in that it has more of a band feel than the others. It contains one of my favorite all time Beach Boys tracks, 'Marcella,' and another, 'He Come Down' … Carl Wilson's hand is much in evidence here, as is his voice, and the addition of Ricky Fataar, who is a superb drummer, enhances the live feeling that pervades the songs. I am a huge fan of The Beach Boys. They have been and still are a major influence on my writing. This album is a step away from *Pet Sounds*, but still has moments of breathtaking genius and experimentation. When this record was released, I remember how different and fresh it sounded. It still does."[8]

But by all accounts, Carl was not pleased with the album that bore his name, feeling it was rushed. And Warner Bros made a huge mistake for a band looking to get back to its rhythm & blues and rock'n'roll roots, releasing *Carl And The Passions "So Tough"* as a double album set with a new release of *Pet Sounds*—pressed in mono, "the way Brian cut it."

Carl had earlier announced that the band had finally located the missing *SMiLE* session tapes and that The Beach Boys would complete the tapes for a fall release. Whether or not Warners had planned on releasing a revisited *SMiLE* album as a package with *Carl And The Passions "So Tough"*, the decision was made to attach *Pet Sounds* instead. For American record buyers looking for the mono *Pet Sounds*, it proved to be a godsend. The American version of *Pet Sounds* had been out of print for years: Capitol had issued *Today!*, *Summer Days (And Summer Nights!!)*, and *Pet Sounds* in a boxed collection—unfortunately in the execrable Duophonic faux-stereo process.

Pet Sounds and *Carl And The Passions "So Tough"* were two albums recorded by two completely different bands, six years apart—a lifetime in popular music terms. When Warner Bros rereleased *Pet Sounds* as a stand-alone album with what is known as the "peanut" cover, two years later, *Carl And The Passions* met the same fate as the Capitol Beach Boys albums—forgotten until its fortunes were revived decades later by the CD revolution.

CHAPTER NINETEEN

The Trader

Over the years, the challenge facing historians of The Beach Boys is that the stories behind every album bear little resemblance to reality. According to the legend of *Holland*, The Beach Boys, enchanted by the Netherlands after an earlier appearance on a European television special called *Grand Gala Du Disque*, decided to crate up their Brother Studios and move it into a barn in Holland, where they duly recorded a masterpiece. But their heartless record company didn't take kindly to their lavishly expensive effort and rejected it, until Van Dyke Parks forced Brian Wilson to sit down at the piano and compose another classic: 'Sail On Sailor.' The new album was released to glowing reviews and gave the band enough new material to record their second (in America) or third (in the UK) live album, which promptly went gold.

The truth is more prosaic but far more indicative of the pressures the band felt after the failure of *Carl And The Passions "So Tough"* to produce a hit. Because the release of *SMiLE* was a condition of their Warner Bros contract, $50,000 (a considerable sum in 1972) was withheld from the band's most recent advance. With drugs becoming more of a problem, especially with Rieley encouraging chemical excess as an adjunct to creativity, Mike and Al embarked on an effort to get rid of the 'old guard' and bring TM devotees on board. Unfortunately, the first casualty was the level-headed and forward-thinking Desper, who went off to produce a stellar body of work with the famously anti-drug Frank Zappa.

With Blondie and Ricky in the band and sharing a love of The Beatles and rhythm & blues, Carl's interest in guitar was reignited. In concerts, when the band closed with 'Johnny B. Goode' or 'Student Demonstration

Time,' Carl would pull out all the stops, often dropping to his knees to close a solo in good old rock'n'roll fashion.[1] As a songwriter, though, he found the piano to be more conducive to his creativity and during this period wrote one of his finest songs, 'The Trader.'

'The Appeal To The Great Spirit,' a 1909 Cyrus Edwin Dallin sculpture of a Lakota chief on horseback with outstretched arms, inspired the symbol The Beach Boys chose for their Brother label. According to Timothy White, Dallin hoped to portray the "Native American's plight as white settlers populated the continent" and "saw the Lakota's gesture as common to all humanity."[2] And with 'The Trader,' Carl sought, with Rieley's help, to tackle the western world's original sin—slavery—as a metaphor for all human injustice.

"Carl was also becoming a strong proponent of speaking out about the fact it's wrong to subjugate a people, as so many people particularly in Africa have been," Rieley later told writer Ken Sharp. "'The Trader' is really about racism; these people who got their orders from the king or the queen and colonized Africa, for example. The tender part of the song asks the Africans to reply. I believe it's quite touching. I wasn't consciously trying to do something political."[3] Ever the family man, Carl opened his most serious work with a recorded "Hi" by his young son Justyn.

The bulk of *Holland*, recorded in that country during 1972, "turned into a pretty mellow, but very nice album," said Blondie Chaplin. "It was also very relaxed to record in an environment like that. You wake up, you come to a place that's not like a formal studio where it can be very cold, and this was nice just to come to."

The sessions, he added, reflected this more laid-back approach. "This was nice to come to, start slow … take it easy, take a walk up to the pub, have a little lunch, work a little bit. Come back to the pub in the evening. That's pretty much what I remember doing. It was a lot of fun and very … easy flowing. So it wasn't heavy pressure to make music."[4]

Carl liked the atmosphere, too. "It's very peaceful here," he told a Dutch reporter. "I'm glad that it's exactly as I imagined it would be when I made the plan to go and live here for a while. I convinced the others that it would be good for all of us to catch our breath in the Netherlands and to get some new impulses. … The truth is that we want to quietly work on a new album, and we think we need about three months for it in a calm environment."[5]

For a band famous for utilizing state-of-the-art technology, recording *Holland* provided a challenge. "I don't know how we did it," Jardine later recalled. "Technically, we were hurting." The differences between American and European electrical power and the lack of outboard effects or echo chambers meant that the album would undergo a great deal of processing later in the States.[6]

Carl found the new circumstances recharged both his creative and his spiritual batteries. "It was a very creative time for me. Brian had me working on the album very hard so he could have some time for himself. He really wasn't up to doing much, as far as going to the studio every day."[7]

In Holland, Brian found a new way to circumvent the pressures of getting 'Brian Wilson product' onto an album to mollify the record company. Drinking a local type of cider called applesap, Brian spent hours listening to Randy Newman's *Sail Away* album—another album by an American artist concerning the slave trade. While Carl stayed with the band in the studio to record the bulk of the tracks that would appear on *Holland*, Brian created a musical fairy tale about a magic transistor radio. He named the piece after the location of Mike Love's high school home at the intersection of Mt Vernon Drive and Fairway Boulevard in Los Angeles.

Carl and Brian produced the album track, with added lyrics by Jack Rieley. Back home, when the record company balked at putting it on the album, it was included as a bonus seven-inch EP inside the sleeve. When Mike Love later made a disparaging remark about it at a concert at the University of California, Irvine, he was met by a shout of, "I think it's bitchin'!" prompting the audience to erupt in applause.[8]

Building a recording studio and housing an entire band and their families drove the costs of *Holland* through the roof, and when the original tapes were submitted to Warner Bros, the company demanded changes—specifically, a hit record by Brian Wilson.

The band returned home and left Rieley in Holland with his lover. Al Jardine, who lived over a bakery, missed the United States, saying "we had enough pastries."[9] They accepted Rieley's argument that he could manage the band long-distance. It had worked for the album, after all: Dennis had successfully made his headquarters in the Canary Islands and flew in for the *Holland* sessions.

Carl and the band returned to Village Recorders in Los Angeles to record 'Sail On Sailor,' a song that by some accounts first surfaced during the *Sunflower* era. Many lyricists have laid claims to co-writing 'Sail On Sailor.' In Van Dyke Parks's account, he went up to Brian's home, and after a series of fits and starts, in which Brian asked Parks to "convince me I'm not insane," they then composed the song on the spot.[10] Soon both Rieley and Brian's friend Tandyn Almer would claim credit. Yet a nearly identical version, with Carl singing lead, exists in Stephen Desper's archives, and Desper left before the *Holland* saga began.[11] Finally, singer Ray Kennedy claimed credit on an earlier version and recorded the song with his band KGB as a simple 'Wilson/Kennedy' composition, in which the first line goes "I am a singer / A gospel singer."

Whatever its lineage, the band delivered 'Sail On Sailor' with Blondie singing lead at Carl's suggestion. It replaced 'We Got Love,' a Fataar/Chaplin/Love number reflecting the new members' experiences in South Africa. When *Holland* was released in January of 1973, the reviewers poured praise on this new Beach Boys and their new music. Yet the album and the 'Sail On Sailor' single stalled once again on the charts at a time when successful singles and radio play were essential to a band's success. There was nowhere to go but back out on tour.

* * *

The new touring Beach Boys were a far cry from the band of the 1964 *Beach Boys In Concert* or *Live In London* and now sported a three-guitar front line. While *Carl And The Passions "So Tough"* and *Holland* may not have ignited the pop charts, the two albums introduced some of the biggest crowd-pleasers into the band's set: 'Marcella,' 'Funky Pretty,' 'Leaving This Town,' 'The Trader,' and especially 'Sail On Sailor.' They also occasionally introduced a combination of The Flame's 'Don't Worry Bill' and *Smiley Smile*'s 'Wonderful.' Switching from guitar to keyboard, Carl now transformed 'Caroline, No' from a quiet, elegant acoustic piece into a Charles Lloyd-esque jazz-rock excursion.

As the band set out on tour during 1973, events conspired to revive their fortunes along with some old controversies. Two films would resurrect the band's standing in the eyes of younger audiences who had, in large part, missed out on the early surfing/hot rod recordings of the pre-Beatles 60s.

The first was the first feature surf film of the 'shortboard' era, *Five Summer Stories*. A new interest in surfing arose along the coast after the innovation of the shortboard, a more compact design that allowed surfers to ride the waves more aggressively. While the bulk of the soundtrack was recorded by the Laguna Beach-based Honk (who would open for many of The Beach Boys' shows), both old and new Beach Boys recordings were featured throughout the film, particularly in one poignant scene in which a disabled surfer rails against the corporate interests ruining the sport against the backdrop of Carl's 'Long Promised Road.'

The film did much to revive The Beach Boys' standing in the surfing community. Before, they were often dismissed as, in champion surfer Greg Noll's phrase, "the Hollywood version." Now, however, they were viewed as battle-hardened survivors who had kept the beach connection in their name and stood fast against Beatlemania. More importantly, The Beach Boys had over the years built up a canon of environmentally conscious art, with songs like 'Country Air' and 'Don't Go Near The Water' sharing the environmental concerns of not only a whole generation but also of a new breed of surfer with increasing concerns about the health of the ocean.

Released in August of 1973, George Lucas's *American Graffiti* was one of the first films to tell its story largely through the music on the soundtrack, featuring 41 tracks by 35 different artists. Yet the two standout tracks in the film were Beach Boys songs—'Surfin' Safari' and the closing number,

'All Summer Long.' One exchange between characters even disparages "that surfin' shit."

As Carl led the band on a tour that would produce their first real hit album in nearly half a decade, Murry died suddenly of a heart attack on June 4, 1973, just a month shy of his 56th birthday. Of his three sons, only Carl attended Murry's funeral in Brian's hometown of Inglewood. Murry had maintained a relationship with Carl, and, through Carl, with The Beach Boys. Only three months earlier, Murry had attended a March 18 performance at Crawford Hall at the University of California, Irvine, and was seen chatting with Carl immediately after the show.[12]

During the summer, Carl brought back tapes of the concert series to Brother Studios, now relocated from Brian's home to Santa Monica. The songs ranged from the early surfing years to *Holland*, all performed by a rough, tough hardworking road unit who could deliver the hardest rock alongside delicate *Pet Sounds*-era songs. Released in November of 1973, *The Beach Boys In Concert* became the band's first gold record in four years (although there were accusations that Warners 'massaged' the actual number to qualify it for a gold record).

At the same time, the band dismissed Rieley and replaced him with Mike's brother Steve as personal manager. Soon after, Blondie left the band, after an argument with Steve, and found himself briefly replaced by James William Guercio, the former Chad & Jeremy guitarist and now the producer of the superstar band Chicago and comedy troupe The Firesign Theatre. Guercio would assume band-management responsibilities just in time to bring The Beach Boys back to being the biggest band in the world.

Carl had little time to bask in the glory of finally delivering a hit album to Warner Bros and leading what was about to become the biggest concert draw in America as the nation sputtered out of the 1973 recession. Without Rieley, Carl found himself in the position of finding a new lyricist for the next Beach Boys studio album. He now had a new sound crew and a new studio still close enough to Los Angeles to accommodate session players.

But 1974 didn't cooperate. In June, Capitol released *Endless Summer*, a compilation of pre-*Pet Sounds* Beach Boys hits. Capitol had deleted virtually the entire Beach Boys catalog in the late 60s and replaced them in the early 70s with truncated versions of their 60s albums with non-chronological band photos. Now, with Mike Love's encouragement, Capitol produced what was probably the first two-disc greatest hits album, supported by a massive promotion campaign and even advertising on television. Warners responded by following the rerelease of *Pet Sounds* with a repackaging of *Smiley Smile* and *Friends* in another two-disc set, followed by *Wild Honey* and *20/20*.

For most kids who grew up after the late 60s, the songs from *Endless Summer* were almost unknown; now, with homages like First Class's 'Beach Baby,' Beach Boys-inspired bands like 10cc, and guest appearances singing backing vocals on hits like Chicago's 'Wishing You Were Here' and Elton John's 'Don't Let The Sun Go Down On Me,' The Beach Boys were back in a big way. In 1962 their rivals were Dick Dale and The Bel Airs. Two years later, The Beatles. Now the 1974 Beach Boys faced a formidable challenger: the 60s Beach Boys.

America needed a break in 1974. It seemed that as soon as the Paris Peace Accords opened the door to ending the Vietnam War, a new scandal called Watergate erupted in Washington DC. An oil crisis and cutting back on defense spending led to a new kind of economic crisis called 'stagflation.' The first wave of baby boomers were pushing 30 and had heard few, if any, of the early Beach Boys hits since the mid 60s. The younger baby boomers now entering the marketplace had seldom if ever heard The Beach Boys' early work.

The drugs of choice changed the way people listened to and made music. Where psychedelic drugs were once used to explore new intellectual and spiritual horizons, drugs had now become a simple rite of passage. A new drug from South America had taken over as the drug of choice among music makers and listeners: cocaine. Combined with the mating ritual of dancing and the now socially accepted sexual revolution, it spawned disco.

Stoned crowds had been docile. The effect of cocaine taking over from marijuana was that people wanted to dance. The drug gave them the confidence and the energy to dance the night away, even if some of them looked like dancing hippos from Disney's *Fantasia*.

Beach Boys fans who bought *Beach Boys In Concert*, released in November 1973, were already on the inside track, as the album delivered a smattering of Beach Boys oldies. Now, thanks to Capitol Records' reissuing of the early hits, The Beach Boys were everywhere. Over the course of the past few years, they had become a new band and won over all of their previous doubters. Now those who once dismissed the band were their biggest supporters.

* * *

In the fall of 1974, Carl and The Beach Boys headed back into the studio, this time to Guercio's new state-of-the-art Caribou Ranch in Nederland, Colorado. Guercio built the studio in a lush valley near the Rocky Mountains to create an environment that would foster greater artistic creativity. The old barn at its center inspired guitarist Joe Walsh to write 'Barnstorm' and Elton John to name an album *Caribou*. Caribou Ranch's rustic surroundings had served as movie locations. Going there, in the words of Nitty Gritty Dirt Band banjoist John McEuen, created an atmosphere in which it was "almost too nice to record."[13]

The relationship between Guercio and The Beach Boys proved mutually beneficial in a number of ways, but most importantly in preparing for an upcoming stadium tour with Chicago that became known as the Beachago concerts. The nation's economic recovery chugged along slowly but surely under the new Ford administration, and rock promoters and managers like Guercio were looking for new ways to put asses on seats. With not one but two hit double albums riding the charts, The Beach Boys had a lot riding on their upcoming tour season and their next Brother/Reprise album.

During the recording, The Beach Boys struck up friendships with the individual members of Chicago, and Carl, Dennis, and Al were invited to sing backgrounds on Chicago's 1974 hit record 'Wishing You Were Here.' After a brief flurry of recording, during which Carl and Brian would put together their later hit 'Good Timin',' the band packed up and returned to their newly finished Brother Studios in Santa Monica.

As Brian Chidester pointed out in his epic essay 'Busy Doing Something,' the years when Brian was rumored to be hiding in his bed were really years filled with songs beginning and ending in fits and starts.[14] Just as The Beach Boys raided the vaults for *SMiLE*-era tracks, now these unused songs, with reworkings from other band members, would form the basis for The Beach Boys' recording career in the three year period between *Holland* and *15 Big Ones*. More importantly, the instrument that Stephen Desper introduced to The Beach Boys had become one of Brian's passions: the synthesizer. Where Carl found in the synthesizer a great tool to enhance old tapes and make them sound new, Brian saw synthesizers as sort of a portable Wrecking Crew. In three years, The Beach Boys with Carl at the helm had produced four very different albums: the airy, naturalistic *Sunflower*, the electronic masterpiece *Surf's Up*, and the funky back-to-basics approach of *Carl And The Passions "So Tough"* and *Holland*.

When the Warner Bros executives heard the tapes for the next album they again expressed dissatisfaction with the results in what was becoming a ritual between The Beach Boys and their record company. As the band's *de facto* producer, the details of dealing with the executives, then returning to The Beach Boys with the dispiriting news of rejections, were left to Carl. However, Warners had signed the band at their lowest point; one could argue that the label's ordering the retooling of *Sunflower*, and the forced inclusions of 'Surf's Up' and 'Sail On Sailor,' were beneficial to the band's fortunes and futures.

Yet even with hits riding the charts for the first time in years, the tours were critically important to the band's own economic and critical recovery. As the end of 1974 closed in, Ricky Fataar quit the band to tour with Joe Walsh, and Dennis's hand injury had healed enough for him to retake his place behind the drum kit. That meant that The Beach Boys' lineup was as close to the original as it had been since the early days, when contracts called for "Carl Wilson and four musicians." Even without an album of new material that year, *Rolling Stone* named The Beach Boys its 'Band of the Year' for 1974.

However, having two hit albums filled with older material now caused a problem for the band. Observers of the band have, over the years, divided into several camps. The most vociferous have propounded the 'art versus commerce' theory of The Beach Boys, in which Carl and Dennis (and, on their behalf, Brian) strove to keep the band producing and playing new material while the non-Wilson faction of the band insisted on the formula—rehashing the oldies and playing on an aging audiences' heartstrings with nostalgic blasts from the past.

"I remember hearing [live] board mixes from the 70s, where they're trying to stay relevant," said later Beach Boys touring bassist and keyboard player Chris Farmer. "The Beach Boys had these original songs, but you couldn't hear them because the audiences were yelling for '409.' Mike was the one who said, 'We can't beat it anymore, we can't buck it. We can do some original stuff, but if we don't give these folks what they want to hear, they won't come back next year.'"[15]

Capitol unveiled plans for a second repackaging of early hits as a companion to *Endless Summer* for 1975. Warners, meanwhile, began putting together a best-of collection of hits from *Pet Sounds* on: *Good Vibrations: Best Of The Beach Boys*. Once again, The Beach Boys found they had to make a choice between critical favorites and popular successes. As the band's set list began leaning more heavily toward oldies, in the post-*Holland* era, they found that, generally, the more ecstatic the audience, the more indifferent the critics. On December 29, 1974, after a concert at the Long Beach Arena, the *Long Beach Press-Telegram* reported that the band worked the audience in a "near-frenzy" and walked offstage after two encores. Yet their hometown newspaper singled out their opening act, Honk, insisting their music was more worthy than the oldies in which The Beach Boys had been trafficking.

In the spring of 1975, The Beach Boys set out on one of their most important stadium tours, with Chicago. The band, with Dennis back on drums, was supplemented by Guercio, Billy Hinsche, Bobby Figueroa, Ron Altbach, and Carli Muñoz. Beginning in Texas in May, they swung through the South and passed through their home state of California, where they performed in front of 50,000 people. Newscasts reported that officials had to rush to the second and third tiers of the newly built Anaheim Stadium to demand that the enthusiastic crowds cease dancing and stomping because they feared they upper levels of the stadium might collapse. At one show, President Gerald Ford's children showed up to scream with the rest of the fans. (Ford's daughter Susan even campaigned to have The Beach Boys play her high school prom, which would take place at the White House, but The Beach Boys and White House staff couldn't come to terms on the contract.)

Backstage at the Anaheim stadium show, Carl spent time with Brian and noted how pleasantly surprised his older brother was that many in the crowd who had been born long after the hits of the early 60s knew all the words to the old songs. By mid summer, The Beach Boys were headlining over some of the biggest acts of 1975, including, at Wembley Stadium in London, The Eagles, Joe Walsh, and Chaka Khan.

Yet the oldies were now haunting The Beach Boys' future. In March, a rereleased 'Sail On Sailor,' now two years old, peaked at number 49. At one show, after performing some material from *Holland*, Carl, who rarely spoke onstage, appeared apologetic and said, "Thank you for listening."[16]

CHAPTER TWENTY

Living With A Heartache

Onstage, Carl Wilson was always the most gracious and professional of musicians. His voice—whether on rhythm & blues rave-ups like 'Darlin'' or the elegant 'God Only Knows'—never broke and his pitch never wandered. His guitars were always perfectly in tune and his chording solid.

"Everybody deferred to Carl, even Mike Love," said Chris Farmer. "Mike deferred to Carl on tempos and parts. He wanted to make sure his cousin was happy too, which is saying a lot for Mr Love. He's the 'Type A' personality who's kept that band going for a lot of years."[1]

The band performed so often at this point that there were few formal rehearsals. Few were needed when the shows were only days—or sometimes hours—apart. Often, soundchecks were expanded to smooth over rough parts.

"Carl probably did the set list but they all consulted each other," said Farmer. "The schedule was that 45 minutes before the downbeat, The Beach Boys arrived for the 'meet and greet.' After about 20 minutes, they would change into their stage clothes and arrive onstage. Generally, the production manager had a set list from the previous show and would consult with Carl. Carl then took the list to Mike and then Al. Of course, the show always went off on time."[2]

Offstage, the Carl Wilson the audiences never saw could be rowdy and rambunctious. Descriptions of his sense of humor range from "dry" to "off the wall." At one point, he began passing out guitar picks embossed with his new nickname, Cookie. Sometimes he introduced himself as Clem.[3] According to Grammy-winning producer Mark Linett, when Carl was asked to sing on David Lee Roth's rendition of 'California Girls,' he had to bring a cassette of

The Beach Boys' original version, explaining with a shrug, "I have to listen to this because we don't do it the original way onstage any more."[4]

The only time his audience really got a glimmer of Carl's humor was in his choice of stage clothes. Beach Boys music was probably the furthest thing from country & western music, yet from the early 70s, Carl chose a selection of jackets, shirts, and pants from the leading tailor of country & western wear: Nudie's Rodeo Tailors of North Hollywood. Nudie Cohn is credited as being the first tailor to affix rhinestones to fabric, and over the years clothed nearly every country artist on note. In 1968, the emerging country-rock bands began using custom-made Nudie outfits as a visual statement of solidarity to the older forms of country. Whether Carl saw himself as a country boy at heart, or just saw the humor in wearing clothing onstage that spoke of a musical style nearly the opposite of The Beach Boys' approach, throughout the 70s Carl was probably Nudie's biggest supporter in rock'n'roll.

Backstage, Carl served as the band's ambassador, especially to the numerous VIPs who showed up to watch the show or during the obligatory meet-and-greets. Always polite, Carl would extend his hand to guests and introduce himself with a disarming "Hi, I'm Carl Wilson."[5]

Onstage, he led a band consisting of both classically trained and self-taught musicians that sometimes varied from one show to the next. The additional musicians served two important purposes in Beach Boys tours. The first was that they were able to successfully reproduce the more complicated arrangements such as 'You Still Believe In Me' or 'Caroline, No.' More importantly, The Beach Boys were getting older, and the teenage vocal chords that propelled the early hits now belonged to grown men entering their thirties. In addition to getting the arrangements right, the touring Beach Boys now 'shadowed' the original members' vocals as well as instrumental parts. As good as The Beach Boys' sound system was, it still couldn't overcome the delirious shouts and applause, with the fans calling out for their favorite hits. Carl had already learned to shadow Brian's voice during the years when he had to rehabilitate old tracks like 'Surf's Up.' Now he had to teach younger band members to shadow The Beach Boys when their voices were overtaxed by screaming fans.

Carl is reported to have complained of some measure of hearing loss during the years when the band played through the massive Fender Dual Showman amps, but with their new PA systems, Carl could now play through a smaller, cleaner amplifier such as a Fender Twin and let the sound engineer bring up the volume.

In October of 1975, Carl finally stepped out of The Beach Boys' shadow after hearing Dean Martin's son (and *Sunflower* cover photographer) Ricci Martin play a song on the piano. Inspired, Carl and Billy Hinsche took Ricci into the studio and produced a single that grew into an album project: 'Stop, Look Around' b/w 'I Had A Dream.' Although the single stiffed, it anchored Martin's 1976 album *Beached*. The album boasted a who's who of Carl's musical circle: Hinsche, Chicago's Peter Cetera, America's Gerry Beckley, and Bobby Figueroa. Of *Beached*, Alan Boyd said, Carl "went to some places that none of the other Wilsons did. You can hear it in the sonic textures on the *Sunflower* and *Surf's Up* albums and I think a spotlight needs to be put on the Ricci Martin *Beached* album … amazing, interesting, and eccentric sonic textures."[6]

Yet even with the massive successes of 1974 and 1975, cracks were beginning to appear in the narrative in which The Beach Boys recaptured America's heart. Back manning the drummer's throne, Dennis irritated Mike at one show when he arrived onstage drunk and riding a motorcycle. The crowd loved it; Mike didn't. Where once the Wilson brothers defended one another from Murry, Dennis's growing alcohol and drug abuse put Carl in the position of defending Dennis from what was becoming known as the TM crowd: Mike and Al. Newfound success brought Dennis back into the spotlight he loved, and while Carl lived quietly with Annie and his sons, jealously guarding his privacy, Dennis over the 70s carried on very public romances, first with Chicago keyboardist Robert Lamm's ex-wife Karen (whom Dennis would marry twice) and then with Fleetwood Mac keyboardist and singer Christine McVie. With Brian still alternating between periods of lucidity and illness, Carl now shouldered the additional burden of keeping an increasingly out-of-control Dennis in line.

Yet there was a glimmer of hope. In October of 1975, Marilyn Wilson hired Dr. Eugene E. Landy to treat Brian and get him back to making music. Landy had treated a number of Hollywood celebrities, including Alice Cooper and Gig Young (who later committed suicide). His treatment involved importing a staff and monitoring the patient around-the-clock to keep Brian away from drugs, alcohol, and food. "I'm outrageously expensive," Landy boasted to writer David Felton in a *Rolling Stone* article called 'The Healing Of Brother Brian.'[7]

In January of 1976, The Beach Boys embarked on recording a new album that would put Brian back in the producer's chair and carry the first 'Produced by Brian Wilson' label since *Pet Sounds*. A new world had emerged since the last time Brian had total control over a session. No longer was recording a simple matter of importing The Beach Boys and the Wrecking Crew into the studio where they would capture magic on four-track machines in a series of three-hour sessions. Now musicians could fiddle endlessly with 24 tracks to make every single instrument sound right before they were combined in a mix.

Brian had also taken to the new synthesizer technology in a big way. No longer would the electric bass anchor the songs; Brian found a whole new world of bass tones literally at his fingertips. Where Carl once produced albums by negotiating with the other band members, he now found himself as Brian's lieutenant. To get Brian back in the producer's role, the band decided early on to start with an album of oldies: cover versions of favorites from their early years, such as Fats Domino's 'Blueberry Hill' and 'Talk To Me' by Little Willie John. The oldies would be supplemented by original songs recorded at, or intended for, the Caribou sessions, such as 'It's OK.'

For *15 Big Ones*, Carl yielded the director's chair and receded back into his original role as singer and guitarist. "I believe that Brian was consciously underproducing the album, and that was his choice—we deferred to him," said Carl later. "But when we voted to do it that way with those particular songs, I left the studio right there on the spot because I was very disenchanted. Thing is, then I came back and worked my ass off because I support my brother professionally and personally."[8]

Carl's voice was particularly important at a time when his brothers had wrecked theirs. The contrast was acute on his duet with Brian on The Righteous Brothers' 'Just Once In My Life,' one of the high spots of the record.

As the album neared completion, the band relieved Guercio of his managerial duties and replaced him with Mike's brother Steve Love. Steve promptly trumpeted Brian's return to the studio in the 'Brian is Back' promotion campaign, and the Beach Boys of 1976 would be as ubiquitous as the Beach Boys of 1975. Once again the band, and Brian, found themselves amidst a whirlwind of concert stops, radio interviews, and television appearances. *15 Big Ones*, released in July, put The Beach Boys back in the Top Ten, peaking at number eight.

In May, the band had unveiled the first Brian-produced single since the odd 'Child Of Winter' Christmas single of 1974. A reworking of Chuck Berry's 'Rock And Roll Music,' it shot up the charts and reached number five in August. 'It's OK,' a Wilson/Love original, breached the Top 30 later that summer.

As *15 Big Ones* raced up the charts, Beach Boys fatigue started to set in. In the November 4, 1976 issue of *Rolling Stone*, Brian admitted having difficulty writing new songs because he'd written "some 250 songs, 300, whatever it is" and said he missed his old method of writing on uppers.

For writer David Felton, "The Beach Boys are probably the most thoroughly written about, mythicized, analyzed, agonized over, and deeply probed pop group in America. And this summer especially we've had Beach Boys up the ass. ... Mainly it's about Brian Wilson, the partially deaf boy-wonder turned mad genius who tuned his one good ear into the drone of middle-class America and heard the lost chord of God until it drove him nuts, and finally silent."

In the article, Brian nearly described Carl when he talks about his mother Audree, whom Felton describes as "a quiet, funny woman surrounded by fighting men" who "spent much of her time and understanding bridging gaps and soothing wounds." In the article, Audree even admitted that, after Murry's death, it was Carl who finally invited her to his home to try the wicked marijuana her late husband so often railed against.

For more critical readers, the article let slip bits of information about the Wilson household that probably had much to do with shaping Carl's and Dennis's personalities. Audree spoke glowingly of Brian's talents emerging at an early age and described the other boys as "slower." When asked about his relationship with Murry, Carl replied, "We had a great relationship," before adding, "He was crazy about Brian, but he and Brian drove each other nuts."[9]

In the days when both England and America were rural societies, families observed a tradition called 'headrights' in which the oldest son would be groomed to take over the family farm or business. After that, it was left for the younger sons to stay home and work the family fields. Clearly, in a house where three sons are all squashed into one tiny room but there was money to purchase pianos and Hammond organs, Murry saw music rather than machinery as the family business, and groomed Brian to take over.

Carl clearly saw his role as serving the family business by serving Brian. And now he had two brothers in various states of substance abuse to deal with as he surrendered much of his leadership role to Brian, who had rejoined the group as a performing member in October and was planning his own solo album. Dennis, too, made plans to record his own solo album, to be called *Pacific Ocean Blue*. The family held out hope for Dr Landy's therapy with Brian, but no comparable effort was made to get Dennis into therapy, even though it was rumoured that he was using heroin by this time.

Carl was the product of the same environment and industry that fueled his older brothers' substance abuse, and he soon fell victim to the two drugs that amounted to currency in the music business: cocaine and alcohol. But with Brian's and Dennis's drug use on public display, Carl's addictions remained unnoticed and untreated until people could no longer look away.

As Brian basked in the love from audiences for the first time since the early 70s, he went back to the studio to make a record, using a new batch of songs inspired by his treatment by Landy, to be called *Adult Child*. Yet The Beach Boys still had bills to pay, and the songs were hijacked by the band for an album that would be called *The Beach Boys Love You* when it was released in April 1977. Carl was relegated to the role of 'mixdown' producer. Ostensibly there to translate Brian's monaural productions to stereo, he basically ended up shaping Brian's new material into commercially viable songs.

"I found the credits interesting," said Alan Boyd. "'Produced by Brian Wilson, mixdown producer Carl Wilson.' Carl was the one who made that album sound as good as it did. He had a very strong sense of dynamics in terms of building a record from beginning to end. And some of his best work in terms of making that work was in what he chose *not* to use. Brian tended to record these things with everything going full steam all the way through … on a song like 'Let Us Go On This Way,' Carl made the aesthetic choice to drop out all the instruments in the first verse, give the lead Moog synth bass a slight left and right delay that kind of it makes it leap out of the speakers. Some of the subtleties and arrangements in the productions are more from Carl's choices in making the mixdown than what had been laid down on tape."[10]

* * *

With only one more album owed to Warner Bros, The Beach Boys signed an $8 million deal in March 1977 with CBS's Caribou label. Then, when manager Steve Love's contract wasn't renewed, Carl suggested a friend of his, named Henry Lazarus, take over the role.

Tensions had been steadily rising in the group since the heady summer of '76. The band was divided between Mike and Al, leading the anti-drug TM axis, and Carl and Dennis, whose substance abuse had been steadily escalating. Under constant watch by Landy's team, and playing in a regular touring band after a decade's absence, Brian had issues of his own to deal with. The two factions now traveled on two different planes and often stayed in different hotels.

Brian's reintroduction to the band created several issues for Carl. For all intents and purposes, Carl was The Beach Boys' acknowledged leader both onstage and in the studio. Yet, with Brian back on board, not only was Carl's leadership position abrogated, he now had to factor Brian's erratic behavior into every decision and improvise around any decisions already made. Brian should have been under prescribed medications, administered by a medical doctor. Landy's 'new age' treatment got him to lose weight and eschew drugs, but Brian was still a severely ill man whose symptoms—rather than their cause—were being treated.

As Carl sought to deal with his own worsening substance abuse, Dennis began spiraling out of control and had escalated to using heroin. Always the good brother, Carl found himself torn between protecting Dennis against Mike and Al and trying to rein in Brian, who might suffer an episode onstage and start playing the wrong song or require the live band members to shadow his vocals when his confidence was low. Plus, as people who have battled substance abuse issues know, drugs and alcohol aren't conducive to making the right decisions in a crisis—and The Beach Boys were in personal and financial crisis.

Bands in which some members take drugs and others don't live in a constant state of crisis management. The Beach Boys were back playing to stadium and festival-sized crowds with the tours—not record sales—supporting a massive infrastructure. Now ticket sales for the events began slipping, and The Beach Boys were looking at committing themselves to a major record label when they were barely speaking to one another.

The Beach Boys always looked to Europe to recharge their flagging spirits and fortunes, and the band promptly planned a major European tour, beginning with a major trade show for their new label's executives and associates. Yet at the last minute, it was discovered that Lazarus had failed to secure the proper paperwork and the tour, save for the appearance at the CBS Convention in London on July 30, 1977, had to be scrapped at an estimated cost to The Beach Boys of $1 million in lost revenues. To worsen matters, when the news broke that the band had canceled everything but a closed industry event, the public perception was that The Beach Boys had abandoned their most dedicated fans to play for a roomful of rich executives in order to curry favor with their new label.

Tensions within the band reached a boiling point. At a meeting in New York over Labor Day Weekend in September there was a move to replace Lazarus by reinstating Mike's brother Steve—a decision that Carl and Dennis vociferously opposed. The bottled-up venom and bile of the past few years exploded into a screaming match.

Carl had become the *de facto* leader of The Beach Boys not because he started the band or because he was chosen or even volunteered; it was because whenever a musical problem or an issue arose Carl would deal with it. Yet, after Mike, Al, and Brian got their way and reinstated Steve Love, the TM axis exhumed every wrong or questionable management decision Carl had ever made and called him to account (Steve meanwhile was later convicted of embezzling nearly $900,000 from The Beach Boys).

Carl responded that he had never been remunerated or credited as the band's producer over the past few years. Brian's decision to vote with Mike and Al left Carl and Dennis outvoted and fuming and put the band's future in doubt.

One of the issues that exacerbated tensions within the band was Dennis's upcoming solo album, *Pacific Ocean Blue*, to be released in August 1977. Those who had heard it realized it was brilliant, and having a brilliant solo artist in a band that was tearing itself apart contributed even more tension.

On September 2, after the crucial meeting, The Beach Boys performed one of the most lucrative yet badly reviewed shows of their career in front of a crowd in Pawtucket, Rhode Island, who had paid up to a record $10 for tickets. Fractured and emotionally spent, The Beach Boys put on a show that critics savaged as a "minimum performance for a maximum payday." Dennis mused quietly backstage that it might be The Beach Boys' final performance.[11]

Boarding a connecting flight back to Los Angeles, they stopped in Newark, New Jersey, for refueling, where a fistfight between Dennis and the

Love brothers exploded on the tarmac in full view of a startled *Rolling Stone* reporter. The rest of the retinue poured from the plane and pulled them apart at the last minute.

Over the next few months, The Beach Boys finished concerts that were already booked, but it was obvious to everyone that the band had disintegrated. Dennis was reported to be rehearsing a band in anticipation of a tour to support *Pacific Ocean Blue*. Mike, Al, and Brian repaired to the Maharishi International University (MIU) in Fairfield, Iowa, to produce their final Warner Bros album. Save for a single lead vocal on 'Sweet Sunday Kind Of Love,' Carl's presence on *M.I.U. Album* is virtually nonexistent.

However, after a meeting at Brian's house, the band patched up things enough to continue touring as The Beach Boys, and in early 1978 they set out to support the new *M.I.U. Album* with a tour of New Zealand and Australia. Carl called the new unity "a truce rather than an armistice."[12] By the beginning of the year, however, Carl was, in Chip Rachlin's words, "on a downward spiral."[13] His marriage to Annie was breaking up and he now suffered from excruciating back pain—a common affliction among guitarists and bassists who stand during performances—that led him to self-medicate. The back problem had started as early as *15 Big Ones*, much of which he recorded lying on the studio floor.

For years, Carl's chief role in the group was quality control, from assessing Brian's new material to overseeing the final mixes in the studio. Now he had one brother undergoing therapies with questionable results (at one rehearsal they found Brian lying underneath the grand piano) and another brother flirting with a heroin addiction and preparing for what looked like a solo career. Dispirited and broken-hearted, Carl simply went through the motions—until he spiraled down too far in front of an audience.

On the flight to New Zealand in February, Brian evaded his bodyguards and managed to score some drugs and exhibited bizarre behavior during the show that night. At a meeting with the show's promoters, Carl made a sarcastic remark to one of Brian's minders—a bodybuilder named Rocky Pamplin—who promptly sucker-punched Carl and knocked him out. With his back in pain and woozy from painkillers, Carl was unable to fight back; when he came to, had to have makeup applied over the bruises for the show. To the shock of many, Pamplin was never disciplined for beating Carl.

Yet it was the show in Perth, on March 14, where Carl finally hit the wall. The show started late after the other band members had to push Carl into the shower to sober him up. Onstage, Carl slurred his words, dropped his guitars, and at one point tumbled into the drum kit. Historically, Carl always counted the songs off and closed them, but now, chemically incapacitated, he missed his cues and the songs lurched out of nowhere and sputtered to awkward halts. When he failed to end 'Good Vibrations,' Brian finally stepped back into his leadership role and managed to bring the song to a halting finish. The others, realizing Carl's distress, cranked up their performances to cover him, and Mike drew the audience's attention with an over-the-top performance that would have done Tina Turner proud.

The next day, however, Carl did something truly astounding—especially for a rock'n'roll band. While rock'n'roll audiences and the entertainment media had for years tolerated aberrant behavior from rock stars, The Beach Boys called a press conference, where a contrite Carl apologized for the evening's performance and explained he had inadvertently mixed his medication with alcohol. The press turned up the heat but Carl, drawing upon his famous diplomacy, managed to mollify the media and outraged fans.

Carl now realized his situation was out of control. He decided he needed to take charge of his destiny, especially after his marriage to Annie fell apart and they eventually separated on July 4, 1978. Yet Dennis had provided an inadvertent and unwelcome distraction in April, when, after a concert in Arizona where he was too incapacitated to perform, he was found in a hotel room with a 16-year-old girl. His subsequent arrest for "contributing to the delinquency of a minor" was plastered all over the papers, but the girl's parents quietly settled with The Beach Boys.

CHAPTER TWENTY-ONE

The Right Lane

For some people, being present at a moment of history can mean a lifetime of repeating the same stories over lunch and having enthralled listeners pick up the check. Few can claim as many moments as Jerry Schilling. He was present at the famous summit where The Beatles met Elvis Presley, in 1965, and at the infamous Elvis and Nixon meeting at the White House, where the president presented Presley with an honorary badge from the United States Bureau of Narcotics and Dangerous Drugs.

Yet Schilling was more than a member of Elvis's Memphis Mafia. He proved to be Presley's most trusted confidante, and his managerial skills and integrity found favor with The Beach Boys when he was brought in first as a tour manager and then as a co-manager with Tom Hulett, after Steve Love was fired after the Australian tour of 1978.

The Elvis connection didn't hurt with The Beach Boys. Carl had been an Elvis devotee from an early age, while on 'Do You Remember,' from *All Summer Long,* Brian had sung, "Elvis Presley is the king / He's the giant of the day / Paved the way for the rock'n'roll stars."

Schilling proved his mettle as The Beach Boys prepared to move from Brother/Reprise to CBS's Caribou Records. Now, with Bruce Johnston, Guercio, and Schilling on board, and two tracks from Dennis's upcoming *Bambu* solo album, they cobbled together the *L.A. (Light Album)* for a spring 1979 release after *M.I.U. Album* stiffed on the charts.

The highlight of the record, a 1974 collaboration between Brian and Carl called 'Good Timin',' brought a new rush of hope to Beach Boys fans after the rough edges of *The Beach Boys Love You* and the polished and very 70s-sounding *MIU* album. Carl delivered a couple of quiet masterpieces with 'Full Sail' and 'Angel Come Home,' which, though sung by Dennis, was a heartbreaking elegy about Carl's separation from Annie, which would be followed by his filing for divorce later in the year. But *L.A. (Light Album)* also contained what may have been either The Beach Boys' boldest track or their worst miscalculation.

Always willing to experiment with new genres, Carl and his friend Curt Becher produced a disco version of *Wild Honey*'s 'Here Comes The Night' that did little to endear them to The Beach Boys' core audience. While some rock critics dismissed its parent album, disc jockeys spun 'Good Timin',' often announcing "The Beach Boys are *back*!" Yet, *L.A. (Light Album)* and its successor a year later, *Keepin' The Summer Alive* (to which Carl contributed two songs co-written with Canadian rock legend Randy Bachman), languished on the charts.

In 1981, after nearly 20 years of nonstop touring and recording, Carl finally left The Beach Boys. With Jerry Schilling as manager and moral support, he decided to test the solo album waters. In Jerry's wife Myrna Smith, formerly of the Sweet Inspirations, Carl found a capable and willing lyricist and extraordinary singer. Movie-star beautiful, down-to-earth, and intelligent (she had once been a high school English teacher), Myrna possessed lyrical gifts, an amazing voice, and an effortless vocal style that perfectly complemented Carl's ability to range from the subdued and serene to spine-shivering soulfulness.

At the house above the Sunset Strip that Elvis bought for Schilling to keep him nearby while he was shooting his movies, Carl brought his acoustic Martin D-76 guitar (a special issue dreadnought that Martin Guitars issued to celebrate the bicentennial) and sat down with Myrna in the living room to write songs for what would become the album *Carl Wilson*, released in March 1981. While much of the lyrical content of the album would reflect Myrna, one song stood out as pure Carl: 'Seems So Long Ago,' which recalled Carl's childhood with Dennis. Meanwhile, 'Heaven' reflected Carl's spirituality in what was ostensibly a love song, and 'Hold Me' underlined Carl's love of good old rhythm & blues.

Now single and sober, Carl left the toxic atmosphere of The Beach Boys and found himself surrounded by a new, more supportive family: the family that surrounded Jerry Schilling. "That was Jerry from the very start," said Schilling's executive assistant, Michelle Beaulieu. "He saw something in Carl, he saw the soulful part of him. Brian gets all the credit for The Beach Boys, but Carl was the soul."

Beaulieu met Schilling through her older sister Priscilla Presley, Elvis's wife. "I actually kind of grew up knowing Jerry because he was Elvis's friend," she said. "To me, they were like uncles." When Schilling found he needed a personal assistant to work with acts such as Billy Joel and The Beach Boys, "He said, 'Maybe you could help me out.'" While The Beach Boys were fragmenting, Schilling "was really good at pulling people together. It was like they were all so fractured it was a real struggle. They were so fractured for so long."

When she met Carl, she was surprised to find not a rock star, but someone who was "really shy, very sweet, but had exuberance like he was as happy to meet me as I was to meet him." Through Jerry, Carl got to know Myrna and found their songwriting partnership a perfect fit.

"That was pretty special," said Beaulieu. "She was more gospel—it came from her background, so she had it in her blood—and Carl had this whole other side to him. It was really just a nice artistic partnership. They were really on their own. As a former school teacher she could guide him and pulled him into different scenarios. So, you got this very thoughtful, uplifting music. He was making a really strong statement and it was important for Carl to be on his own at that time." In Schilling, Carl found a "good friend who had a chance to help out a friend."

Socially, the only Beach Boy Carl interacted with at the time was Dennis, who was also close to Jerry. "I think Dennis really felt safe with Carl," Beaulieu added. "Dennis was his own worst enemy." Yet in all of Carl's relationships, music was always at the center. "Carl was a huge Elvis fan. Jerry had lots of stories to tell. It was a creative time."[1]

As Carl and Myrna polished the songs for recording, he now looked to forming a band. As most of the songs were written on an acoustic guitar, with Carl employing a fingerstyle picking technique more akin to jazz artists like Joe Pass than 'fingerpickers' like John Renbourn, he would need a rhythm section with a lead guitarist. With Myrna's help, he found one.

John Daly started playing guitar at the age of six and later studied with noted guitarist Al Colombo. He then took music theory at Rutgers University before moving to California in 1976. "I was working with a band called Salvage with [drummer] Alan Krigger and [bassist] Gerald Johnson, doing some pretty jive places, when Gerald walked in and said, 'Hey guys, we're going to do an album with Carl Wilson.' It was a moment of serendipity that got me into the band. Gerald had worked with Myrna in Las Vegas and when she sought him out, he said, 'I have a drummer and a guitarist.'"

Playing lead guitar in a band headed by one of the most well-known lead guitarists in the world seemed like a daunting enterprise. "The first record I ever bought was 'Help Me, Rhonda,' because I really liked the guitar solo." But in Carl, rather than a hotshot, demanding bandleader, Daly found "a sweet and gentle and generous man. I never saw him angry or perplexed or confused."

For the first rehearsal, they all got to know one another and learned a couple of tunes. "Audree was there—what a wonderful woman," said Daly. At another rehearsal, Dennis pulled in driving a sports car and nearly ran over some of the band members. Carl smiled and said "That's my brother."

"The next thing I knew, we were flying to Caribou Ranch to record an album. Jim Guercio was another of my idols and to see that ranch was just amazing. The whole time it was a mind-blowing experience," Daly added. "What was really exciting was how comfortable they made me feel." For one track, Daly didn't manage to get his solo on the first take. Guercio shrugged it off and told him [Chicago founder] Terry Kath—another one of Daly's guitar heroes—seldom got his solos on the first take either.

Carl's first order of business was to have Daly's Ibanez guitar and Fender Vibrolux Reverb amp reconditioned for the recordings. He offered Daly two Epiphone guitars (one six-string and one 12-string) to use on stage as well.

"There was a comfort level that he knew how to give someone. He let me be the lead guitar player, which was the biggest honor." Daly particularly enjoyed 'The Right Lane,' a rocker to celebrate Carl's newfound sobriety. "That was *the* song—I loved playing it so much. Carl let me stretch out on that one."[2]

Now, with Billy Hinsche on keyboards and occasional guitar, the band finished recording the album and embarked on Carl's first solo tour, which included his famous debut at the Roxy on the Sunset Strip and television appearances on programs like *Solid Gold*. In public, Carl's official line was that he wanted to try his hand at a solo career when The Beach Boys decided to take some time off; although they would tour for the best part of a year without him, to some of the worst reviews of their career. The atmosphere was not helped by a fist-fight between Mike and Dennis at the Greek Theatre in Los Angeles in July.

Carl had left The Beach Boys not for selfish reasons but for artistic reasons, said Schilling. After an initial solo tour in April, he spent the summer of 1981 supporting The Doobie Brothers. He told the *Omaha World Herald*, "I haven't quit The Beach Boys but I do not plan on touring with them until they decide that 1981 means as much to them as 1961."[3] Mike, predictably, was not sympathetic. "I think that people that come to see The Beach Boys want to hear our old stuff. I think you're doing them and yourself a really big disservice if you kid yourself they don't want to hear those songs."[4]

Daly found Carl an impressive leader. "He was extraordinarily precise. He did not make errors. I never heard him misplay a note." On tour, there were few road tales and little discussion of The Beach Boys. "He didn't speak much of The Beach Boys, and Billy spoke well of them. If there were any conflicts, both were honorable and said nothing. When you're in a band from the 60s through the 80s, and they are a family, I knew that part of Carl's heart would always be in The Beach Boys no matter what."

Yet the album and subsequent touring did much to rehabilitate Carl's mental health. "He pretty much said what he wanted and did what he wanted to do. We were thrilled to do anything he asked. I think it gave him a comfort level in his career." Now he was able to act out of choice, not responsibility. "One of the things we ran into is we were just 'Carl Wilson.' Only the cognoscenti knew who Carl was, whereas with The Beach Boys, Carl was a rock star. The crowds were considerate and effusive, but they knew who they were listening to."

Daly found Carl to be as playful as he was professional. "My greatest influence was Jeff 'Skunk' Baxter," he recalled. While opening for The Doobie Brothers, Carl escorted Daly into the hospitality suite, led him toward what appeared to be a tall, long-haired blonde standing by a table, and said, "John, I have somebody I want you to meet."

"The tall blonde turned around," Daly recalled, "and it was Jeff Baxter." After the show, he added, "We talked for three and a half hours before security threw us out. I have Carl to thank for that as well."[5]

While *Carl Wilson* did deliver one bona fide hit, 'Heaven,' its misfortune was to be released at a time when the record business found itself battered by a major international recession, a rise in niche musical styles, and the advent of independent record labels to accommodate a newly fragmented audience. Recession and oil shortages hit the record industry hard in the final years of President Carter's administration, which ended in 1981. And the introduction of Dolby sound-processing equipment gradually turned record buyers away from vinyl albums to the handier cassette format. These were widely used to make copyright-infringing copies of albums, and that affected sales of many records, including *Carl Wilson*.

In May of 1982, Carl rejoined The Beach Boys after laying down conditions requiring the band to rehearse more, bicker less, and eschew the Las Vegas-style 'showbiz' engagements he loathed. Yet he still didn't blow off all of the musical steam pent up over the decades.

As the one Beach Boy always searching for new musical horizons, Carl sought out Jeff Baxter to produce his second solo album, *Youngblood*, released in 1983. "To me, 'Skunk' Baxter had been chosen to produce Carl's follow-up album both for his skill as a musician and also for his wizardly command of the recording studio on a technical level," Hinsche wrote later of *Youngblood*. "Not only was he a world-class guitar slinger ... he had recently moved into the area of design and development for the Roland Music Corporation. With the possible exception of the gadgeteer and progenitor of 12-string electric folk-rock, Roger McGuinn, Baxter had more electronics, cutting edge technological hardware, and special effects than anyone I knew."[6]

Moving into Cherokee Studios in the Fairfax District of Los Angeles, Baxter surrounded Carl with some of the most respected musical talent in Los Angeles. Along with his touring band, *Youngblood* boasted session stalwarts such as guitarists Baxter and Elliott Randall, pianist Nicky Hopkins, and trumpeter Lee Thornburg, just to name a few. On vocals, Carl, Myrna, and Hinsche were joined by Poco and Eagles bassist Timothy B. Schmit, Guess Who lead singer Burton Cummings, Phyllis St. James, and Billie Barnum. For their background efforts on the title track, Carl, Schmit, and Cummings called themselves 'Zoot & The Carlettes.'

Youngblood is a collection of searing rockers (like John Fogerty's 'Rockin' All Over The World'), jumping rhythm & blues numbers, and ballad performances to match 'God Only Knows.' It is, wrote Hinsche, "a rock'n'roll album fused with Carl's love of all the great Motown artists, along with a healthy portion of rhythm & blues combined with a rich sprinkling of his own blue-eyed soul, a touch of good humor, and more than just a dash of tenderness, all rolled up into one remarkable aural feast."[7]

Youngblood yielded one Top 20 Hit: 'What You Do To Me.' Meanwhile, back in The Beach Boys, a new storm was brewing—and this time the problem was Dennis.

* * *

By the summer of 1983, Dennis Wilson was at a low ebb. Drinking relentlessly, he made half-hearted efforts to lay down tracks for his prospective second album, *Bambu*, a follow-up to the acclaimed *Pacific Ocean Blue*. On December 28, five months after his fifth marriage, to Shawn Marie Love, allegedly the child of Mike Love, he dove into the Marina del Rey and drowned. Jerry Schilling broke the news to Brian.

In the wake of the loss, the remaining Beach Boys made one more serious attempt at pulling together a new and vital Beach Boys album. Carl had no doubts about how difficult it would be. "We're damned if we do and damned if we don't," he said. "If we do a record that sounds like the others, it's the same old thing. If we do something new we'll be attacked because it doesn't sound like us."[8]

Through Bruce Johnston, Carl met British producer Steve Levine, then one of the most successful in the business, having recorded The Clash's first album along with hits by Culture Club and others. "They wanted to make a record like that," Levine said. He suggested the band employ the latest in computer and synthesizer technology—a suggestion that resonated with Carl. The two bonded right away. "He was very, very funny," said Levine. "We started in the studio at Westlake Audio [in Hollywood] and we were having conversations about making sure the vocals were cool and not 'cabaret-esque.' He would do a take in a Las Vegas style just to be funny. Carl showed up one day in a full gold lamé suit—that is what I miss a lot."

Levine had worked with Brian earlier in Jamaica, and had introduced him to some local musicians there. "I remember Brian at the piano singing 'Surfer Girl' with all of the Jamaican players harmonizing. I had my Fairlight Series One [one of the most cutting-edge sampling synthesizers of the 80s, the grandfather of today's digital-audio workstations] and we sampled Brian's voice. Brian was blown away."

Levine introduced this new concept to The Beach Boys. They would build the tracks using the state-of-the-art Fairlight rather than by trucking the whole band into the studio. "Once we got going with the tracks, the two mainly in charge were Carl and Bruce. Carl understood the technology really well. Carl played a lot of the parts."

Working on the album that would become The Beach Boys was a two-way street. "[Carl] taught me a lot about harmony balance because he was the ears of the group," Levin recalled. "The vocals on 'Getting Late' are as good as anything I've ever done."[9] Mark Linett, who would later master the tapes for The SMiLE Sessions, noted that Carl was "somewhere between obsessive and perfectionist—but you see that a lot in my business."[10]

Released in June of 1985 after a year of gestation, *The Beach Boys*, like *Youngblood*, featured a star-studded lineup of guest talent, including Stevie Wonder, Culture Club guitarist/keyboardist Roy Hay, Ringo Starr, and one of Carl's favorite guitarists, Gary Moore, on guitar and Synthaxe. While Moore overdubbed his parts later in London, Levine said Carl was "thrilled" to have him perform on a Beach Boys record. Carl wrote three tracks for the album, while there are one each from Stevie Wonder and Culture Club's Boy George and Hay. Carl's singing throughout is exceptional, on the originals and the covers, perhaps the best examples of a great blue-eyed soul singer at the height of his powers. Brian's tracks, meanwhile, included credits to his psychologist Dr Eugene Landy, which were removed when the album was rereleased on CD.

Even though the album yielded a minor hit, 'Getcha Back,' and reached the band's highest album chart position in eight years, CBS declined to renew the band's contract. But Carl's and Bruce's efforts to make The Beach Boys more contemporary at least garnered them some new respect as pioneers. "He came back and he made a difference," said Jerry Schiling, "And he was right."[11]

Although *The Beach Boys* was filled with excellent vocals and wonderful songs, the response of critics and fans alike was lukewarm, most likely because it fell into the 'orphan' category of albums, like *Surfin' USA*, that were produced by neither Brian nor The Beach Boys. However, viewed as a swan song by Carl Wilson, one of the world's most important artists, *The Beach Boys* provided a proper closing act.

* * *

By the time *The Beach Boys* was released, Carl was approaching 40 years old; the rest of The Beach Boys had already crossed that border. After nearly a quarter of a century, they had attained the status of legends. Now, instead of producing Beach Boys records, Carl would spend the next decade guesting on albums for artists such as Olivia Newton-John and recording with Chicago keyboardist Robert Lamm and America's Gerry Beckley.

Of the Beckley-Lamm-Wilson album, *Like A Brother*, critic William

Ruhlman said, "This is far and away Wilson's best non-Beach Boys work, and some of the best work of his career. His songs are full of a sense of a generous love, the kind one feels for family rather than a romantic partner. 'I Wish For You' might be written for a child, while 'They're Only Words' warns that love must be acted on, not just spoken about. The album's most striking song is 'Like A Brother,' Wilson's tribute to his brother Brian, in which he discusses the oddity of earning applause every night for performing music written by his usually absent sibling. 'Like A Brother' deserves a place in any Beach Boys fan's collection."[12] After a gestation lasting almost a decade, *Like A Brother* was finally released in 2000.

Two things were central to Carl Wilson's life: music and family. And in Carl's case, music was family and the family was music. The key to Carl's willingness to serve his family and his music was his spirituality, which affected all of the people around him and bonded him to the people in his life. In 1988, the year he was inducted into the Rock and Roll Hall of Fame, Carl became an ordained minister in the Movement of Spiritual Inner Awareness (MSIA), which combines elements of many faiths and spiritual paths, including Christianity. Along with the rest of The Beach Boys, Carl had been drawn into TM and later, during the mid 70s, he became a popular supporter of the self-help movement known as EST (Erhard Seminars Training). But MSIA seemed to connect all of the dots for him.

In July 1987, the band became one of the first rock groups to move into hip-hop territory by backing The Fat Boys in a humorous rap version of The Surfaris' 'Wipe Out.' It reached number 12 on the *Billboard* Hot 100, and number two in the UK. That November, after nearly a decade of bachelorhood, Carl tied the knot with Gina Martin, another dark-eyed beauty, who was singer Dean Martin's daughter and the sister of Ricci Martin. With two sons by Annie Hinsche, he was now related to two-thirds of his former opening act, Dino, Desi & Billy. That same year, The Beach Boys celebrated their 25th anniversary with a television special highlighted by Ray Charles singing 'Sail On Sailor.'

In January 1988, The Beach Boys, along with The Beatles, were inducted into the Rock and Roll Hall of Fame, where their biography reads, "The Beach Boys at times have appeared to be rock and roll's longest-running soap opera. At the same time, they've been responsible for some of the most perfect harmonies and gorgeous melodies in the history of popular music, and it is for this vast legacy for which they are remembered and celebrated."

At the ceremony, which the band attended with champion boxer Muhammad Ali, Brian read an elegant message of gratitude and Carl edged to the microphone long enough to memorialize his brother Dennis. Mike Love, however, employed the time-honored football coach's technique of rousing the team onto greater victory by impugning his audience's talents and their courage, calling on them to mobilize their star power in the service of a yet-to-be-determined charitable cause. However, he ran over time and his speech was interrupted, leaving him sounding like little more than a cranky old man.

In November 1988, The Beach Boys scored their first US number one hit since 'Good Vibrations' with 'Kokomo,' from the soundtrack of the hit film *Cocktail*. Mike and Terry Melcher had rehabilitated John Phillips's dismal hippie lament about looking back on happier times and turned it into an upbeat single that resonated with fans of both the movie and The Beach Boys. The Grammy-nominated song succeeded in large part due to Carl's soaring and eternally young falsetto vocal on the choruses, and was certified platinum (for sales of one million copies or more) within six months of its July 1988 release. But even with Brian's former lyricist Van Dyke Parks performing on it—on accordion—there was no trace of Brian either on the single or in the video.

The month 'Kokomo' was released on Elektra Records also saw the release of Brian's critically acclaimed *Brian Wilson*, an album *Rolling Stone* called a "stunning reminder of what pop's been missing all these years." Yet, the album's bejeweled centrepiece, 'Love And Mercy,' failed to chart. Critical acclaim for Brian and lavish sales for The Beach Boys simply fueled the long-running 'art versus commerce' debate that had divided Beach Boys fans since *Pet Sounds*.

On the strength of the success of 'Kokomo,' executives at Capitol pulled together a series of old and new Beach Boys songs that had been featured in films plus a handful of unreleased new songs to make an album called *Still Cruisin'*. It breached the Top 50 and became their best selling album since 1976, but it is not regarded with affection by fans. Carl takes one lead, on Al Jardine's 'Island Girl,' and shares lead duties on 'Somewhere Near Japan,' by John Phillips, Terry Melcher, Mike Love, and Bruce Johnston.

The Beach Boys, with Carl, did make one last stab at an album of new material in 1992, with the release of *Summer In Paradise*. Carl contributed neither songs nor instruments, although he did sing, notably a cover of The Shangri-Las' 'Remember (Walking In The Sand).' It became the lowest-selling album of their career and quickly vanished from record store bins. And yet the following summer, the release by Capitol of a boxed set, *Good Vibrations: 30 Years Of The Beach Boys*, gave them a new lease of life on the road, interspersing unexpected tracks with the time-honoured oldies. Carl's vocals on such rarely heard songs as 'It's Over Now' and 'The Night Was So Young' were a particular delight.

Much of Carl's time in these years was spent extracting Dr Eugene Landy from Brian's life. In 1975, Marilyn, with the support of the rest of The Beach Boys, had brought the psychologist in to treat Brian and turn him back into a functioning artist. It worked well enough to bring Brian back into the studio for *15 Big Ones* and *The Beach Boys Love You*. But after 18 months, and following clashes with Brian's manager, Landy was dismissed.

Then, in 1983, Landy was rehired by Carl. The 24-hour therapy began again, long enough for Brian to produce his first solo album, *Brian Wilson*, and collaborate in an unreliable autobiography that brought defamation suits from Mike Love, Audree Wilson, and Carl. But while Landy had certainly rescued Brian from the clutches of substance abuse, he had inserted himself into Brian's artistic life by taking credits as co-writer and co-producer. Carl, Audree, and Brian's daughters Wendy and Carnie now took action to remove Brian from Landy's clutches: it was even alleged that Landy had prepared a new will for Brian making him the chief beneficiary. (Landy denied this.)[13]

In 1990, various actions began to remove Brian from Landy's control. Landy became the subject of an investigation by the California Board of Medical Quality Assurance. According to the *Los Angeles Times*, the state board accused Landy of "grossly negligent conduct," including the sexual abuse of a female patient. Most of the accusations concerned his relationship with Wilson, alleging that his multiple business entanglements had caused the singer "severe emotional damage, psychological dependence, and financial exploitation." In early 1992, Landy was finally served with a restraining order prohibiting continued interference in Brian's life.

Touring was the one constant in The Beach Boys' career. In the early days, it toughened up the band and turned them into the level of musician necessary to assist Brian in his greatest flights of creativity. During the lean years, touring paid the bills while The Beach Boys dealt with issues that would have easily broken lesser bands—or men.

For the next five years, Carl continued to tour with The Beach Boys, often finding a quiet corner prior to the show where he could do vocal exercises to keep his voice in shape. Then, in early 1997, doctors informed him he had lung cancer. Like the trouper that he was, Carl went out for the band's 35th anniversary tour. Physically drained from the treatments, Carl now often sat rather than stood when he sang, save for when he sang 'God Only Knows,' where, no matter how exhausted he was physically, he summoned the strength to perform the song that had touched so many people over the decades. In his final concerts, he even invited his doctors to bring up their guitars and jam on the final songs.

Carl kept his condition hidden from the band and the fans for as long as he could. "I never saw a physical deterioration from Carl," said Chris Farmer. "He had it, but he kept it hidden. He was very proud." Carl recovered from the performances by quietly repairing to the sleeper coach he shared with Gina. "We didn't know the extent of the cancer, but we knew Carl 'the rock' had done everything he could to keep playing with his band," said Farmer.

People in the industry and fans of Roy Orbison know that Roy never cracked a note. Like Roy, Carl could belt, sing low, and sing falsetto. But people knew the end was near when Carl gave his final performance of 'God Only Knows,' on November 29, 1997. "He cracked a note once on 'God Only Knows.' Just once," recalled Farmer. "I remember his last day onstage in Atlantic City. He said, 'This is my last show, I've got to go home. But I'll see you in November.'"[14]

Carl Wilson died quietly on Friday, February 6, 1998, surrounded by his family and his friend Jerry Schilling. He rests today not far from his mother Audree in Westwood Memorial Park near the University of California, Los Angeles. His simple headstone is emblazoned with the legend 'The heart and voice of an angel' above his dates of birth and death, and 'The world is a far lesser place without you.'

In death, as in life, Carl's legacy remained one of healing. The family set up the Carl Wilson Foundation, shepherded by his sons Jonah and Justyn, to fight the cancer that took his life. Because Carl's reputation in the family was as the Papa Bear who looked after all of the children in the family and especially Mike's eight offspring, his cousin and onstage partner became one of the foundation's biggest supporters.

Over the decades, most people have come to concur with Sir Paul McCartney's assessment of 'God Only Knows' as one of the greatest songs ever composed. Today it is ranked number 25 on *Rolling Stone*'s list of the 500 Greatest Songs of All Time. During The Beach Boys' 50th anniversary Reunion Tour in 2012, all the surviving members of the band, including David Marks and Bruce Johnston, paid tribute to Carl by synchronizing their performance of 'God Only Knows' to a widescreen presentation of him singing the song in 1980 at Knebworth, England.

The original Beach Boys began with Carl's lead guitar as their entrée into a new music explosion; his death effectively ended The Beach Boys as a band and turned them into a brand. Today, Mike Love leads a Beach Boys touring band, along with Bruce Johnston. It brings the message of fun and sunshine that Carl did so much to create to new audiences, year after year.

Notes & Sources

Chapter 1
1 Tom Nolan *Rolling Stone*, October 1971
2 Author's interview with David S. Gold, October 2014
3 *Goldmine* magazine, September 1992
4 Leaf
5 Author's interview with David Marks, October 1997
6 Carlin
7 Carlin
8 Author's interview with David Beard, April 2015
9 Carlin
10 Stefano Belli 'Psychobiographical Analysis Of Brian Douglas Wilson,' 2009
11 Year: 1930; Census Place: Los Angeles, Los Angeles, California; Roll: 154; Page: 4A; Enumeration District: 0573
12 Carlin
13 Steve Eidem liner notes to Murry Wilson *The Many Moods Of Murry Wilson* (2008 reissue)
14 *Rock Influences*, November 1984
15 Ken Sharp *Rockcellar* magazine, 2013
16 White
17 Tom Nolan *Rolling Stone*, October 1971
18 Marv Goldberg *The Hollywood Flames*, uncamarvy.com
19 rockabillyhall.com

Chapter 2
1 Leaf
2 *Carl Wilson: Here And Now* (MFM Productions 2011)
3 Steven Rosen *Player*, 2005
4 Author's interview with Justyn Wilson, May 2015

5 Author's interview with David Marks, October 1997
6 Preiss
7 Author's interview with David Marks, October 1997
8 Author's interview with Chris Montez, April 2010
9 *Rock Influences*, November 1984
10 Antonio Rios-Bustamante *Mexican Los Ángeles: A Narrative and Pictorial History* (Floricanto Press 1992)
11 Lee Stacy (ed) *Mexico And The United States* (Marshall Cavendish 2002)
12 Gilbert Estrada 'Brief History Of The Ports Of Los Angeles And Long Beach,' kcet.org 2014
13 David S. Gold and Stan Ross *The Gold Star Album* (unpublished manuscript)
14 Author's interview with David S. Gold, October 2014
15 David S. Gold and Stan Ross, *The Gold Star Album* (unpublished manuscript)
16 Author's interview with David S. Gold, October 2014
17 Author's interview with David S. Gold, October 2014
18 Author's interview with Bob Keane, November 1997
19 Geoffrey Himes 'Fun, Fun, Fun: Carl Wilson's Life As A Beach Boy,' guitar.com
20 Author's interview with John Stebbins, September 2014
21 Author's interview with John Stebbins, September 2014
22 Andrew Ruskak, *Composites Fabrication* magazine, May 2001
23 Author's interview with Chris Fleming, May 2010

24 *Guitarist* magazine, October 2010

25 Author's interview with Nick O'Malley, May 2010

26 Author's interview with Dick Dale, June 1989

27 Author's interview with Dick Dale, June 1989

Chapter 3

1 Author's interview with Billy Hinsche, September 2014

2 Author's interview with Stephen W. Desper, May 2015

3 *Carl Wilson: Here And Now* (MFM Productions 2011)

4 *Carl Wilson: Here And Now* (MFM Productions 2011)

5 Author's interview with Jon Stebbins, September 2014

6 Gaines

7 Williams and Lydon

8 Author's interview with Justyn Wilson, May 2015

9 Author's interview with Bob Keane, November 1997

10 Ed Ward *Michael Bloomfield, the Rise and Fall of an American Guitar Hero* (Cherry Lane Books 1983)

11 Liner notes The Beach Boys *All Summer Long* (Capitol 1964)

12 David Felton, *Rolling Stone*, November 1976

13 White

14 National Institute of Mental Health, nimh.nih.gov

15 National Institute of Mental Health, nimh.nih.gov

16 Liner notes to The Beach Boys *All Summer Long* (Capitol 1964)

17 Craig Slowinsky, 'Analysis Of Beach Boys Session Tapes,' *Endless Summer Quarterly* 2007/08

18 Author's interview with Jon Stebbins, September 2014

19 *Let's Go To Hawthorne CA With David Marks!*, documentary produced by Chuck Kelley

20 Author's interview with Jon Stebbins, September 2014

21 Stefano Belli 'A Psychobiographical Analysis Of Brian Douglas Wilson'

22 *Let's Go To Hawthorne CA with David Marks!*, documentary produced by Chuck Kelley

23 Badman

24 'Cuckoo: A Celebration of Mr Laurel and Mr Hardy' (BBC *Omnibus* 1974)

25 Author's interview with Marilyn Rutherford Wilson, January 2015

26 Author's interview with Stephen W. Desper, May 2015

27 Jim Delehant *Hit Parader*, February 1967

28 Author's interview with Bob Keane, November 1997

29 Author's interview with Bob Keane, November 1997

30 Author's interview with Bob Keane, November 1997

31 Author's interview with Chris Montez, April 2010

32 Author's interview with Chris Montez, April 2010

33 Author's interview with Chris Montez, April 2010

34 Author's interview with Jon Stebbins, September 2014

35 Anthony Reynolds *The Impossible Dream: The Story Of Scott Walker And The Walker Brothers* (Jawbone Press 2009)

36 Geoffrey Himes 'Fun, Fun, Fun: Carl Wilson's Life As A Beach Boy,' guitar.com

37 billyhinsche.com

38 Author's interview with David Marks, October 1997

39 billyhinsche.com

40 Author's interview with David Mark, October 1997

41 Author's interview with David Marks, October 1997

Chapter 4
1 *Beautiful Dreamer: Brian Wilson And The Story Of 'Smile'* (Showtime Networks 2004)
2 Author's interview with David Marks, October 1997
3 Author's interview with Jim Pash, October 1991
4 Del Halterman *Walk-Don't Run: The Story Of The Ventures* (lulu.com 2009)
5 'A Psychobiographical Analysis Of Brian Douglas Wilson,' 2009, by Stefano Belli
6 Author's interview with Stephen W. Desper, May 2015
7 *Carl Wilson: Here And Now* (MFM Productions 2011)
8 Author's interview with Dick Dale, June 1989
9 Author's interview with Nick O'Malley, May 2010
10 Author's interview with Nick O'Malley, May 2010
11 Author's interview with Dick Dale, June 1989
12 Author's interview with Bill Medley, October 2008
13 Author's interview with Richard Delvy, September 1997
14 Teagle and Sprung
15 Blair
16 Author's interview with Dick Dale, June 1989
17 Author's interview with Dick Dale, June 1989

Chapter 5
1 Einerson and Furay
2 Geoffrey Himes 'Fun, Fun, Fun: Carl Wilson's Life As A Beach Boy,' guitar.com
3 Author's interview with Bob Berryhill, September 1997
4 Carlin

5 *Al Jardine In-Studio* (The Artie Lang Show, Direct TV 2014)
6 billyhinsche.com
7 surfermoon.com
8 Tom Nolan *Rolling Stone*, October 1971
9 surfermoon.com
10 Author's interview with Bob Keane, September 1997
11 Blair
12 White
13 Preiss
14 Author's interview with Nick O'Malley, April 2010
15 Carlin
16 *Beach Boys' Party!* (Capitol Records 1965)
17 Tom Nolan *Rolling Stone*, October 1971
18 Liner note to *All Summer Long* (Capitol Records 1964)
19 Author's interview with Chris Farmer, December 2014
20 Craig Slowinski 'Analysis of Beach Boys Session Tapes,' *Endless Summer Quarterly* 2007/08
21 *Al Jardine In-Studio* (The Artie Lang Show, Direct TV 2014)
22 *Al Jardine In-Studio* (The Artie Lang Show, Direct TV 2014)
23 Author's interview with Mark Guerrero, November 2014
24 Author's interview with Dr Leroy 'Zag' Soto, November 2014
25 Rusten and Stebbins
26 Author's interview with Dr Leroy 'Zag' Soto, November 2014
27 Author's interview with Jim Pash, October 1991
28 Author's interview with Dr Leroy 'Zag' Soto, November 2014
29 Author's interview with Dr Leroy 'Zag' Soto, November 2014
30 Author's interview with Jim Pash, October 1991
31 Author's interview with David Marks, September 1997

Chapter 6
1 Rusten and Stebbins
2 Author's interview with David Marks, September 1997
3 Author's interview with David Marks, September 1997
4 Rusten and Stebbins
5 Blair
6 Author's interview with Jon Stebbins, September 2014
7 Author's interview with David Marks, September 1997
8 Blair
9 Jeff Lear in correspondence with John Blair
10 Preiss
11 Tom Nolan *Rolling Stone*, October 1971
12 Tom Nolan *Rolling Stone*, October 1971
13 Author's interview with Bob Berryhill, September 1997
14 Blair
15 Tom Nolan *Rolling Stone*, October 1971
16 Tom Nolan *Rolling Stone*, October 1971
17 *The Beach Boys In Studio Q* (CBC 2012)
18 Author's interview with Jon Stebbins, December 2014
19 Author's interview with Jim Frias, February 1998
20 Author's interview with Jim Pash, October 1991
21 bigvjamboree.com
22 Author's interview with John Blair, April 2015
23 Peter Reum liner notes to The Beach Boys *Surfin' Safari* (Capitol 2001)
24 Tom Nolan *Rolling Stone*, October 1971
25 *Rockcellar* magazine 2013
26 Peter Reum liner notes to The Beach Boys *Surfin' Safari* (Capitol 2001)

Chapter 7
1 *Rockcellar* magazine, 2013
2 *Rockcellar* magazine, 2013
3 Author's interview with Jim Pash, October 1991

4 Author's interview with John Blair, April 2015
5 Author's interview with John Daly, March 2015
6 David Marks interview, *Rockcellar* magazine, 2013
7 Author's interview with David Marks, October 1997
8 Author's interview with Jon Stebbins, January 2015
9 *Carl Wilson: Here And Now* (MFM Productions 2011)
10 Rusten and Stebbins
11 *Al Jardine In-Studio* (The Artie Lange Show, Direct TV 2014)
12 Stebbins and Rusten
13 *Beach Boys' 50th Anniversary Interview* (Google 2012)
14 *Al Jardine In-Studio* (The Artie Lange Show, Direct TV 2014)
15 Jon Stebbins *Dennis Wilson: The Real Beach Boy* (ECW Press 2000) and Tom Nolan *Rolling Stone*, October 1971
16 *Brian Wilson On Phil Spector And Be My Baby* (YouTube)
17 David S. Gold and Stan Ross *The Gold Star Album* (unpublished manuscript)
18 David S. Gold and Stan Ross *The Gold Star Album* (unpublished manuscript)
19 Author's interview with Larry Levine, March 1998
20 David S. Gold and Stan Ross *The Gold Star Album* (unpublished manuscript)
21 jananddean.com
22 Author's interview with David Marks, October 1997
23 Rusten and Stebbins

Chapter 8
1 Geoffrey Himes 'Fun, Fun, Fun: Carl Wilson's Life As A Beach Boy,' guitar.com
2 White
3 Jack Rieley *Rollling Stone*, November 1970

4 Rusten and Stebbins
5 billyhinsche.com
6 Author's interview with Jim Pash, October 1991
7 Author's interview with Jon Stebbins, September 2014
8 Carlin
9 Rusten and Stebbins
10 *The Beach Boys: The Lost Concert* (Image Entertainment 1999)
11 *Newsweek* magazine, May 2012
12 Rusten and Stebbins
13 White
14 earcandymag.com, October 2003
15 Author's Interview with Stan Ross and Dave Gold, January 2000
16 Author's Interview with Rick Henn, February 2015
17 earcandymag.com, October 2003

Chapter 9
1 Author's interview with David Beard, April 2015
2 Rusten and Stebbins
3 Author's interview with David Beard, April 2015
4 *Guitar Player* magazine, April 1976
5 David S. Gold and Stan Ross *The Gold Star Album* (unpublished manuscript)
6 Author's interview with Carol Kaye, October 1997
7 Author's interview with Hal Blaine, April 2010
8 Craig Slowinski 'Analysis of Beach Boys Session Tapes,' *Endless Summer Quarterly* 2007/08
9 Craig Slowinski 'Analysis of Beach Boys Session Tapes,' *Endless Summer Quarterly* 2007/08
10 'Marshall Amps,' guitar-bass.net, November 2013
11 Author's interview with Bob Keane, November 1997

12 Author's interview with Henry Diltz, May 2008
13 Craig Slowinski 'Analysis of Beach Boys Session Tapes,' *Endless Summer Quarterly* 2007/08
14 Author's interview with Jon Stebbins, September 2014
15 Author's interview with John Blair, March 2015
16 Author's interview with Billy Hinsche, January 2014
17 Author's interview with Jon Stebbins, September 2014
18 Author's interview with Stephen W. Desper, May 2015
19 Author's interview with John Daly, February 2015

Chapter 10
1 Preiss
2 Leaf
3 Siegel
4 *Beautiful Dreamer: Brian Wilson And The Story of 'Smile'* (Showtime 2004)
5 Preiss
6 Craig Slowinski 'Analysis of Beach Boys Session Tapes,' *Endless Summer Quarterly* 2007/08
7 Murry Wilson letter to Brian Wilson, May 1965, lettersofnote.com
8 *Phil Ochs In Concert* (Electra Records 1966)
9 John Teagle *Vintage Guitar* magazine, January 1999
10 Author's interview with Stephen W. Desper, May 2015
11 Author's recollection
12 *Goldmine* magazine, March 2011
13 *Goldmine* magazine, July 2010
14 Liner notes to The Beach Boys *Summer Days (And Summer Nights!!)* (Capitol 1965)
15 *Goldmine* magazine, July 2010
16 Geoffrey Himes *Musician*, September 1983

Chapter 11

1 'Solid Gold' (Operation Prime Time June 1985)

2 Brian Wilson liner notes to The Beach Boys *Beach Boys' Party!/Stack o'Tracks* (Capitol 1990)

3 Rusten and Stebbins

4 Author's interview with Larry Levine, March 1998

5 Geoffrey Himes *Guitar* magazine, September 1983

6 Author's interview with Billy Hinsche, January 2015

7 Author's interview with Chris Farmer, December 2014

8 Author's interview with Chris Farmer, December 2014

9 billyhinsche.com

10 Author's interview with Chris Farmer, December 2014

11 Einerson and Furay

12 Author's interview with Chris Farmer, December 2014

13 beachboysfanclub.com/ps-liner.html

14 *Rockcellar* magazine, 2013, Tony Asher interview by Ken Sharp

15 *Al Jardine In-Studio* (The Artie Lange Show, Direct TV 2014)

16 Rusten and Stebbins

17 Craig Slowinski 'Analysis of Beach Boys Session Tapes,' *Endless Summer Quarterly* 2007/08

Chapter 12

1 Author's interview with Billy Hinsche, January 2015

2 billyhinsche.com

3 Author's interview with Billy Hinsche, January 2015

4 billyhinsche.com

5 *Carl Wilson: Here And Now* (MFM Productions, 2011)

6 Brad Elliott liner notes to The Beach Boys *Pet Sounds* (Capitol 1999)

7 *Al Jardine In-Studio* (The Artie Lange Show, Direct TV 2014)

8 Rusten and Stebbins

9 *Carl Wilson: Here And Now* (MFM Productions 2011)

10 Author's interview with Chip Rachlin, August 2014

11 *Carl Wilson: Here And Now* (MFM Productions, 2011)

12 *Beach Boys Stomp* magazine, August 2007

13 Rusten and Stebbins

14 Rusten and Stebbins

15 Craig Slowinski 'Analysis of Beach Boys Session Tapes,' *Endless Summer Quarterly* 2007/08

16 *Rockcellar* magazine, September 2013

17 *Al Jardine In-Studio* (The Artie Lange Show, Direct TV 2014)

18 Brad Elliott liner notes to The Beach Boys *Pet Sounds* (Capitol 1999)

19 Brad Elliott liner notes to The Beach Boys *Pet Sounds* (Capitol 1999)

20 Jim Delehant *Hit Parader*, February 1967

21 Eric Boehlert *Rolling Stone*, March 2000

22 Rusten and Stebbins

Chapter 13

1 *Rolling Stone* '500 Greatest Songs Of All Time'

2 Leslie Coffin, *Lew Ayres: Hollywood's Conscientious Objector* (University Press Of Mississippi, October 2012)

3 *New York Times*, June 1967

4 Author's interview with Daryl Hooper, January 2015

5 Author's interview with Jim Pash, October 1991

6 Michael Buchanan 'Beach Boy Carl Wilson Becomes A Draft Dodger,' reasonabledoubt.org

7 Author's interview with Marilyn Wilson

Rutherford, January 2015
8 Michael Buchanan 'Beach Boy Carl Wilson Becomes A Draft Dodger,' reasonabledoubt.org
9 Rusten and Stebbins
10 Rusten and Stebbins
11 *Inside Pop: The Rock Revolution* (CBS News Special, April 1967)
12 Michael Buchanan 'Beach Boy Carl Wilson Becomes A Draft Dodger,' reasonabledoubt.org
13 Rusten and Stebbins
14 Author's interview with Chris Farmer, December 2014
15 Liner notes to The Beach Boys *The Smile Sessions* (Capitol 2011)
16 'Psychobiographical Analysis of Brian Douglas Wilson,' 2009, by Stefano Belli
17 *The Beach Boys: An American Band* (Eagle Rock Entertainment 1985)
18 Author's interview with Dick Dale, June 1989
19 David Leaf liner notes to The Beach Boys *Smiley Smile / Wild Honey* (Capitol 2000)
20 Author's interview with Stephen W. Desper, May 2015
21 *Los Angeles Times*, June 2012
22 Rusten and Stebbins
23 Rusten and Stebbins
24 Michael Buchanan 'Beach Boy Carl Wilson Becomes A Draft Dodger,' reasonabledoubt.org
25 'Military Obligations Waved For Tours,' United Press International, September 1971
26 Author's interview with Stephen W. Desper, May 2015

Chapter 14
1 Author's interviews with Alan Boyd and Mark Linett, April 2015
2 Lambert
3 Author's interview with Stephen W. Desper, May 2015

4 Preiss
5 Rusten and Stebbins
6 David Leaf liner notes to The Beach Boys *Smiley Smile / Wild Honey* (Capitol 2000)
7 David Leaf liner notes to The Beach Boys *Smiley Smile / Wild Honey* (Capitol 2000)
8 Author's interview with Bill Halverson, December 2014
9 David Leaf liner notes to The Beach Boys *Smiley Smile / Wild Honey* (Capitol 2000)
10 Preiss
11 Nick Kent *New Musical Express*, July 12 1975
12 Williams
13 Rusten and Stebbins
14 Author's interview with Bill Halvorson, December 2014

Chapter 15
1 Dave Zimmer (ed), *Four Way Street* (Da Copa Press 2004)
2 *The Beach Boys: An American Band* (Eagle Rock Entertainment 1985)
3 Dave Simpson *The Guardian*, July 4 2013
4 *Back To Godhead*, Number 21, 1968
5 David Leaf liner notes to The Beach Boys *Friends / 20/20* (Capitol 2000)
6 David Leaf liner notes to The Beach Boys *Friends / 20/20* (Capitol 2000)
7 neilyoungnews.thrasherswheat.org 2005
8 Rusten and Stebbins
9 *Goldmine* magazine, April 2010
10 neilyoungnews.thrasherswheat.org 2012
11 Rusten and Stebbins
12 'Revolution Blues' by Neil Young, songfacts.com
13 Leaf
14 Gaines
15 Author's interview with Jon Stebbins, September 2013
16 Scotty Wilson *Son Of A Beach Boy* (CreateSpace Independent Publishing Platform, January 2015)

Chapter 16

1 Barney Hoskyns, *Waiting For The Sun: A Rock 'n' Roll History Of Los Angeles* (Backbeat Books 2009)
2 Author's interview with Stephen W. Desper, May 2015
3 Gaines
4 *Cease To Exist* (Saguaro Pictures 2007)
5 Rusten and Stebbins
6 *Paste* magazine, March 2014
7 Rusten and Stebbins
8 Ken Sharp *Goldmine*, July 2000
9 Author's interview with Stephen W. Desper, May 2015

Chapter 17

1 Rusten and Stebbins
2 *Paste* magazine, March 2014
3 Carlin
4 Rusten and Stebbins
5 Author's interview with Alan Boyd, April 2015
6 *Paste* magazine, March 2014
7 Rusten and Stebbins
8 *Endless Summer Quarterly, Sunflower* edition, Winter 2010/11
9 Author's interview with Stephen W. Desper, May 2015
10 Author's recollection
11 Author's interview with Gary Griffith, December 2014
12 Author's recollection, February 1971
13 Author's interview with Daryl Hooper, January 2015

Chapter 18

1 Author's interview with Chip Rachlin, August 2014
2 *The Grateful Dead Meet The Beach Boys At Fillmore East*, April 1971 (Fire Power: unofficial release)
3 Author's interview with Chip Rachlin, August 2014
4 *Record Collector* magazine, October 2013

5 Tom Nolan *Rolling Stone*, October 1971
6 Author's interview with Stephen W. Desper, May 2015
7 AndrewHickey.info, January 2014
8 Liner notes to The Beach Boys *Carl And The Passions/So Tough / Holland* (Capitol 2000)

Chapter 19

1 Author's recollection
2 White
3 Record Collector magazine, October 2013
4 *Endless Summer Quarterly, Holland* edition, Spring 2013
5 Rusten and Stebbins
6 *Endless Summer Quarterly, Holland* edition, Spring 2013
7 *Endless Summer Quarterly, Holland* edition, Spring 2013
8 Author's recollection
9 *Endless Summer Quarterly, Holland* edition, Spring 2013
10 Leaf
11 Author's interview with Stephen W. Desper, June 2015
12 Author's recollection
13 *Daily Camera*, July 2013
14 *Paste* magazine, March 2014
15 Author's interview with Chris Farmer, December 2014
16 Rusten and Stebbins

Chapter 20

1 Author's interview with Chris Farmer, December 2014
2 Author's interview with Chris Farmer, December 2014
3 *Carl Wilson: Here And Now* (MFM Productions 2011)
4 Author's interview with Mark Linett, April 2015
5 Author's interview with David Beard, April 2015

6 Author's interview with Alan Boyd, April 2015
7 *Rolling Stone* magazine, November 1976
8 White
9 *Rolling Stone* magazine, November 1976
10 Author's interview with Alan Boyd, April 2015
11 Rusten and Stebbins
12 Rusten and Stebbins
13 Author's interview with Chip Rachlin, August 2014

Chapter 21
1 Author's interview with Michelle Beaulieu, March 2015
2 Author's interview with John Daly, March 2015
3 Rusten and Stebbins

4 Rusten and Stebbins
5 Author's interview with John Daly, March 2015
6 Liner notes to Carl Wilson *Youngblood* (Iconoclassic 2010)
7 Liner notes to Carl Wilson *Youngblood* (Iconoclassic 2010)
8 Rusten and Stebbins
9 Author's interview with Steve Levine, January 2015
10 Author's interview with Mark Linett, May 2015
11 *Carl Wilson: Here And Now* (MFM Productions, 2011)
12 allmusic.com, June 2010
13 White
14 Author's interview with Chris Farmer, December 2014

Interviews
Michelle Beaulieu, David Beard, Johnny Black, Hal Blaine, John Blair, Dick Dale, John Daly, Henry Diltz, Chris Farmer, David S. Gold, Gary Griffith, Mark Guerrero, Bill Halvorsen, Rick Henn, Billy Hinsche, Darryl Hooper, Carol Kaye, Bob Keane, Larry Levine, Steve Levine, David Marks, Steven McParland, Bill Medley, Chris Montez, Nick O'Malley, Jim Pash, Chip Rachlin, Stan Ross, Marilyn Wilson Rutherford, Ken Sharp, Richard Sherman, Dr. Leroy 'Zag' Soto, and Jon Stebbins.

Radio/television interviews
Brian Wilson: Jim Pewter interview KRTH-101 1974
Dennis Wilson: Pete Fornatale interview 1976
Carl Wilson: *This Day Tonight (The Beach Boys In Perth)* 1978

Carl Wilson: *Rock Influence* 1994
Carl Wilson: *American Bandstand* 1981, Dick Clark Productions

Unpublished manuscripts
David S Gold and Stan Ross, *The Gold Star Album*
Jim Pash, untitled history of The Surfaris

Documentary Films
Carl Wilson: Here And Now (MFM Productions 2011)
1974: On The Road With The Beach Boys (MFM Productions 2011)
The Beach Boys: An American Band (Eagle Rock Entertainment 1985)
(Let's Go To) Hawthorne CA With David Marks! (Produced by Chuck Kelly)
Beautiful Dreamer: Brian Wilson And The Story Of SMiLE (Showtime Networks 2004)
The Wrecking Crew (Magnolia Pictures 2015)

Cease To Exist (Saguaro Pictures 2007)
Brian Wilson: Songwriter 1962–1969 (Sexy Intellectual 2010)
Brian Wilson: Songwriter 1969–1982 (Sexy Intellectual 2012)
Dennis Wilson: The Real Beach Boy (BBC Legends Series 2009)

Internet sites
beachboys.com
beachboysarchives.com
beachboysfanclub.com
billyhinsche.com
brianwilson.com
smileysmile.net
surfermoon.com

Papers, essays, etc.
Belli, Dr Stefano Roberto 'A Psychobiographical Analysis Of Brian Douglas Wilson: Creativity, Drugs, And Models Of Schizophrenic And Affective Disorders,' *Personality And Individual Differences* (2009), hosted at researchgate.net
Slowinski, Craig 'Analysis Of Beach Boys Session Tapes,' *Endless Summer Quarterly* (2007/2008)

Magazines and periodicals
Endless Summer Quarterly (issues 82, 87, 99, 100, 103, 104, 106, 108)
Rolling Stone magazine (various issues 1968-2015)
Guitar.com 'Carl Wilson Interview,' 1982
Guitar magazine 'Carl Wilson Interview,' 1976

Online educational resources
Stephen W. Desper Study Videos (swdstudyvideos.com) Stephen W. Desper and Mike Connor (Will C. Music Productions 2015)
David Marks Guitar Clinic At Hawthorne High, sponsored by Hawthorne Historical Society, 2011 (YouTube)

CD liner notes and booklets
The Beach Boys 'Two-Fer' Reissues (2000 Brother Records, Inc., under exclusive license to Capitol Records, Inc.); liner notes by David Leaf
The Beach Boys *The Pet Sounds Sessions* (Capitol 1997); liner notes by David Leaf
The Beach Boys *Pet Sounds* (Capitol Records 1999); liner notes by Brad Elliot
The Beach Boys *The Smile Sessions* (nine-disk boxed set)
Pet Projects: The Brian Wilson Productions (ACE 2002); liner notes by Bob Pennis
Cowabunga—The Surf Box (Rhino Records 1996); liner notes by John Blair
Dick Dale *Better Shred Than Dead* (Rhino Records 1997)

Books
Badman, Keith *The Beach Boys: The Definitive Diary of America's Greatest Band On Stage And In The Studio* (Backbeat Books 2004)
Blaine, Hal, David Goggin and David Schwartz *Hal Blaine And The Wrecking Crew* (Rebeats Press 2010)
Blair, John *The Illustrated Discography Of Surf Music 1961–1965* (John Blair 2008)
Carlin, Peter Ames *Catch A Wave: The Rise, Fall, And Redemption Of The Beach Boys' Brian Wilson* (Rodale Books 2007)
Chidester, Brian, Domenic Priore, and Kathy Zukerman *Pop Surf Culture: Music, Design, Film, And Fashion From The Bohemian Surf Boom* (Backbeat Books 2008)
Davis, Francis *The History Of The Blues: The Roots, The Music, The People* (Da Capo Press 2003)
Einerson, John and Richie Furay *For What It's Worth: The Story Of Buffalo Springfield* (Cooper Square Press 2004)
Fein, Art *The L.A. Musical History Tour: A Guide To The Rock and Roll Landmarks Of Los Angeles* (Faber & Faber 1990)

Gaines, Steven *Heroes And Villains: The True Story Of The Beach Boys* (New American Library 1986)

Hartman, Kent *The Wrecking Crew: The Inside Story Of Rock And Roll's Best-Kept Secret* (St. Martin's/Griffin 2013)

Lambert, Philip *Inside The Music Of Brian Wilson: The Songs, Sounds And Influences Of The Beach Boys' Founding Genius* (Bloomsbury Academic 2007)

Leaf, David *The Beach Boys And The California Myth* (Grossett & Dunlap 1978)

McParland, Stephen J. *It's Party Time: A Musical Appreciation Of The Beach Party Film Genre* (John Blair 1992)

Morrish, John *The Fender Amp Book* (Miller Freeman 1995)

Preiss, Byron *The Beach Boys* (Ballantine Books 1979)

Priore, Domenic and Becky Ebenkamp *Look, Listen, Vibrate, Smile* (Last Gasp 1997)

Priore, Domenic *Smile: The Story Of Brian Wilson's Lost Masterpiece* (Sanctuary Press 2007)

Rusten, Ian and Jon Stebbins *The Beach Boys In Concert! The Complete History Of America's Band On Tour And Onstage* (Backbeat Books 2013)

Siegel, Jules *Record* (Straight Arrow 1982)

Stebbins, Jon and David Marks *The Lost Beach Boy: The True Story Of David Marks* (Virgin 2007)

Stebbins, Jon *Dennis Wilson, The Real Beach Boy* (ECW Press 2000)

Stebbins, Jon *The Beach Boys FAQ: All That's Left To Know About America's Band* (Backbeat 2011)

Teagle, John and John Sprung *Fender Amps: The First Fifty Years* (Hal Leonard 1995)

Unterberger, Richie *Urban Spacemen And Wayfaring Strangers: Overlooked Innovators And Eccentric Visionaries of '60s Rock* (Backbeat Books 2000)

Webb, Adam *Dumb Angel: The Life & Music Of Dennis Wilson* (Creation Books 2001)

Wheeler, Tom *The Stratocaster Chronicles: Celebrating 50 Years Of The Fender Strat* (Hal Leonard 2004)

White, Timothy *The Nearest Faraway Place* (Henry Holt 1996)

Williams, Paul and Michael Lydon *Outlaw Blues: A Book Of Rock Music* (Entwhistle Books 2000)

Wilson, Scott and Karen Lesley Powell *Son Of A Beach Boy* (CreateSpace Independent Publishing Platform 2015)

Acknowledgments

First and foremost, special thanks go to my wonderful family: my amazing children Billy, Chelsey, and Courtney; my brilliant grandchildren Kennedy, Sean, and London, and their beautiful mom Leslie. Thanks also to my Mom, my brother Keith, who rushed home one day in 1962 to tell me about this great new band called The Beach Boys, and my sister Kathleen, who threatened grievous bodily injury if I did not do right by Carl; and to Debby Crowley, Danny Wippert, Tawny and Jay Delgado, Jimmy and Jessica Wippert, Brian, Emily, and Reagan Crowley and Joyce Planeta. Very special thanks go to Alyssa Adamson, Corky Colbert, Steve Eastis, Steve O'Sullivan, Brannon Mitchell and of course the dynamic duo, Richard Peraza and Robbie Soriano.

My two most important guides to the world of Southern California music are the world's two greatest living engineer/inventors and wonderful human beings: David S. Gold of Hollywood's Gold Star Recording Studio and Stephen W. Desper. Thank you!

I am also tremendously grateful to Billy Hinsche, Chris Farmer, Gary Griffith, Alan Boyd, Mark Linett, Steve Levine, David Marks, Hal Blaine, Robb Starr, Darryl Hooper, John Blair, Mark Guerrero, Rick Henn, Bill Halverson, Nick O'Malley, Don Randi, Marilyn Wilson Rutherford, Michelle Beaulieu, John Daly, Chip Rachlin, Chris Montez, Richard Sherman, David Leaf, Dick Dale, Henry Diltz, Jim Frias, Fred Stuart, Chris Fleming, Don Randi, Carol Kaye, Dr LeRoy 'Zag' Soto, Jeffrey Foskett, Norman and Gerald Sanders and Jonah and Justyn Wilson. Special thanks also to the late and much lamented Stan Ross, Paul Buff, Larry Levine, and Jerry Cole.

I also want to express my gratitude to the 'keepers of the flame,' the Beach Boys and California music historians. First among these is author and historian Jon Stebbins; I consider this book an adjunct to his stellar work. Likewise, special thanks go to David Beard and his cohorts on Endless Summer Quarterly who have done an amazing job over the years of keeping the flame burning while keeping peace in the valley. Special thanks also go out to Ken Sharp, Tom Wheeler, Johnny Black, Stephen McParland, Craig Slowinski, Dr. Jim Murphy, Andrew G. Doe, Art Fein, Domenic Priore, Bob Dalley, Russ Wapensky, Elliot Kendall, and Pat Woertink.

And one more round of thanks goes to the BIA Baldy View Chapter: Jonathan Weldy, Terry Kent, Jim Perry, Carlos Rodriguez, Cassandra Kristensen, and Billie Petty; and to everybody out at the Cooper Museum in Upland.

Most of all, I am greateful to everybody at Jawbone Press, especially my sainted editor John Morrish: thank you again!

Finally, to my beautiful wife Wendy, Dad, Danny Quam, and Jeffrey Ingersoll (who stole Carl's nameplate off the door of the Roxy dressing room), I miss you all.

Index

Photo Credits